THE ART OF
LEGAL RISK
MANAGEMENT

A GUIDE TO MANAGING LEGAL AND CORPORATE RISK

BRYAN E. HOPKINS

PARTRIDGE

To order additional copies of this book, contact
Toll Free 800 101 2657 (Singapore)
Toll Free 1 800 81 7340 (Malaysia)
orders.singapore@partridgepublishing.com

www.partridgepublishing.com/singapore

To my wonderful wife Yeong Hee, my son Geoffrey,
and daughter Christine and their families who are
always in my thoughts-thank you for your love

To Rod Manning, Esq., a fabulous lawyer and good friend

To Won Young, Won Kyung, and others I have mentored or
helped along the way- keep up the good work and pass it on

To Rodney Johnson and my good friends at Erudite
Risk Management- thanks for everything

CONTENTS

Part III: Legal Risk Management Strategies: Pre-litigation

Part IV: Legal Risk Management and Litigation

Part V: Legal Risk Management: Evaluation of the Process

Preface and Request

When I wrote my first book on legal risk management, I never thought it was a topic that I would revisit on a regular basis. However, due to the interest in the topic I 've been asked by colleagues to update it as a number of risks facing companies today has not only increased but grown in complexity. For instance, cyber-crimes are now front and center of any risk management department. Companies must now be more pro-active than ever in order to survive, let alone weather the multitude of crisis that they face on a regular basis. So, I've updated sections of my first book that I thought needed more attention in today's corporate environment. However, since I decided to add a series of chapters at the beginning (chapters 1-17 of the book) based on a fictional case study to walk the reader thought the basic framework of legal risk management I view this as really a complete revision of the book. Some of the old chapters have been deleted and some new chapters have been added, including chapters on antitrust and trade secrets.

It should be noted that this book covers a lot of material and combines legal risk concepts with ERM and other risk management ideas. Part One of the book contains a fictional case study that walks the reader through not only all stages of risk management analysis but important concepts as well. Part One of the book introduces the reader to Eunice Kim and of course, Mr. Lee, the two main characters of the case study. Please consider each chapter carefully as Mr. Lee will throw a lot of concepts out quickly.

Risk management of course has become popular in recent years due to various corporate scandals, government investigations, disasters, and fines. Though some in the risk management industry often refer to enterprise risk management (ERM) when discussing risk management, it is in my opinion that risk management is in reality a process to reduce and minimize the legal risk that is found in many areas. Such legal issues include class actions, product liability claims and lawsuits, government investigations and fines, shareholder actions, and often other legal-related matters. Hence, this book is really about the study of legal and corporate risk or legal risk management (LRM) and what issues, concerns, processes, and procedures should be discussed and implemented when instituting a legal risk management program.

The main role of in-house counsel in corporations or legal entities is, of course, to mitigate legal risk in connection with the sale of products or services provided by the company. In essence how the company protects its success will be based in part on its ability to manage, control, and minimize legal risk, especially in a litigious society such as the US marketplace. Legal counsel must take an active effort in developing strategies, systems, and processes that will minimize the legal risks faced by the company on a daily basis.

In order for the LRM program to be successful in any organization, management must be involved. It is hoped that corporate managers will also take an interest in this vital area, as a successful risk management program or LRM program greatly depends on executive ownership of risk management. Only with the buy-in of executive management will legal risk management be embedded in the strategic decision-making processes of the organization.

I hope, therefore, that this book will not only aid in-house counsel when dealing with legal risk management issues but will also help educate managers and corporate managers as to the issues and concerns of legal risk they face, but also potential strategies, processes, and procedures when dealing with legal risk management or LRM.

This book describes many of the processes and activities that have been developed through my experience to manage and control legal risks faced by most companies today. It is not meant to be exhaustive or all-encompassing, but to describe the basic LRM processes a risk manager, corporate manager, or in-house counsel should consider when trying to minimize legal risk and exposure. I do not cover financial risk management issues in this book but many of the concepts can be used. Financial risk management is really a topic for another book.

It should be noted that I will often refer to legal risk management as the acronym LRM throughout this book. I cannot emphasize enough the fact that risk management itself is interconnected with legal risk. All risk management issues at the end are connected to and quantifiable by the legal exposure faced by a company. Therefore, for a company to protect its bottom line, an aggressive LRM program should be implemented on a daily basis.

This book is intended as an introduction to legal risk management to be used by corporate counsel, risk managers, or mangers in general. I refer to risk management principles, insurance concepts, and basic corporate concepts throughout the book as issues that intersect and connect with legal risk management. The concepts of course intertwine with each other.

The concepts in this book reflect my experience in managing the numerous legal risks for multinationals. This book is not intended to be an exhaustive legal treatise or a legal hornbook but merely a guide to be used by those in-house or corporate managers. I leave a detailed legal analysis one would expect in a treatise or hornbook to others. Because this is an introduction to legal risk management and not an exhaustive textbook or treatise, I will not refer to the multitude of books and articles written on the various topics of this book but will limit the references I use. Nonetheless, I obviously owe a great deal to the practitioners and authors who have influenced me. However, I must state that the greatest teacher I have had over the years has actually been experience. It is my experience that I offer to you, the reader. Needless to say, I hope this book becomes the basis for further discussion and analysis on the topics presented.

At the beginning of many chapters in Parts Two, Three and Four of this book I list certain proposed forms, checklists, and other tools that should be used when implementing a LRM program. A few will be set forth in the appendixes of this book. However, as the forms I list are quite numerous and in some cases very lengthy, most of them cannot be included in this book. They have been included in another book I wrote on the use of forms and checklists in case any of you are interested in using them- *Agreements, Forms and Checklists for Risk Managers.*

Like the first book, this book is divided into several parts. However, in this book, as I mentioned above, Part One introduces LRM through the use of a fictional case study set forth in Seoul, Korea. As the characters in the case study are based in Seoul, it is only fitting to add Korean law and content to some of the areas I touch upon in the book. I think it best to introduce legal risk management issues and concerns as well as strategies via a fictional case study as it helps to understand what everyone should be thinking and why. And of course, as I am based in Seoul, I think it fitting for the fictional case study to take place in Seoul as well. Please remember it is fictional. However, there is an art to the proper use of risk management concepts.

The other parts of the book discusses the LRM process as it pertains to various areas departments of an organization as well as the legal issues a company faces on a daily basis. Corporate governance is popular these days and is addressed in the book as is compliance, crisis management and other topics such as antitrust. Besides the case study in the first section of the book, I have also added several hypothetical case studies as well as a few real case studies at the end of some of the major chapters to help put legal risk in some context and help the reader appreciate the seriousness and complexity of LRM processes and procedures that one faces in an attempt to mitigate and control legal risk.

To help consider the implications of this book, discuss the main concepts of this book with your colleagues. Consider how the concepts impact your organization. Ask yourself how your company addresses risk management concepts. Thinks about the status of risk management in your organization and how it can be effectively used.

Remember, the fate of a company or organization in today's world is tied to how it handles legal risk and whether it manages risk effectively or fails to appreciate the consequences of disregarding it. So, it is you the reader that must fully understand and appreciate the legal risks your organization faces and how to handle such risks.

It is in this spirit that I humbly offer this book.

B. E. Hopkins

Part One

Discovering All About Legal Risk Management

1   Eunice Kim's Dilemma

Eunice Kim, the newly appointed Senior Counsel and compliance manager for FIVE STAR GROUP (an up and coming hedge fund specializing in pharmaceutical, telecommunications, and leading-edge technology related acquisitions) had only just landed in Korea when she began to feel out of her depth. As the only Korean-American working for the Corporate Management Division (CMD) of FIVE STAR GROUP, which was headquartered in NY, her boss (the GC) assumed she would be a natural fit to help monitor FIVE STAR's newly acquired pharmaceutical division in Seoul, Korea, but she now wondered if accepting such an ambitious mission had been a good career move.

Maybe this time, I've gone too far, she thought.

FIVE STAR specializes in picking up distressed companies and had just purchased all of the assets of SilverStar Pharma (a local Korean-owned pharmaceutical company), which included a factory outside of Daejeon as well as a sales and marketing office in Seoul. This was FIVE STAR's first foray into the international marketplace as it had previously concentrated only on the US market. The acquisition of SilverStar's assets was just too tempting to pass up, though no one at HQ had any direct experience running a company in any Asian market. In essence, FIVE STAR now found itself in possession of a pharmaceutical company in Korea: FIVE STAR PHARMA.

FIVE STAR's factory produced a well-known heart medication used for treating blood pressure and heart attack victims. Though FIVE STAR's legal team and outside lawyers did a yeoman's job of handling the due-diligence investigation on the assets before closing the transaction, Eunice suspected there were a lot of unknowns when it came to liabilities. Besides purchasing the assets, FIVE STAR had to enter into *Key Employee Agreements* with the factory manager and his team as well as several of the scientists and engineers that helped produce the main products. FIVE STAR also entered into Key Employee Agreements with the former president of FIVE STAR and his management team, thinking preserving continuity was the most prudent short-term operating strategy.

FIVE STAR's plan upon acquiring SilverStar's assets was to create a new pharmaceutical company that could not only service the local Korean marketplace but also Asia as well. It seemed to FIVE STAR's management that despite any cultural differences, the newly acquired pharmaceutical division would be a good fit in the heart medication market.

The trouble was, there were some issues that had not been uncovered in the investment due diligence. For instance, the remaining employees at the Daejeon factory had recently formed a union and announced they would hold a work stoppage if their demands were not met. The manufacturing equipment had not had the latest safety and certification inspections completed as required under Korean law as well. And of course, no one at FIVE STAR in the US knew anything about the pharmaceutical business, so no one at HQ was prepared for the increased regulatory scrutiny that normally follows a foreign acquisition of this type.

Enter Eunice Kim.

As a member of the CMD's Compliance Team, and fluent in Korean, Eunice Kim was dispatched to Korea to look at the union problems as well as any regulatory and compliance issues FIVE STAR's new pharmaceutical division was facing. She was expected to come up with a game plan to help resolve any legal issues facing FIVE STAR PHARMA prior to its planned expansion into the rest of the Asian market. If this worked out, she could spearhead the launch of other FIVE STAR companies and divisions in Korea, including a cell phone business currently being acquired. And of course, she could expect a nice promotion and perhaps stock options as well as the respect and admiration of the executive team if she did well.

Now on the ground and faced with a largely blank sheet of paper, Eunice was already at a loss over how to proceed. Should she just outsource everything to local outside counsel? Surely that strategy had its own problems. An outside advisor wouldn't understand FIVE STAR's culture, or know what leadership wanted, or understand how to get work done there. It was a suboptimal option, and besides, she had been sent here to do it herself.

I'm going to do this or die trying, she thought.

Was it all about compliance? What about legal and financial issues? Who was looking at things from an operational standpoint? What about regulatory issues? She heard rumblings about the anti-trust regulator, the KFTC, and wondered if there was also pricing and competition related issues to deal with. The potential angles risk could come at them seemed truly daunting.

Prior to arriving in Korea, Eunice heard from a friend about a former CLO living in Seoul, who applied risk management principles to legal problems and had started his own consulting firm, called Lee and Associates. Apparently, he headed up law departments of not only US companies but handled major legal issues for Korean conglomerates as well. Mr. Lee had a reputation of pro-actively handling many legal issues facing his clients before such issues spiraled out of control. Perhaps Mr. Lee could give her a little advice on how to wrangle all the risks she and FIVE STAR faced. It couldn't hurt to talk to him.

Not a week into her assignment, after reviewing the situation on the ground and meeting with the local leadership team, (including talking to the former president of SilverStar Pharma, who was now an employee of FIVE STAR Pharma Korea), Eunice's first call for help was to Mr. Lee. She called to see if he was available for a quick consultation. He was.

2 Eunice Kim's Introduction into Legal Risk

Lee was enjoying an iced Americano coffee (one of his favorite drinks) as Eunice came into the lobby of one of the hotels near Namsan Mountain. Upon seeing a young lady scanning the faces of the people in the lobby, Mr. Lee assumed it must be Eunice and waved at her. Eunice walked over to the table where Lee was staying.

"Ms. Kim" he said, while motioning to a chair. "Have a seat." Eunice took a seat at the table opposite Mr. Lee. "Well" Lee said shaking Eunice's hand, "To what pleasure, do I owe your visit on this fine day?"

Eunice wondered how to approach the matter, but finally blurted out "Well, I've been dispatched from my company in the US to get a grasp on the legal and compliance issues facing our newly acquired pharmaceutical division we acquired. You may have heard of the company, SilverStar Pharma."

"Yes," Lee said, "I saw your acquisition in the newspaper. Congratulations. That was a nice catch."

"Thank you," Eunice replied. "It is now FIVE STAR PHARMA and I've been dispatched to ensure it doesn't blow up on us."

"Blow up on you?"

"Well, I'm not saying there are any problems, but there may be problems. What I'm really saying is that I don't know for sure. No one knows for sure what risks we've just acquired."

"I see," Mr. Lee said, taking a long drink on his coffee.

"There is no in-house counsel at the pharma division, and I am the only compliance manager and lawyer. I don't know where to begin.

The lawyers back home are more interested in the next acquisitions than helping me. I heard you are an expert in managing legal risks for companies and hoped you could help give me a few pointers."

"Pointers?" Lee inquired.

"Tell me where to look," Eunice said, just jumping to the chase. "Tell me how to get a handle on all the risks before they get a handle on me. Is that possible?"

"Possible?" Lee smiled. "With money, leadership, and a lot of luck, anything is possible." He laughed heartily at his own joke, until he noticed that Eunice didn't find it so funny.

"What about with distant leadership, limited funds, and fickle luck?"

"Well then you better have processes", Lee said. "Good processes can make up for a lot of weaknesses in other places."

"Processes? What processes?"

"Well, in this case, I'm talking about risk management processes, of course."

"Of course," Eunice echoed.

Lee continued. "The acquisition of SilverStar by FIVE STAR, made the news" he said. "So, did the fact that a number of employees quit for other jobs including the only in-house lawyer SilverStar had. I don't know if he quit over the acquisition or saw issues he didn't want to address or deal with. Due to the nature of the pharmaceutical business in Korea and elsewhere there are probably a number of issues facing your newly acquired pharma division including some contractual, some regulatory, and legal in nature. But of course, legal issues or even compliance issues are not your only problem. I assume a legal risk audit was conducted prior to the acquisition and all legal risks, as well as operational, financial and regulatory were fleshed out. Correct?"

"No," she said. "A legal risk audit was never done." She neglected to mention that no one at FIVE STAR had ever even heard of a legal risk audit.

Why am I not surprised, thought Lee.

"It is not that surprising one wasn't done. That is often the case. Even most in-house counsel and compliance managers confuse legal risk audits with compliance audits or think due diligence handles everything. Legal risk management is a relatively new topic for in-house counsel and managers, even though it shouldn't be."

"In reality, it is all about legal risk management or LRM as I like to call it. If you really want to get a grip on the issues facing your company here in Korea as well as abroad you need to understand legal risk management, what it is, how to implement it and how to use it for the benefit of the company. The focus of LRM is to control and manage an organization's legal risks, which in countries like the US can be diverse and challenging. Legal risk management processes are primarily designed and implemented to engage in preventative projects, such as counseling the organization regarding insurance matters, developing risk management processes, and administering training programs."

Taking a sip from his coffee, Lee continued. "Also of course, the processes are used in conjunction with legal defense activities, such as coordinating the company's defenses against product liability litigation and claims, responding to product-related investigations, and analyzing governmental reporting responsibilities. In fact, a compliance program can be considered part of the LRM process, as it can be an effective tool to monitor and prevent actions that are either against corporate policies or that are illegal. As you can see, it is a broad and important function that encompasses many areas."

Eunice replied "I heard about ERM, but not legal risk management. I don't think the pharma division has a risk manager. Its lawyer left after the acquisition. He may not have been too involved with risk anyway."

"What most in-house lawyers don't understand is that they are in fact risk managers or legal risk managers. Most lawyers are not trained to be pro-active or think in terms of risk, but they really have to be if they want to survive. When in house lawyers or even managers think about risk they usually think in terms of insurance. It is a great deal more than insurance, though insurance plays a part. Of course, compliance plays a part too."

Lee went on to explain that legal risk management was a core enterprise of any company. "How a company manages its legal risks (whether it mitigates them, transfers them, or accepts them) will in fact dictate its fate. And to manage risks you have to properly identify and understand them."

"That's the part I'm worried about," Eunice said.

"Many companies have gone bankrupt because they neglected their legal risk. By controlling and managing legal risk, an organization is able to control its future. Without adequate LRM processes, a company is exposed to claims, lawsuits, fines, and investigations. Not a day goes by where some governmental investigation or lawsuit is not reported in the local newspaper.

"The main issue facing many companies when dealing with legal risk management, whether through the Risk Management Department or RMD, Legal or Compliance, is that divisions and/or departments within a corporation often fail to effectively partner with RMD or Compliance. This, in turn, leads to improper handling of major legal and sensitive issues, which can lead to legal claims, fines, and liabilities. Remember, a $100 Million fine can destroy a company."

Lee looked at Eunice. "You need to be very pro-active. You can't wait for the legal risk events to arise…it would be too late. Before you can fully understand and appreciate LRM, you should understand the basics of risk management and how they are applied to the legal function of a company. Does your company have a risk manager or chief compliance officer back home who can help you?"

Eunice was embarrassed to answer, but she knew needed to face the facts. "No," she said. "I'm all alone in this."

Lee thought to himself for a few minutes. Eunice Kim's case was certainly interesting. She was doing exactly what he would have wanted to do if he was a younger man. Perhaps he could tackle this vicariously through Ms. Kim.

"You're a brave soul," Lee said. "I'd hate to see you fail."

"I'd hate to see me fail more," she said.

"I'll help," Lee said.

"I have a limited budget," Eunice said.

"It's okay," Lee said. "I have enough clients to keep me busy for the rest of my days. I'll do it for you pro bono, but you have to play by my rules. Number one, you do all the real work. I just sit here and drink coffee and be philosophical. We meet once every two or three weeks at 2 pm. This time works for me. And you pay for the coffee. That's it."

"I think I can handle that," Eunice said, happy at her unexpected boon.

"We'll start tomorrow. For now, go and prepare some background information for me."

"Such as?"

"The questions are: What is risk? Do you know your company's risk appetite or tolerance? What are the main risks facing the pharmaceutical division that you should be concerned about? What areas of risk are being supervised in the company such as the monitoring of safety issues, the monitoring of compliance programs, oversight of the company's product safety department and insurance coverage issues? What about manufacturing and risk protocol issues?"

"That's a lot," she responded as she wrote down the items.

"Ask your pharma division's president or operations manager about them. Or if they unavailable, maybe someone in the insurance department or contracts can help you. Remember, legal risk management processes and procedures must be applied to provide to prevent loss due to claims, litigation, and investigations and fines. LRM must be properly applied in a corporate setting, whether under the control of the company's law department or under the control of a separate division such as compliance or insurance. In order for LRM to be properly applied in a corporate setting, legal and management must take an active role in applying LRM in all areas of responsibility."

"You're a life saver," Eunice Kim said, standing up to leave.

"I'm merely going to tell you how to build a life preserver. It's up to you to make it and wear it. That's the hard part."

"I'll follow up on these questions and see you tomorrow then," she said.

"Pay at the cashier," Lee said and downed the last drink of coffee.

3   Eunice Considers Various Kinds of Risk

Eunice found Lee at his favorite table contemplating the view of the Han River. "Well" he said. "Did you get answers to the questions?"

Eunice hesitated before she spoke. "In a word, no. I asked the president who seemed not to understand the questions except that he thinks the main risk facing the pharma division is lack of sales due to the competition."

"And that was lesson number one" Lee remarked and smiled.

"Risk is not well understood by most managers. Leaders are rarely, if ever, congratulated for all the bad things that never happened, even though without their affirmative action bad things are likely to have occurred. When a car accident doesn't take place, we wonder why we paid for insurance, right."

"Maybe," Eunice said, biting her lip. She knew she was sometimes guilty of the same thinking.

"We all do it. Even me," Lee opined "But when the big one comes, everyone stands back and says, why didn't we take precautions? It's selling the problem of taking precautions that is the tough part, right? Well, you don't have to worry about that because you are here. Your company has already decided to do what's necessary. Half the battle is already won."

"I didn't think of it like that," Eunice said. "That really lightens my mental burden!"

"Good," Lee said. "Risk is the probability that a certain event will happen in the future and that the event will have a negative or positive impact on the company business objectives. More often than not, the event or risk event as we sometimes say will be a negative event. What do I mean by 'probability'?" He asked, looking at Eunice.

Trying to remember her statistics class from college, Eunice finally spoke. "You mean the likelihood of an event occurring."

"Yes" acknowledged Lee. "Actually, the likelihood of the cause of risk occurring that results in a risk event that will negatively impact the company. There are many kinds of risks" he continued. "Many kinds of risks and of course causes. Operational, financial, environmental, and so on. But most can be lumped into legal risk because at the end of the day, all risk events will lead to lawsuits, government investigations, fines and penalties and of course litigation, which especially in the US can be very expensive. Remember, they say USA stands for *you sue anyone*."

Eunice realized Lee was starting to get warmed up on the topic. She quickly flipped through her notebook to be sure enough blank pages remained.

"The key to thinking about legal risk" he said, "is that you have to think about events that may have a probability of happening. Too often companies think about risk events that have no actual likelihood of happening. A potential catastrophe that has a zero percent chance of occurring is really a much smaller risk than it appears to be at first glance. On the other hand, risks with medium to large impact and a high likelihood of occurring may merit extreme mitigation measures. You have to map out each risk you face and see where it lies on the graph of severity and likelihood."

Lee had an idea. He pulled out a tablet from his briefcase near the table. Looking at Eunice he asked, "Can you list out business risks that you think most companies face?"

Taking the tablet Eunice listed them as follows:

1. Credit risk
2. Financial risk
3. Operational risk
4. Regulatory risk

"That's a good start" added Lee. "But there are others." Taking the tablet, he filled in a diagram listing most risks that companies face. The diagram looked something like this:

Figure 3-1

Eunice was shocked. "I never thought so many kinds of business risks exist" she admitted.

"Well" Lee continued, "the problem many companies face is that they don't address all of or even most of the potential risks out there. That includes the law department. Most lawyers think in terms of insurance or in transferring risk via contract like an indemnification clause. They don't understand that for most types of businesses, related risks eventually become legal risks. Nor do they try and get their hands around the risks they do see. Either they are too busy defending a lawsuit, which is not proactive at all – it is fighting yesterday's battles, or they think the insurance department or maybe the compliance department will handle it and look the other way."

"There is a good book on legal risk by Bryan Hopkins called *Legal Risk Management for In-House Counsel and Managers*. That's where you should start. It may be hard to find so I brought my copy for you. Please read the first few chapters and I'll see you next week at this time. Oh, it's not a gift, I'll expect that copy back."

4   Eunice Learns About The Steps In Managing Risk

Two weeks later at 2:00 PM on the dot, Eunice Kim found Lee sipping an ice Americano coffee at the same table as always. Eunice wondered how he managed to always secure the same table. *Did he live here*? She asked herself.

"This coffee is expensive" he commented when he saw her, "but it's really good and I'm sure FIVE STAR can afford it."

"We're not against investing in something if we see a good deal," Eunice retorted and sat down in her usual spot.

"Well played," he said, admiring her ability to take him on. "Very well played. Learn anything about risk?"

"I am surprised how many risks there are" replied Eunice. "How do you get a handle on it?"

"It's about managing legal risk at the end" Lee remarked. "Or in our case LRM. As you read a few chapters in Hopkins' book I presume, why not diagram it out for me on how you think you should manage it."

Eunice admitted to Lee she was uncertain. She hadn't covered that many chapters in the book.

Okay Lee offered. "Managing legal risk or LRM is using the risk management process to manage legal risk. Think of it as a process. It's actually all about processes and procedures." Lee pulled out a paper tablet and began to draw a diagram. Once he finished, he showed Eunice the steps in managing risk. "Here it is" he said.

Figure 4-1

"Risk management is a series of steps or phases. It is a process" Lee opined. "Legal risk management or LRM is managed the same way. You have to be able to assess, identify, quantify & evaluate and then manage it. The processes or steps, once mastered, are fairly easy to implement if you know your industry. Thinking in terms of risk will help you think proactively not reactively. Come back next week and we will talk about the first step- assessing risk. Be prepared to talk about it. By the way, check the weather before you come. The rainy season will start soon. You may need an umbrella."

5   Risk Assessment-A Plan

"Hello Eunice" Lee said cheerfully.

"Hello Mr. Lee," Eunice said placing her wet umbrella on the floor next to the table. She was not a fan of rain in the city.

"I hope you read up on risk assessment."

"I did," she said.

"Tell me about it," Lee said.

"Well, establishing a risk assessment plan is really the first step in a risk management process. Sometimes it is combined with risk identification as well but is primarily the first step. It involves recognition of risks and can be used to review corporate goals and objectives, core processes and event stakeholder issues."

"Wow," Lee said. "You're a quick study. I see they sent the right person. Please do go on."

Eunice continued. "The purpose of a risk assessment plan or a process is to identify major risks that can be analyzed and evaluated. It is really the starting point of the whole legal risk management process."

"And if done improperly—" Lee began.

"If done improperly," Eunice interrupted him, "the risk assessment plan or the resulting processes could be flawed, which could skewer the risk identification process and then, even if execution is perfect, a company will be planning its way to failure."

"Wow again," Lee said. "Should I just pay for my own coffee now or wait till later?"

"I'm done," Eunice said, proud of herself. "Your turn."

"Okay, I'll just add some color to what you said. As an example of how risk assessment processes can fail to truly uncover risks, just think of the companies that already have certain controls in place, whether financial or otherwise, and assess risk while considering those controls. That's a great start, but in reality, by assessing risks without taking controls into account, you really get a better picture of the true value of risks that are out there. Why is that?"

"Because controls may or may not actually function as designed,"

"Exactly," Lee said. "And once you assess risk without looking at the controls you can really determine if the controls in place are actually working or not, right?"

"How do you approach risk assessment then?" questioned Eunice, writing in her notebook as fast as she could.

"Look at a company's approach to risk assessment itself. If a company uses a top-down approach to assess risk, such as the BOD or the CEO looking at risk, the BOD or CEO may not be very concerned about many of the internal risks as much as they would be about the external risks. If a company uses a bottom up approach, whether individual or departmental, it will look more at internal risks and processes and less about external risks."

"So, in other words" Eunice concluded "risk assessments will be influenced by the risk assessment process used. So certain individuals or managers may be needed to perform a particular kind of risk assessment. I would think that to do a proper risk assessment someone concerned about or knowledgeable in internal company processes should be in charge of the risk assessment, or at least involved in it."

"Right" said Lee. "If you look at a non–technology focused company, such as a company that is still in many ways' analog, paper reports may still be the norm while a high-tech company may look at electronic reporting as more appropriate. A trucking company or transportation company could be more analog than a computer software company, for instance."

Eunice started nodding in agreement. "So, a bottom–up risk assessment will focus on compliance and basic internal risks, but a top-down assessment will focus on strategic and tactical related risks.

So, if you are worried about compliance or internal risks or processes you really need a bottom up approach as opposed to a top to bottom approach."

"But isn't it all about perception of legal risk?" Eunice asked. "People may have different perceptions of legal risk based on a number of factors such as their seniority or their concerns. Some will be more concerned with low level risks that have a high probability of occurrence as opposed to high level risks with a low probability of occurrence."

"That's right" Lee affirmed. "Good answer. That's why to get a good picture of a company's legal risks, a company needs to draw upon all levels of management for a better understanding. A company may want to come up with its own definitions of risk based on its risk appetite as well as its size and complexity or even the nature of its industry. A nuclear power company will have a different perception of risk than a paper manufacturing company or a company that designs greeting cards for instance. Management's perception of risk will be different as well as the rank and file's perception."

Lee was happy that Eunice seemed to understand where he was going. She nodded as if a light bulb went off in her head, so he continued talking." In fact, certain organizations have come up with risk assessment techniques to provide information on risk assessments including ranking risk, risk assessment techniques and basic risk assessment programs and processes. The two most popular are ISO 31010 Risk Management and the COSO Standard. COSO is popular in the US and is a standard many accounting firms use, and ISO is more popular in the EU.

Lee continued he discussion of risk standards. "The COSO standard became popular in the US and elsewhere in the 2000s because of the Sarbanes Oxley Act and is popular amongst most finance related companies. It is a joint initiative of a number of organizations including the American Accounting Association sometimes called the AAA, as well as the Institute of Management Accountants or the IMA to name a few. Of course, it has been updated to reflect the new risks and the changes in corporate governance trends."

"What about ISO?" Eunice asked.

"Well, ISO 31000 seeks to provide a structured methodology to standardize risk management as well as taking a more global approach. ISO of course means International Organization for Standardization and ISO 31000 attempts to provide a true global risk management standard. It is recognized in some countries as the natural risk management standard. From a risk management standard, ISO 3100 consists of three primary stages: principles, framework and processes. Obviously, it is really the processes you are more interested in."

Pulling out a piece of paper from his briefcase, Lee showed Eunice a basic chart outlining the ISO 3100 conceptual risk management process. He got it from Erudite Risk Management, one of Lee's favorite risk management consultants.

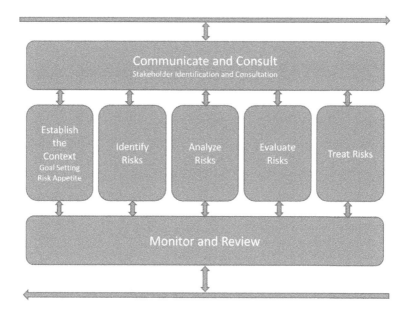

Figure 5-1

"Here" he said handing Eunice the paper. "This is what the ISO standard proposes a risk management process look like."

Eunice noted the diagram. "It looks like the risk assessment process really consists of risk identification, risk analysis and risk evaluation. It's getting confusing. What do those things mean?"

"It can be confusing," Lee admitted. "It uses the term 'establishing the context' in essence as how I describe 'assessing the risk.' In looking at legal risks or LR, I view risk identification, risk analysis, and risk evaluation separately. To me, assessing the risk is really assessing the context and situation of risks. Once you understand the context and situation you are assessing the risk environment. You can then identify, analyze and evaluate the important legal risks a company faces. So, coming up with a risk assessment plan or process is key. Here look at this matrix from Erudite. It helps identify risks and the severity of risks. It can be expanded of course to include as many risks as many as you want to focus on."

Identified Risk	Likelihood	Severity	Risk Rating
Contractual	Possible	Moderate	Low
Regulatory	Unlikely	Severe	Acceptable
Intellectual Property	Likely	Medium	Minimal
Litigation	Likely	High	Not Tolerable

Matrix used to help identify risks, likelihood and severity.

Figure 5-2

Eunice looked at the diagram. "So, a company needs to come up with a process to assess risks which includes its own definition of risk to clearly identify the major legal risk sit faces."

"Right. When thinking in terms of LRM, ask yourself some questions. First, what is the degree of risk your company or division or department is comfortable with? Also, what perception of risk does the various levels of management in your company have towards risk? Remember, as an in-house lawyer, you should talk to all departments and the various department heads as well as middle managers, etc. to get a good grasp of their perception of risk or at least their perception of legal issues facing them. Once you do that, you can assess the legal risk environment and then proceed with your risk analysis. Of course, the accounting department may be looking at things under COSO and the HR department may be looking at risks under the ISO standard. You will have to get a handle on that. Compare and contrast them perhaps."

"Also," Lee pointed out, "you may want to do a risk assessment of areas that are important to your company. Such areas you may want to think about I've written down on a piece of paper for you." Taking the paper from Lee, Eunice gasped realizing how detailed a risk assessment could be.

The paper read as follows:

- All insurance matters, including the renewal of insurance carrier and recommending obtaining additional or different types of insurance when needed.
- Handling all product liability claims, including product safety claims, subrogation claims, investigations, discovery, and product liability lawsuits for the organization.
- Reviewing product warranties, warnings, and manuals to ensure compliance with US laws and regulations.
- Reviewing processes regarding product recalls, government-related complaints, and government investigations and inquiries, including the FDA, and FTC in the United States, Korea's FDA, etc.
- Working with the Service Department or QA Department and other departments to analysis potential safety issues and report the findings to the loss-control committee in order to prevent problems before they can expand.
- Performing due diligence reviews of safety-related issues and evaluating such findings.
- Reviewing PR/marketing processes, other departments and outside PR on responding to the media with respect to safety-related issues (media crisis team/crisis management team).
- Assessing the training given to the service/call center (if any) personnel on how to handle consumers complaining about

safety issues and how to recognize product liability issues and escalate them to the proper people.

Lee added, "Review and assess processes and procedures of any testing labs or facilities the company may have, as well. Remember, government agencies in most countries, such as the FDA, do not give companies much time to respond to inquiries and expect testing facilities to conduct tests in a timely and efficient manner."

6   Identifying The Various Kinds of Risk

Eunice was confused. Of course, risks needed to be assessed.

Lee knew Eunice was thinking about risk assessment and processes. "Well," he said. "any questions?" While he waited for Eunice to answer, Lee stirred his iced tea. He thought he needed to inject some variety into the proceedings.

Eunice looked at Lee thoughtfully. "I am wondering how a company that wants to do a risk assessment plan actually evaluates the risks?"

Lee thought for a moment. "Good question" he stated. "I am glad you are thinking about it. To evaluate risks, you need to identify them. Risk identification helps a company in determining its exposure to risk. Of course, that requires knowledge of a company's products or services as well as its objectives and the markets it is involved in. So, the first or second phase of any risk management plan, as part of the initial risk assessment, is risk identification. Identifying risks, helps you categorize the risk that may impact your business."

"Ok. But I still wonder how you identify them" queried Eunice.

"There are many ways to identify risks" answered Lee. "To be honest, a company should identify as many potential risks it can from the greatest number of sources it can. It can then evaluate and analyze them. Sources can consist of surveys, questions to employees, focus groups, benchmarking, checklists, audits and even business process reviews, to name a few. The more sources the more risks you can identify."

Lee continued talking. "There could be hundreds of risks facing a company, but by coming up with a well-developed, defined process, the task of identifying risks becomes easier. In fact, you may want to categorize legal risk that your company may face to make it easier to use processes to identify them. The categorization of potential legal risks can be used as an effective tool to initiate or facilitate discussions with management and employees to help identify the risks that your company actually faces."

Lee emphasized, "Actually, by using this tool, you or the subject matter experts your company may be using for any particular area, can effectively guide discussions to identify the legal risks your company faces. However, the problem facing some companies is that they don't use legal counsel, or an SME, or even a facilitator such as a 3rd party professional such as Erudite Risk to lead discussions. When they don't use professionals, who are used to discussing or identifying the issues, but instead use managers or employees who are not used to identifying issues, the finger-pointing and shouting starts because no one wants to admit that risks exist in their area."

Lee looked at Eunice. "Remember, to avoid having a risk identification meeting becoming a chaotic mess, have a process in place."

Lee pulled out a chart from his briefcase. "This could in fact be as simple as a sample tool categorizing legal risks that should be identified."

Kinds	Examples	Severity
Contractual	Damages	Moderate
Regulatory	Compliance	Minimal
Non-Contractual	Unintentional Liability	Moderate
Litigation	Class Actions	Severe
Reputational	Negative	Some
IP	Loss of IP	Heavy

Figure 6-1

Eunice looked at the chart. "This could be an effective tool" she admitted. "Obviously, it will have to be customized for the pharma industry."

"Right" said Lee sipping his iced tea. "Create a chart and use it. Maybe you create several charts. Come back in two weeks to discuss risk analysis and evaluation. Risk analysis and evaluation will in fact help you determine how likely it is that a risk event will occur and the consequences of such an event."

Lee pulled out a book from his briefcase and handed it over the table to her. "Here is a good book on risk management by Paul Hopkin called *Fundamentals of Risk Management*. Read the chapters on risk assessment and evaluation."

"Also" added Lee, "why not use confidential interviews as a tool to identify legal risk? I have found that the use of confidential employee interviews is one of the most effective ways of identifying legal risk. This is because employees may not only need certain internal corporate processes explained to them in order to evaluate the probability of risk or legal risk; confidentiality is often needed in order for employees to really open up and talk to management about issues and concerns. Remember, when conducting a risk assessment of any department within the company, the Risk Management Department or Law Department must not only try to identify risks but must also find out why the risks exist and how to mitigate or resolve them. Feedback from employees is essential when trying to identify and resolve legal risks."

Eunice pondered Lee's statement. "So, you advise using a number of ways to identify legal risks," she concluded.

"Yes" Lee continued. "I advise using a number of tools—interviews, workshops, surveys, document reviews, industry information, or even focus groups—to identify risk as well as decide how to respond. Once the legal risks are identified, it is easier to decide how to address such risks, whether through training, workshops, new processes, etc. Obviously, legal risk can be identified through a series of legal audits using risk modeling tools, interviews, and surveys to name a few processes. Once potential risks or risk factors have been identified, an action plan can be put together. Only through a legal audit or review will legal risks become apparent."

Lee had an idea. He pulled out an old report from his briefcase. "This is a summary of a legal risk audit I did for an in-house law department of a multinational company who will remain nameless. I was asked to help the in-house law department audit the HR Department of its US subsidiary as they thought that coming from the outside, I could offer a fresh opinion. My findings of risk and the status of the investigation are summarized in this report."

Lee opened the first few pages and Eunice could see what the audit revealed.

<u>Audit of XYZ HR</u>

The audit of XYZ HR has identified numerous areas of legal risk. Such areas and recommended actions to mitigate risk are as follows:

Lack of effective partnering with XYZ Law Department:

- Description: Critical legal issues are present in HR function. XYZ HR needs a process to escalate these issues to XYZ Law Department for handling.
- Risk factors: Improper handling of sensitive issues—liabilities, investigations, fines, penalties, etc.
- Status: Ongoing.
- Recommended action: Develop standards and processes for escalation, handling, and control of HR legal matters.

Employee handbook:

- Description: The employee handbook is an important document, which communicates policies to the workforce.

- Risk factors: Policies not communicated properly and not followed.
- Status: Ongoing.
- Recommended action: Review and approve XYZ Legal Department's revisions to handbook.

Lack of training re US legal requirements:

- Description: A US training program is needed for managers, especially for non-US citizens who rotate to other branches or offices around the world.
- Risk factors: Liabilities, investigations, fines, penalties, private litigation, etc.
- Status: Ongoing.
- Recommended action: Develop and implement a US training program.

Wage and hour issues:

- Description: Lack of systematic characterization of job titles as "exempt" or "nonexempt."
- Risk factors: Fines and penalties; responsibility for unpaid overtime across entire job classifications; a Department of Labor (DOL) investigation or IRS investigation could be triggered by violation.
- Status: Ongoing.
- Recommended action: Develop standards and process for escalation, handling and control of HR legal matters.

ERISA Audit-US:

- Description: Identified critical missing documents; lack of ERISA processes.
- Risk factors: Significant liabilities, fines, penalties, investigation by DOL and IRS.

- Status: Pending review by board of directors.
- Recommended action: Devote resources to find missing documents, implement critical processes and tools to implement processes, and create a risk management plan going forward to follow ERISA regulations.

Other issues:

- Description: Inadequate documentation of employee discipline; lack of document retention, and lack of workplace advisory posters, etc.
- Risk factors: Potential employee termination issues, administrative issues, fines, penalties, and litigation.
- Status: Investigation ongoing.
- Recommended action: Develop document retention program; order workplace advisory posters and initiate managerial training regarding documentation of employee discipline.

EPLI insurance program for US:

- Description: Shifting legal risk of employee-related litigation to insurance company by obtaining employee litigation insurance.
- Action: Discussing RFPs from insurance broker in effort to obtain favorable EPLI insurance coverage.
- Status: EPLI insurance expected in one month.

"You see," Lee asserted, "the above legal risks identified by my audit of XYZ's HR Department are typical of a corporation's legal risk audit. The LRM process, including legal risk shifting strategies, can be successfully used to control and mitigate legal risk. I think a legal risk audit should first focus on those departments that frequently come into contact with employees or customers, as those departments or divisions have some of the greatest legal exposure or immediate exposure of any group."

7   Risk Assessment and Evaluation

Rainy season was in full swing. It had been raining in Seoul a lot and the Han River was rising.

Lee was busy reading a paper when Eunice arrived. Seeing Eunice walkover, Lee raised his hand to greet her. "Hello" he said happily and put down his paper.

"Hello," she said, putting down her umbrella and books and taking her usual seat opposite him.

"Wet enough for you?" Lee asked.

"No more, no less of a risk than I assessed," she retorted.

"Good, good," he said, nodding his admiration at her ability to go toe to toe with him. "In that vein, let's talk risk assessments."

"Let's," Eunice said. "Risk assessments should include a review of all critical corporate processes and procedures, with an evaluation of weaknesses of current processes. Such assessments could include areas like insurance, product liability issues, a review of PR materials, loss control, etc. But in order to properly evaluate risks that you've identified, you need an objective or goal to evaluate the risk assessments. Such goals could be to contain or minimize a company's legal exposure or expenses or to implement a strong auditing program or to review product related complaints or to prevent product recalls. Or even to audit a department for risks."

"Do I even need to be here?" Lee joked.

"Only to explain to me what I just said," Eunice joked back.

"Well, once you have a goal in mind, you can take the risks identified and do a risk assessment and evaluation on them. The assessment and evaluation may be more quantifiable in nature and would cover a process such as the creation of a risk assessment project plan covering the assessment of risks that have been identified, whether through workshops or surveys, scoring of risks including how severe the risks will be and a critical risk analysis which would cover the severity of the impact of the risk or risk event. The legal risk analysis would primarily focus on estimating the potential impact of the risks you identified and whether they are financial in nature or not. The risk evaluation part will consist of the prioritization of the legal risks you identified and assessed."

"The trouble of course" Lee continued, "is that the assessment and evaluation of risks are highly data dependent. What is the quality of data that you are using? That's the question to ask. The more reliable the data is, the more reliable the assessment and evaluation."

Looking at Eunice, Lee asserted "In assessing your risks, you need to estimate the likelihood of a risk event and the consequences of the event. How do you do it?" he asked.

Eunice thought a moment. "Well" she said, "you can use industry data but that may not be complete. You can also come up with a tool such as a matrix that can show the impact and severity."

Excellent. She is really getting it. "Yes," he said. "Come up with a tool such as a matrix that can be data driven. What would the matrix or chart look like?"

Eunice drew a chart

Risk	Impact	Unlikely	Likely	Certain
Contractual	Heavy	1	2	5
Regulatory	Moderate	1	5	4
Operational	Heavy	1	4	5
Litigation	Likely	1	2	3
Reputational	Moderate	1	3	2

Figure 7-1

Lee looked at the chart. "Right idea. Obviously, you can expand the chart to cover all sorts of legal risks and plug in data from your company using past events. You can come up with a pretty good idea of the likelihood and impact of each event.

"But" he countered, "Remember the data you use needs to be good. So, remember the process I outlined at the beginning. Risk identification, risk assessment, risk evaluation, creation and implementation of a risk management plan and last of course, a review of the risk management plan."

8   Risk Evaluation and Scoring

"How is FIVE STARS Pharma doing?" Lee asked. Two weeks had passed since they had last met.

"Well" Eunice replied, "It's hard to get the company focused on the top risk issues and priorities. It is always hard, especially if a company is not used to doing it. You need a corporate culture driving it before it becomes easier. Can we talk about risk scoring?"

"Sure," Lee said. "As you know, risk analysis will of course, if done properly, create or generate risk scoring tools to help generate decisions about the top risk that a business faces. Such tools can be a heat map or risk map as well as a risk register. A heat map is a quantitative analysis of the identified risk using a red-yellow-green color-coding process that uses color to denote the risks the company faces. The highest priority or most severe risks are in red with the least or most minor are in green. A risk register serves as a detailed chart or outline of risk that contains the identified risk, a heat map, the planned management of each risk and maybe the outcomes of the risk plan, if known. A heat map normally is in color, but you can use shades of grey and black as well."

"What about risk scoring itself?" asked Eunice.

Lee looked at her. "I thought you would never ask! Risk scoring is at the word implies, a numerical score. Risk scoring uses algorithms, statistics or other methods to create a calculated number or 'score.' The score reflects the level of risk. For instance, when dealing with a credit report, the system will assign a number to late payments, outstanding debt, past experience and so on to come up with a score. Other scoring methods might use the weighted average when assigning numbers to the probability of risk, risk tolerance, the cost of risk, and so on for a score."

Eunice thought a moment. "So, in essence, the risk score is a tool to determine the degree of risks that were identified when evaluating the risks."

"Yes" replied Lee. "The scoring method can be used in many applications. Think about cost justifications. When a pharmaceutical company, like yours, is thinking of developing a new drug or treatment, it may want to use risk scoring to justify the cost. For instance, look at the probability of occurrence times the magnitude of loss. If it costs $1 Million USD to develop a new drug that has a ten percent chance of failing in the drug trials, any response to the risk of failure shouldn't cost more than $100,000 USD."

Lee continued "Remember, you can provide a number or score when looking for the severity of risks. Risk professionals use a risk matrix with scores that reflect the three main components of severity, probability, and risk assessment values. At the end of the day, risk scoring can be a valuable tool to evaluate the severity and probability of risk by providing a good risk assessment number or value."

"But remember" Lee once again cautioned, "it really depends on the data that is plugged into the process. That's why it is so hard to provide a realistic risk score or number in an insurance setting if there is no reliable data or if the industry or company is so new that legacy data does not exist. Insurance brokers will always ask you about data before getting quotes in the marketplace."

Lee looked at Eunice. "I think you are understanding the process. Risk scoring or rating can be a valuable tool as is a risk matrix. Once you analyze potential risks via risk scoring, it's time to evaluate potential risks by conducting a critical risk analysis. This is the last step in the risk management process before you come up with a risk management or risk mitigation plan. Come back in two weeks and we will discuss. Prior to that, why don't you read the chapters from Tony Norma's book- *Corporate Risk Management* covering critical risk analysis techniques? See you next week."

9 Critical Risk Analysis-A Discussion

The following week, while walking to the coffee shop in the lobby of the hotel near Namsan Mountain, Eunice realized she missed Lee. The meetings every two weeks as well as discussions covering the full gamut of legal issues, made her realize she looked forward to the meetings. Eunice found Lee at the coffee shop sipping an ice Americano. Lee looked thoughtful. Lee looked up and smiled. His smile told Eunice that Lee missed her too.

Eunice sat down. Pulling out the book on critical risk analysis she commented on it to Lee. "There seems to be various ways to do a critical risk analysis. You can use heat maps, risk modules, a loss frequency chart or even a GAP analysis to look at the risks you've scored to determine how critical they are or could be in the scheme of things."

"You are right" Lee replied." But, don't forget you could also use risk models that are fact-based scenario models taking into account the data or facts you have at hand to provide an analysis. Legal risk models sometimes run two basic scenarios: a regular or typical loss scenario and a severe or catastrophic loss scenario. A typical loss scenario can be based on a company's usual loss frequency chart such as what basic losses a company will suffer if a normal risk event happens over a one- or two-year period of time. You can call it residual risk or minimal risk. The other model is a severe loss model which takes into account a severe loss caused by a major risk such as a worst-case scenario. Think major crisis such as an environmental catastrophe or major product failure. Or governmental investigation."

"So" concluded Eunice, "the whole idea is to run fact-based scenarios based on the company's data to determine the average every day legal risk at hand as a baseline while also using the severe or critical loss scenario to provide an understanding of the potential worst-case environment that a company faces at any time."

"Yes" said Lee. "Remember, however, the worst-case scenario is hard to quantify as is rarely happens. No matter how accurate the data is, it will always be harder to calculate the worst-case scenario than it will the typical everyday garden variety loss scenario. Think about it. A typical loss scenario covers usual everyday risks. Say for a pharmaceutical company, the risk that one of the machines producing medicine or drugs needs maintenance and goes offline for two or three days. Ok, how often does that happen and what risk does a company have in fulfilling its orders if a machine needs maintenance? The worst-case scenario would be that the machine doesn't appear to need maintenance, but for some unknown reason it breaks down or the machine suffers a critical part failure that can't be fixed requiring the machine to be replaced. In some cases, the machine can't be replaced. Or even worse, the FDA decides to ban the drug because of machine failure. Then what? Looking at those two scenarios you can analyze the risks and determine what financial impact each event would have. You can then take steps to mitigate or plan for each impact."

"What about legal risk itself?" asked Eunice. "There is always a financial component to legal risk, or even vice a versa. I can see a company using models or even heat maps or a GAP analysis to look at risk scores and ultimately a risk scenario."

"You are right. Think about it this way. A company looks at typical everyday losses caused by normal risk events, such as the cost of a governmental investigation or audit that happens on a normal basis. Normally, audits or investigations lead nowhere but audits can cost money. But what happens if the audit or investigation uncovers major criminal conduct or gross negligence leading the government to levy an extremely large fine or penalty against the company or it goes after an executive officer or BOD member? Or even cause the government to file criminal charges? In an antitrust situation, if a company has provided employees and managers with appropriate antitrust training, an investigation will probably lead to nothing. That would be a typical everyday scenario. But what happens if despite training, an antitrust investigation leads to the finding of criminal conduct causing the government to levy a large fine: such as one hundred million or two hundred million dollars? So, you have two scenarios. The first is rather easy to quantify, the latter harder to quantify."

Lee continued. "The scenarios provide an analysis of the potential risks and the environment the risks could occur in. With that in mind it is then up to you as the legal risk manager to come up with a plan to mitigate them or manage them. Once you have analyzed the risks, what steps do you take? What corporate resources do you need to handle them? The risk models and or heat map can all be used to go management to ask for resources to implement a plan. So, once you assess, identify, score and analyze risks you can then go to management with a plan or a proposal to mitigate or manage risks. Some companies, depending on the industry, use charts that evaluate numerous legal risks in many forms, such as contractual risk, financial risk, operational risk, environmental risk and so on. So, for instance the legal risk model could look at contractual risk on a typical basis and quantify legal risk exposure to cost approx. ten thousand dollars while the extreme model could allocate a financial exposure of five hundred thousand dollars. Based on the critical risk evaluation you do; it is then up to you to propose plans to mitigate or manage the risk exposure."

"Also" Lee continued as he pulled out a chart from his briefcase, "why don't you look at the following legal risk scoring chart provided by Erudite Risk to get an idea about scoring legal risks and the tools to use. It is in the form of a heat map."

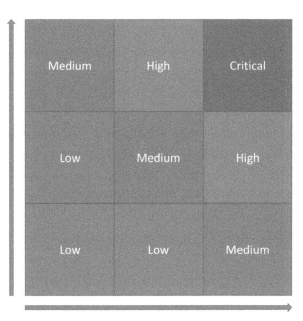

Figure 9-1

"What if your company has issues with its manufacturing line?" Lee asked.

"So many issues to think about" Eunice declared.

"Ah, I see. Well" said Lee, "I hope you have read chapter four on critical risk analysis techniques."

"Yes," replied Eunice. "Very interesting, it put things into perspective."

This meeting was the longest session Eunice and Lee had to date. Lee looked out over the Han River from the lounge. Lee pondered how long it would take for Eunice to really get it. *So much to teach her,* he thought. It was very important for companies to realize how important legal risk management is and what processes to implement. Even a company's corporate culture had to embrace it.

"You know" Eunice piped up, "we are having problems in operations. Too many losses. Maybe I can use a heat map to point that out."

"Right, you can. Conduct a comprehensive risk analysis of the operation processes you are interested in. Brainstorm with your team-ask yourself what risks are inherent in operations. Look at the data, controls in place, if any. Based on that identify the main risks and score them. Use a heart map to identify the major risks you scored and take it to Management."

Lee sipped his coffee. I think she is getting the risk management concepts. *Let me hope she understands it.* he thought.

"Well, I know you are busy. Come back in two weeks and we will talk about the next process in a legal risk management: program-developing and implementing a risk management plan. Remember, once you've assessed, identified, scored and evaluated risks, what do you do? What process or processes do you come up with to handle the situation? How do you manage the legal risks you've identified? Let's discuss next week after you have had time to think about it."

10   Responding to Legal Risk Issues-The Risk Management Plan

It had been two weeks, since Eunice had met with Lee. For some reason Lee had decided not to meet at the normal lounge coffee shop but the restaurant of the hotel instead. "I wonder why we are not meeting at a coffee shop." Eunice thought as she saw Lee looking at a menu. Sitting down across from Lee, she realized the restaurant was also famous for green tea, also one of Lee's favorites. Sure enough, he ordered green tea.

"Well" said Lee, looking up. "Anything going on?"

Eunice paused. "Yes. Management has asked that I prepare a legal risk management report or registry outlining risks and what to do about it."

"It looks like your management is interested in a briefing on risk" Lee said.

"Maybe, but I am not certain."

"How so"? Lee asked.

Eunice shook her head. "I don't think they completely understand what the risk issues and concepts are. I don't know if they are really taking this seriously or not, but just going through the motions. It looks like they are."

Lee pondered Eunice's statement. "It will be very interesting to see what your management has to say about your presentation. I think your management has to take risk seriously, especially the Board of Directors. The Board has a fiduciary duty to consider risks. What prevents a major crisis if a customer hears the risk issues facing FIVE

STAR which it hasn't been addressed and it then decides to change suppliers or vendors?"

"Nothing, I guess. But if FIVE STAR moves quickly on risk, won't it be considered a supplier of choice by most customers?"

"Perhaps they would." Lee answered. "FIVE STAR has to be seen in the industry as a company with not only good products but a company which has not only addressed all of the risks it faces or may face but risks to the supply chain and any risk that could affect its customer base. One of the questions you should ask FIVE STAR is whether it is in a position to assert itself in the marketplace without addressing the risk issues or not? Many companies have thought they are immune to investigations, audits or even bad press or PR coming out of risk events only to find out they were not. For instance, a company is never really prepared when it finds out it is subject to a cartel investigation. What happens if its export license gets revoked? Fines levied by regulators could be in the hundreds of millions of dollars. No company is really immune to risk"

"We will see if I can persuade them to address the risk situation" Eunice countered.

"By the way" she added "I've been thinking about the latest session including the charts you showed me up until now. The tools appear to be usable in almost any industry across product lines. It seems to me I can use the chart to brainstorm processes need across FIVE STAR's multiple product lines."

Lee nodded cautiously. "You can use it across industries or product lines as long as your data is up to date and you understand the risks each industry or division may face. Anyway, have you thought about the last assignment?"

"You mean the next process in a legal risk management program such as developing and implementing a risk management plan?" she countered.

"Yes, once you identify, access and analyze the risks your company faces, what is the next step? The answer of course, is to come up with a process or processes to manage the risk or risks. That is part of your job as in-house counsel or as a risk manager."

"Well, I guess that is what a risk management plan is all about. Once you identify, access and analyze the risks you need to come up with a way to address them. So, the plan would include recommendations on mitigating, transferring, eliminating or even accepting the risks that have been identified and analyzed. I am not certain really how to come up with a plan that does it though."

"Remember, what I said about ISO 3100 and other risk management models. They address risk management and lay out the steps. So, under ISO 3100 the step after risk analysis is treating the risk. By treating risk, you are to implement controls or processes that treat the risk by mitigating, eliminating or transferring the risk. So, the key is really to come up with the controls or procedures that addresses the risks at hand. The COSO standard calls for risk assessment and then risk response. In other words, what you will do in response to the risk such as accepting it, reducing it, sharing it or avoiding it. That is what a risk management program is about under COSO."

Lee looked at Eunice hoping she was in fact getting it. "You know what? I was going to wait until next time to show you this chart, but it might be very useful now. This chart lays out the basic process including the risk management plan and I think can give you some ideas." Lee pulled out a chart from his briefcase that Erudite Risk provided him and gave it to her.

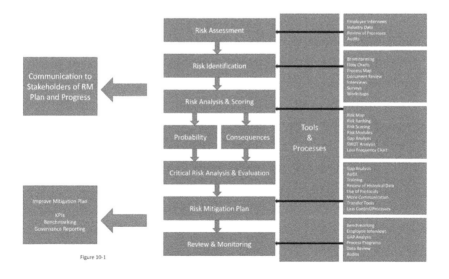

Figure 10-1

"This chart shows it all" he explained. "Besides looking at the chart, why don't you read chapter six and seven of Hopkins' book on legal risk management. I think that will help you understand. Let's meet after your presentation to management. It covers the basic principles at hand and helps pull things together."

Eunice looked at the chart and understood what he meant. She was suddenly excited about the possibilities it presented. She realized the complexity of the issues. "It appears that in first phases of the risk assessment plan, it is important to identify categories of risk, which may also identify the kinds of risk and their severity."

"Yes" admitted Lee. "Such categories could include be strategic, operational, financial, HR and regulatory. By looking at the categories of risk and identifying the major areas of risk, it is easier to manage the risk and come up with solutions. Perhaps the risks consist of weak internal controls or an absence of protocols or systems when dealing with the public or even a failure to appreciate governmental regulations."

Lee continued. "By using risk tools set forth in the chart, it will obviously help to identify the probability of risk and severity of the risk. Each business unit may want to develop tools to identify the risk and its severity within its own unit. Once the risk assessment is accomplished and the risk scoring tools are used to determine the probability and severity of such risk, a critical risk analysis must be conducted. And then you can formulate an action plan. It shows many tools you can use."

Eunice agreed. "It seems to me that the most important phase of a legal risk assessment is the implementation of an action plan. It can consist of training, audits, enforcing existing processes, and developing new processes and tools, as well as other procedures. It is the plan that will mitigate the legal risk a company faces not the processes themselves. And so, the risk management plan must be monitored."

"You are getting it" said Lee rather happily.

"Still" Eunice countered, "I wonder if this can be used in all uses, take employment or HR issues or risks for instance. Because of the Me Too movement, we have a large number of complaints. I wonder if a risk mitigation plan would work."

"Of course," opined Lee. "Remember the first step for any risk manager is to ask the hard questions such as -what management processes are in place that relate to employment issues? Go from there, go through all the steps and use tools to help mitigate risks. Processes are helpful tools especially in HR. Check with your HR team if it is aware of risk management processes and who handles them. What you may find out, is that since the acquisition, many people in HR left the company. Institutional memory maybe gone. Look into the processes. Maybe some have not been implemented."

11 Monitoring the Risk Management Plan

Eunice was on her way to the hotel near Namsan Mountain. Getting out of the taxi she realized not only how much she enjoyed her talks with Lee but that soon she would no longer have her talks with Lee to look forward to. She hoped there was at least two or three more talks

Seeing Lee sip his coffee, Eunice waived and sat down beside him. *How does he always get the table near the window?* she asked herself.

"Well" said Lee. "How did management take your ideas?"

"I think they were surprised at the number of risks I identified and the potential severity of the risks too. They were also concerned about the possible consequences of doing nothing, but the expense of handling the risks are also of concern to them. Some of the management liked my ideas and in fact one of the VPs asked that I become head of the loss control team. But, most of the Board of Directors were not really excited like I thought they should be. In fact, I think they are really weighing the cost of doing nothing as opposed to addressing the risk."

"Well, that's not surprising. Normally, management tends to think more about profit and the company's business plan, not the risks generated by the business plan or even the business. You need to sit down with them and really show them why they need to follow your proposals. In fact, now you can put everything together and make concrete proposals to mitigate the risks. It's hard to talk to the Board if you don't have a seat at the table. That's why I push the GCs I know or the VPs of Risk Management in organizations to demand a seat at the table or to at least have direct communications with the Board via an audit committee. Have you thought about your risk management plan and recommendations to address the risks you pointed out to them?"

"You are right" said Eunice. "I really need to sharpen my proposals."

Eunice continued. "Looking at the chart you gave me last time and reading Hopkins' book, I realized it's about using tools to come up with the right processes to address the risk, whether it is to avoid risk, mitigate risk or even transfer risk. The tools I saw in the chart were very helpful to think about what processes I should develop or at least think about. Each risk will require a different response or process to address it."

Eunice sipped her coffee and continued." So, I think it's about developing processes and coming up with action plans to implement the policies that address risks. Of course, once the right policies or procedures are in place they have to be implemented. This requires identifying the right departments or people to handle the implementation. So, if HR has a risk, the right person in HR has to be identified that can implement the processes to manage the risk. It also means that management has to agree with the risk management plan so the right resources can be given if needed to implement the plan and the plan's priority can be made known to all ranks of management though out the company. Everyone has to be on board with the plan or at least the implementation of the plan."

Lee looked up from his coffee and chuckled. "Maybe I should pay for the coffee today." Looking at Eunice, he continued. "Remember, there are trade-offs for everything. You have to quantify the risks or potential risks and come up with responses that are not only timely but cost effective. What good is a risk management process that costs more to implement than the potential cost of the risk event itself. You must also remember that you need to always keep the appropriate stakeholders in the communication loop when discussing the implementation of the processes. You must of course, identify those stakeholders. As you may know, in order to really tie everything together you have another step. Any idea on what it is?"

Eunice though for a moment." I need to monitor the plan to make certain it is working. Otherwise, there will be no way to calculate how effective the proposed process is until the risk event itself happens."

"Right you are" said Lee happily, thinking that she is really understanding the process. "You have to monitor or audit the plan after implementation. It depends of course on what kind of processes you are auditing, and the risks being considered. In some plans, the processes may be audited or monitored on a weekly or monthly basis, some plans need to be reviewed or audited once a year. It depends. Pulling out another chart, Lee pointed to it. This chart I showed you before. But looking at it in context with more detail shows it all- all the processes including the monitoring of the risks."

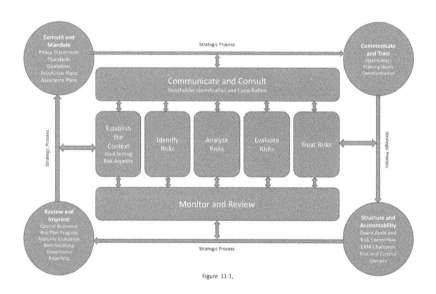

Figure 11-1,

Lee continued. "How do you know the action plan is working? What to you look for?"

"Well" said Eunice. "I think you were right in talking about the data. You have to look at the data, operational or otherwise. What does the data in fact say? So, if you are looking at potential antitrust risks or HR risks, and you put a policy in place of training, look at whether training was in fact accomplished. The data should tell you. Also, you may want to issue a questionnaire to the employees about the training to confirm they understand it."

"That's right" Lee said enthusiastically. "You're right. Look at the data. You may also want to review processes to see if they were in fact implemented. Create tools such as a checklist or memo in order for the people in charge of implementation to let you know if the process was implemented and how it is working. Look at business events that could be exposed to the risks you identified…what was the underlying result of the risk management process you put in place? Did it achieve the required result? If not, why not? Do you need to change the process or update the process? Look at the techniques and processes in place. You will only know if the work if you monitor the risk management processes that have been implemented. So, the last but perhaps most important piece of the overall risk management plan itself is the review or monitoring piece. Only then you know if you are right or if you are wrong."

Eunice suddenly grasped the issues. "This also means there has to be sufficient communication throughout the enterprise or the relevant division or even department to provide a realistic review of the data and processes involved to show whether the risk management processes implemented actually works or not. Communication is always an issue for most companies especially those that have a communication structure based on silos. So, the monitoring piece of the risk management process is very important and can't be taken for granted."

Lee was very happy Eunice was getting it. "True. So, when you develop your risk management plan and come up with a response, what tools do you use to adequately monitor or review the results of the implementation? That is a major question you have to think through as in each company and even in each division or departmental communication processes could be different. If you have employee turnover, major processes could be lost. Responsibilities of staff could be different. How data is collected and reviewed could be different. All this has to be thought out. Maybe a GAP analysis would help show you where you are."

As time wound down and Lee continued to sip his Americano, Eunice wondered if that was the last lesson from Lee. She was hoping for at least one or two more lessons but wasn't sure. She learned a great deal about risk and how to manage it but wondered if this was going to be the final meeting. Eunice's fears proved to be unfounded as Lee looked up from his coffee.

"Well" he said. "We have covered a lot of territory, but I think we need at least one or two more meetings. You see, managing risk, especially legal risk covers a lot of ground. Most risks are quantifiable and can be addressed through proactive risk management like we have been discussing. But some risks can't. These risks tend to result in a major crisis that could threaten the existence of a company. It is worthwhile to spend at least one more session discussing crisis management. Why don't you look at Denzenhall's book on crisis management- *Nail'Em!* It is an excellent little book. Steven Fink's book *Crisis Communications* is good too. I think it offers good advice on handling a crisis. Let's meet in several weeks near downtown Seoul for lunch and a discussion around managing a crisis. I will pick a place that makes a good club sandwich."

Lee pondered for a moment and then continued. "By the way, let me tell you about a friend of mine from my past. He was always taking a pro-active stance towards risk. His aim was to put in processes that could mitigate and even prevent class actions that were being filed time and time again against his company. He knew that if the class action issue was not resolved the company would go under. After an exhaustive review of the company's processes and an audit of the departments involved in the class action litigation, he realized that most class action litigation could be prevented if a number of preventative steps or processes were put in place starting from the beginning- the design stage of the product and going through all stages including the after-service stage of the product. It was a twenty-five-step process. He was so successful that he teamed up with me when my company began experiencing a rash of clash actions in the US. He came over from the division he was with to head up the risk department in my division. Again, it took a while to get our hands around what was happening. But by going through the risk management process and using all the tools available, as well as the processes he identified, we came up with the right processes for mitigating and preventing class actions. It also had a great impact on the company's loss control reserves."

"Wow" Eunice exclaimed. "Both of you were heroes."

"Yes and no" countered Lee. "I realized that risk management principles could be used to not only reduce the risk of class actions but could be used throughout a company to reduce all forms of legal risk. So, I decided to leave the company and start my own consulting company."

"Lee & Associates" Eunice confirmed.

"Yes, indeed. My friend however went back in-house at a major electronics company hoping to help apply risk management principles in the company. He found a great deal of resistance internally as each department had its own processes and of course people in various divisions had their own viewpoints and past history on how to handle problems. You can't expect division heads to just roll over without a fight when you challenge their ideas. So, he started from the ground up and tried to meet with various department heads about risk management principles. He eventually became a star and in fact the Assistant General Counsel and Director of Risk Management. You know why?"

"No" Said Eunice, looking perplexed.

"He realized that the company was set in its ways and he would have to wait for the right moment. It happened a year after he joined the company. A massive governmental audit that resulted in a DOJ investigation hit the company. In other words, a teachable moment! So, he ran with it. The company's management was so scared it gave him the resources he needed to put a full-scale risk management program in place. He is still there though I think he will retire soon."

Lee paused. He realized he had been talking longer that he should and hoped Eunice would start asking questions.

"It was smart to use the investigation as a teachable moment!" Exclaimed Eunice.

"Well, he had studied risk management from his class action days and saved the company millions of dollars. But he never made GC."

Eunice was surprised. "Why not?" she asked.

"He never made GC because he was too successful at what he did. So much so, he ruffled the feathers of some upper management folks. Being a GC in a large company sometimes entails a certain amount of politics. So, he made it to Assistant GC but could go no further."

"That's crazy" said Eunice. "He saved the company millions."

"You are right. But remember, it's easy to look back and expect he would rise to the top. But looking back I think he realized he made too many enemies and ruffled too many feathers. Maybe he didn't satisfy enough stakeholders. Remember, if you step on too many toes, no matter how right you are, sooner or later politics will take a toll, regardless if you are prepared or not. After all, you are in a corporate setting."

12 Managing a Crisis-Lee Points Out The Issues

Eunice was running late. The traffic into the northern part of Seoul was heavier than she expected causing her to miss the 12:00 pm appointment with Lee. She hoped he wasn't too upset.

Rushing into the lobby of the hotel, she found Lee at the lobby coffee shop enjoying a club sandwich. She thought it was odd he wasn't drinking any coffee.

"This is the best club sandwich in Seoul" Lee remarked as Eunice sat down at the table. "Why don't you have one? The other items on the menu are tasty as well. And of course, the deli in the basement has a very good bakery in case you want pastries or bread to take home."

Eunice ordered a club sandwich and coffee. She looked around the lounge realizing how crowded it was.

"I read Fink's book on crisis communications. You are right, crisis management is really different from managing risk on a regular basis. I didn't realize the issues that must be addressed while managing a major crisis."

"Yes, managing a crisis can be complicated. Let's remember however, if not successfully managed, a crisis can lead to the end of the company. It's that serious."

Lee continued. "The problem with managing a crisis is that a crisis could be a major unpredictable event or an in fact a major predicable one. Either way, the crisis event could be a catastrophe that has disastrous consequences if it is not managed properly. Some companies fail to manage a crisis until it is too late."

Eunice thought for a moment. "You are right. I've read about companies collapsing because of crisis that were not properly handled." She remembered the aftermath of Enron, WorldCom and even Toyota with its past brake issues. Many stakeholders, inside and outside the companies were affected. Of course, Enron never recovered and Ebbers at WorldCom went to jail.

Lee looked at Eunice. Knowing she was getting to where he was going. He continued, "Think about events that could cause a crisis. There are many kinds of events including financial, environmental, product related and so on. And if they happen in an international setting, another layer of complexity is added."

"Why do you think crisis are so hard to manage?"

"Well" began Lee. "Several reasons, I think. These days, because of the internet, companies have to get out in front of a crisis, or the bad PR will kill them quickly. It used to be companies had time to react and get out front. Now they don't. So, if companies don't have a strategy in place to address the crisis, it's hard to get out in front. In fact, by most accounts, a company has twenty-four hours to put a crisis management strategy in place once it becomes aware of the underlying event. This twenty-four-hour period is sometimes referred to as 'the golden hour.' If a company isn't prepared, twenty-four hours is not long enough to think things through. Of course, In-house counsel have to understand their roles in a crisis as well. They have to manage legal liability of course but they have to balance it with business considerations. They also have to help the PR team educate the public on the case and make certain all legal regulations are followed."

Lee sipped his coffee. "Another issue is that many companies refuse to acknowledge the existence of a crisis until it is normally too late. Remember, a crisis unfolds in a series of stages and not in a vacuum. First, there are early indications of a crisis brewing followed then by actual warnings of a crisis followed by the crisis exploding and overwhelming management. It is at this stage that most companies try and resolve the crisis, but it is usually too late. The crisis morphs, PR gets really bad, the impact of the crisis deepens, the stakeholders and shareholders get very worried and upset and then it's curtains. The key to properly managing a crisis is to acknowledge the existence of a crisis at the beginning and to have a crisis management plan in place."

Eunice began to get worried. FIVE STAR Pharma Korea had not considered how to handle any kind of crisis that she knew of. It had been lucky up to this point. But could it weather the storm if a major crisis happened tomorrow?

Lee continued. "The major problem with handling a crisis is that communications play an important role. When you look at the timeline of the average crisis: a company not only has to determine what need for communications exist (internally and externally) but also must have the communications drafted and ready to go within twelve hours of the start of the crisis. Within twenty-four hours, Management should have a plan in place including a communications plan and should be talking to the media or have a third party talking to the media for it. If you don't have a crisis management plan already in existence before the event, you probably won't get your hands around it in time. It's that simple."

Lee had an idea to drive the point home. He pulled out a chart from his briefcase. "Look at this chart from Erudite. Here is a chart showing the three sides of managing a crisis within a company. Look at what it shows."

Figure 12-1

"Wow. The chart puts things into perspective." Eunice replied. "You can see there are three major sides to managing a crisis and how it impacts the business plan and goals of a company. Communication is one of the tree sides. It's important as is the legal/regulatory side of things. Of course, operations too. To manage the crisis, you have to think about all three sides of crisis management."

Eunice sat back and pondered the slide then asked. "What do you think FIVE STAR should be doing?"

"It has to come up with a crisis management strategy plan. Normally a plan consists of steps including planning for a crisis, appointing a crisis manager, establishing a crisis management team, creating a crisis communication plan and in some cases appointing an international crisis manager."

Lee continued, "FIVE STAR should be thinking about all the crisis events it can imagine and run simulations on them to understand the impact and consequences of the impact. And then prepare!"

"For instance, what happens if one of the machines in your company's main manufacturing line that is used to find defects in the drug manufacturing process breaks down? How long would it take to come back online? Also, say you can cover by finding alternative sources of supply, how long would that take to do? How long to cover the losses? Remember, if you lose productivity and can't supply customers on time you could lose everything or at least major contracts. If you lose a month of revenue because the line is down, not only would you lose revenue but the trust of the market. So, run a scenario and see what happens. The longer it takes to handle a crisis, the fewer options you have to pull things out. You should be doing this already by now."

"Who should be the crisis manager?" Eunice asked, grasping the enormity of the concept.

"I think the crisis manger needs to be someone who thinks out of a box. He or she shouldn't be part of the existing management team, especially if the team helped cause the crisis. He or she wouldn't know what to do or how to resolve it. You really need someone who is practical, pro-active and thinks out of the box."

Lee was worried. He had heard rumblings that FIVE STAR Pharma Korea had manufacturing issues and hoped it would not blow up. He thought for a moment. "I think you need to sit down with management and map out basic crisis scenarios for your industry, whether it is a manufacturing related crisis, environmental one, etc. You need to do it soon. Any problems give me a call. Before you leave today, I want to ask a question that I think is relevant."

"What's that?" asked Eunice.

Lee was silent for a second and then piped up. "In case of a crisis do you know all of the relevant insurance policies and the appropriate notification deadlines? Also, if a crisis involves regulators, are you aware of the basic time frames in which to notify and or involve the regulators? And, who are the appropriate regulators?"

"You see" stated Lee. If you don't or if the crisis management team that is created doesn't, once a crisis happens it may be too late. You have to be on top of it before a crisis develops. So, from an in-house perspective I would advise you think in terms of civil liability, as there will probably be a great deal of litigation at the end. So how do you minimize civil liability and perhaps criminal liability too? That is what you should be thinking about."

Lee suspected Eunice was getting overwhelmed. Looking directly at her he continued.

"I know you are busy. You have a lot on your table. Let's meet next month to consider the implications of crisis management. As you can see, there is a lot to consider. By the way, pay for the sandwiches."

13 The Crisis-Eunice Puts Things Into Perspective

Lee was enjoying his coffee in Myeong-dong, one of Seoul's main upscale shopping areas in the northern part of Seoul. Unlike Gangnam, Seoul's most famous shopping district located south of the Han River, Myeong-dong was a smaller and more centralized area. But like Gangnam, Myeong-dong had its fair share of world class coffee shops, and so Lee was enjoying a coffee latte that morning. He had read about FIVE STAR Pharma in the news the week before and hoped things had not spiraled out of control.

True to form, Eunice arrived at the agreed upon time. Looking a little harried, Eunice sat down across from Lee.

"Well" said Lee, looking up from his morning paper, "Tell me what happened. Did you resolve it?

"You were right" Eunice replied. "A crisis did happen. One of our two main production lines for the heart medication 'Viathoel B' went offline as the optical quality control unit or OQCU broke down. We were unable to fix it in time and failed to meet out production quota. Not only that, but someone notified the press about it, we still don't know who. Then, we were contacted by a major customer who heard about it and of course HQ in NY called me as well. As we are the only producer of Viathoel B in Korea, it looked like we would have a catastrophic quarter. If the news got out that we couldn't meet our production quota, our parent company's stock could take a nosedive."

"I saw something about it in the press last week but since then I haven't seen anything" Lee confirmed.

Eunice replied, "I was able to get a crisis management team together like we discussed last time. Fortunately, I got it assembled just before the crisis hit. We had a safety engineer lead the crisis team as he knew about the manufacturing process and our VP of Communications handled the communications portion. I was concerned about the legal and regulatory portion. I reviewed all of the insurance contracts, so I knew our reporting obligations to the insurers as well as the local regulators. Viathoel B is very important in Korea. I didn't know how important until I started doing research."

"Great" Lee replied. "What else happened?"

"Well, you know about the crisis stages we talked about. I went back and found Service Department reports discussing the issues with the line that collapsed. No one addressed it because of the cost but Management had been warned about the possibility the line would stop working. I was able to argue to Management however, using the reports to outline how the manufacturing line could break down, so they took their collective heads out of the sand in time to notice a crisis could happen."

Eunice sipped her coffee and continued. "Luckily, just before the line broke down, we went through several crisis scenarios and figured out the potential financial impact if the line broke down and we lost our major customers. That was enough to spur management to allocate funds on trying to repair the line as well as considering ways to find alternative sources of supply to cover our customers. We were also worried about the time needed to recalibrate the OQCU as it could take up to one week to recalibrate once it was fixed."

"So, what was the outcome?" Lee inquired.

"We were able to come up with an alternative source of supply two days after our line went down. So, covering our lack of supply quickly worked out this time. And we faced no regulatory liability as we filed the appropriate paperwork with the Korean FDA on time. It took much longer to find the appropriate parts to fix the line, but we eventually found the parts to repair it with. Luckily, we were prepared to recalibrate it quickly once it was fixed. It didn't take as long as we thought it would."

Eunice took a breath and continued. "The Service Department reports which had remained unread until I looked at them in detail actually contained enough information for the line engineers to figure out what parts were failing and why. No one in Management read the reports until I stepped in. They assumed engineering would simply tell them. Had we not conducted a crisis scenario at the beginning and figured out the impact and next steps, there was no way we could have recovered within two days. It would have taken at least three to four weeks which would have been catastrophic for us. We also reported the potential claim to our insurance company, and we informed Korea's FDA about the issue in a timely fashion, so we had no issues from a regulatory standpoint. Once recalibrated we had the FDA certify the calibration and we were able to get back up to speed."

"Ah" said Lee. "You were able to get a handle on it quickly. That's good. Remember, the longer it takes to handle a crisis the greater the impact. Here, look at this chart that Erudite created on the impact of a crisis. It will give you an idea on the legal impact of a crisis and puts crisis management of the crisis into perspective."

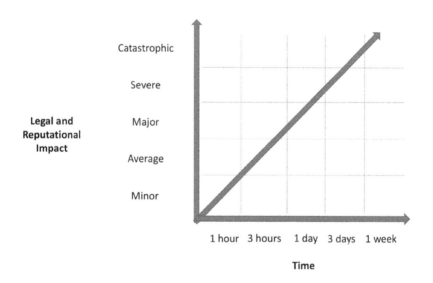

Figure 13-1

Eunice looked at the chart and nodded, "we were lucky. But we still lost a few customers we shouldn't have. They apparently weren't notified in time to keep the contracts in place with us. They opted to go a different route."

Lee sipped his coffee and thought for a second. "I think you did a great job in solving the issues that caused the crisis. Kudos. But some of your customers or stakeholders didn't know it in time. Have you looked at your communication processes? Who is communicating to your regulators and other stakeholders? What communication protocols are in place? You may also want to check the basics of your communications plan again. Did your PR department get a budget approved that allowed them to pay for social media or send out the necessary letters or notifications? Sometimes, the communications piece plays second fiddle to solving the crisis- which can be disastrous. Think about what happened to a local hamburger franchise in Seoul lately. Horrible communications.

14 Lee Discusses Communications As Part of Risk Management

Eunice was tired. She had been working non-stop to help manage the recent crisis FIVE STAR Pharma Korea had faced. With helpful advice from Lee she was able to put processes in place just in time though they lost a few important customers. Now she was running late to see Lee two weeks after the crisis. She knew her meetings with Lee were wrapping up. "Maybe this will be the last meeting" she thought.

Eunice saw Lee at the usual lounge coffee shop. She settled down in the chair next to him. Lee looked at her for a second and continued sipping his coffee.

"Our usual meetings are wrapping up." he said. "I think you have grasped most of what I had to say or at least I would like to believe that."

"I can always use more advice" Eunice said with a grin. "You know I thought our crisis was resolved but…"

Lee looked at her. "Well, there are a few more things I want to talk to you about if you have time that may actually help answer your questions. Actually, it covers lessons you may have already learned during the crisis last month."

"What's that?" Eunice asked.

"Think about the risk management processes and steps that we have discussed including the crisis you recently went through. What is the common denominator in all the steps? What determines how successful you will be?"

Eunice thought for a moment. Something finally dawned on her. "I think communication is very important part of every process we looked at."

"Precisely" said Lee. "Think about it. Each process you go through, whether risk identification or risk evaluation and so on requires a certain degree of communication. Companies that have a great deal of internal communication tend to handle risk or the job of managing risk better than those that don't."

"Why is that? Asked Eunice, happy that she was right about communication but perplexed that it was so important."

"When it comes to legal risk management or risk management for that matter, it depends on the data. It also depends on how the data is used or processed. This is determined to a certain degree by a company's internal communication structure."

Lee continued. "Think about the risk management chart and the tools that can be used to come up with a mitigation plan. Each and every process, to a certain degree, required communication, whether it's communication between departments or communication between divisions or even communication between profit and cost centers. And of course, to and from management such as top to bottom or bottom to top. The more communication there is, the better. For instance, think about the Board of Directors. How does Management communicate to the Board and how does the Board communicate to the Management?"

Eunice thought for a moment. "Isn't there a cost factor too?" she asked.

"You are right" replied Lee.

"The more communication, the easier and more efficient it is to come up with risk management processes and strategies as well as to implement them. This includes audits, training and other processes and tools. Communication will determine how effective it is. And of course, if it is effective and efficient, the costs to implement it are lower than otherwise."

"So really, managing legal risk also takes into consideration communications" she concluded out loud. Eunice was ecstatic over the idea.

Lee was happy that Eunice appeared to be getting it. "So, in your opinion, how do you increase communications in your company?"

Eunice pondered it for a moment. "In my last position on the compliance team I worked on compliance issues. I noticed that the compliance team or department had set up an internal mailbox for employees to post questions or concerns anonymously. Maybe something like that."

"Good idea" Lee replied. "Why not expand it out and have an internal website for all employees to ask questions or post ideas as well as to receive communications from your Management. Maybe you can ask your IT department to come up with that or something like that. In fact, why not start a loss control committee with people from Service, HR, Legal, Engineering, Risk, Quality Control, etc. They can meet once a month to address loss control issues or even quality control issues. Communications between the departments will increase rapidly once people start talking to each other and share ideas, especially on how to save the company money."

Lee pulled out a familiar chart but showing the importance of communications in a risk setting. Look at the chart we used in the past to discuss the risk management process. I've added communications in the chart to show how important communications really is.

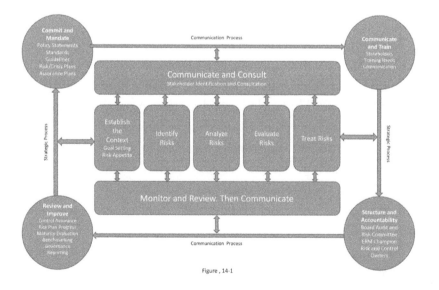

Figure , 14-1

"Doesn't the concept of communications deserve a few more meetings? I mean it is a large topic."

"It is a broad topic." Lee replied. "Many books have been written about it. It is taught in college classes as well. But more emphasis is placed on PR communications these days, not internal communications. That's why I brought up the idea of a crisis communication plan when we discussed crisis management. Many companies simply think a PR plan is enough which misses the point. So, for risk management purposes, internal communications happen to be very important. How you communicate a risk management plan to internal stakeholders is also of great importance. Of course, during a crisis, communications is very important. There are a number of communication steps that have to happen for a successful outcome during a crisis. It is very important during a crisis that the crisis management team realizes that it must communicate with stakeholders, communicate with shareholders, communicate with regulators, communicate with business partners and creditors and of course communicate with the public. Winning the hearts of the public is important."

"Here is another assignment if you want it" offered Lee.

"What is that?" asked Eunice.

"When you go back to your office think about all the ways to improve internal communications. Do a risk audit on that too. You will be surprised on the ideas that get generated. Brainstorm with your communications department or PR team if you have one. Remember, it is not only about the adequacy of that data but how and when the data gets communicated throughout the organization."

Eunice thought for a moment. "Ok. Good idea."

But then she continued. "But haven't you heard? I am leaving the office soon. Upper Management liked my ideas so much that they want me to take over the risk department of DR Telecoms- the telecoms company they just acquired."

"Congratulations!" exclaimed Lee. "I hope you realize that your hard work has paid off."

"Yes" Eunice replied. "But who knows how long I will stay with DR Telecoms or FIVE STAR? I may ruffle some feathers. As you pointed out, you always have to consider politics."

Eunice looked at Lee. "It's time for me to be going. I have a driver coming to pick me up. Perks of the new position."

"You know what?" Lee admitted. "I think there is one or two more issue to discuss. Why don't you come back in a few weeks if you have time for a meeting?"

Eunice nodded. "Sounds like a plan."

Lee looked around the lobby after Eunice left, contemplating the last few months and the impact his lessons had on Eunice's career. Knowing he made another risk management convert he slowly finished his ice Americano.

15   Corporate Governance and the Impact of Corporate Culture

Eunice was rather sad the meetings with Lee were about to end. Still, after all this time she had yet to receive an invoice from Lee despite the time he spent with her. *Maybe he really meant he would do it pro bono*, she admitted to herself.

Eunice found Lee at the lobby of the hotel, where they first met. Where it all began. He was reading the newspaper for a change instead of sipping a coffee. Looking up, Lee greeted Eunice.

"Well, you may have wondered why I decided upon another meeting." Lee said.

"Yes" Eunice replied

"I decided to offer another meeting, because we really didn't spend much time on the topic, I think is very important. Corporate governance and how LRM fits in with it." Lee put down the paper.

"You see, corporate governance not only implies corporate structure and corporate leadership, but in essence it also covers corporate culture. When you think of corporate governance you also think of corporate culture as well…i.e. not only the corporate management structure and associated obligations such as disclosure requirements but corporate vision, values and ethics that help define the company's working environment and moral values."

"Well we talked about it briefly but not too much" Eunice said.

"So, when thinking about LRM, as company has to think about how it fits in the company structure and culture. Corporate culture is being looked at more and more as an important part of corporate governance. Think about the scandals in the past involving the misuse or failure of corporate governance and how culture played a part. Think about WorldCom for instance. Yes, Ebbers played a major role in the fiasco, but the Board received blame as well. Why? Because the Board failed to adequately control Ebbers. It had a fiduciary obligation to protect its shareholders but failed to confront Ebbers and gave in to the loose corporate culture that was prevalent under Ebbers. That resulted in a corporate governance failure."

Eunice pondered what Lee said. Corporate governance was key to the implementation of a robust LRM program, but corporate culture also had a role to play.

"You are telling me then, that the beginning of any legal risk management or LRM assessment in a corporation, you have to also assess the corporate big picture. Is the company ethical, are corporate values clearly defined, is the company operating as ethically as it should, etc.?"

"Right" said Lee. "We can discuss the various stages of LRM, but it will be hard to implement an LRM strategy throughout the company if a careful assessment of corporate culture in not undertaken as well. The leaders at the top should have an understanding of corporate culture which should be reflected in corporate governance. So, you need to ask the hard questions at the beginning, such as how employees handle conflict in the organization, do employees work well together, does the company value performance and whether the company encourages its employees? After all, in a compliance setting, if employees know they will be punished if they report violations, what good is a reporting system? Your legal risk management tools might not be as effective as they should because not many employees will use them."

Eunice pondered Lee's assertions. "I really need to not only think about LRM programs, but also how they get rolled out depending on the corporate governance of the company including the prevailing corporate culture."

"Yes" said Lee. "The processes we discussed are very important. But so is corporate governance and culture. There has been a great deal of research on corporate culture and its effects on corporate governance.

To get a good introduction to corporate governance consider how enterprise risk management or ERM as we call it impacts it. Why don't you get a copy of Lam's book on ERM called *Enterprise Risk Management*? An interesting read. Read the chapters that cover corporate governance".

16   Eunice Considers Insurance and Its Uses

Lee found himself at his favorite table near the window of the hotel lounge in Seoul. He realized he had enjoyed his discussions with Eunice and hoped she had gotten something out of his thoughts on legal risk management of in his own words LRM. Today may be the last time they would probably meet Lee thought. Lee knew that Eunice will not only be promoted but will probably be transferred out of the country as most expat managers leave Korea after a few years. There was of course a chance he could be wrong, and she would stay longer than he thought. But handling the risk of the newly acquired telecoms company was a big job that would eventually require her to probably leave. Sipping on his ice Americano Lee saw Eunice approach and sit down next to him.

"How are you doing today?" asked Lee.

"I am a little worried about FIVE STAR." Eunice replied.

"I know they are looking at my suggestions on managing legal risk, but I think they still don't get it or really don't care. The crisis is over and that all they care about."

Lee looked at her thoughtfully. "That's really not unexpected. They failed to put a basic risk management process in place even though they are in the pharmaceutical business and their only lawyer left."

"True, but I thought they would take a closer look once we overcame our crisis several months ago."

"You may have to talk with them not only about processes but a few basic risk management tools to get them thinking more about risk.

Which is why I wanted to talk with you at least one more time." Lee stated.

Eunice nodded.

Lee continued. "Though we have covered everything in some detail, it is always useful to think about risk management strategies that a company should consider." Lee pulled out a chart and showed it to Eunice.

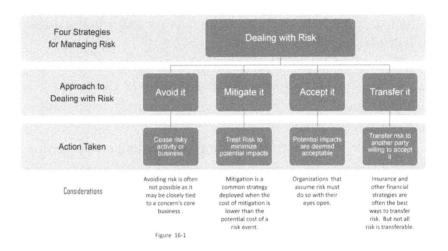

Figure 16-1

"What is this?" Eunice asked.

"It's a chart outlining the four basic or standard strategies dealing with risk management. My friends at Erudite Risk created it. Mainly, avoidance of risk, transfer of risk, mitigation of risk and acceptance of risk. Each strategy requires a company to make a conscious decision to use processes or tools to implement the risk management strategy. One of the basic strategies a company can use is the transfer of risk. As you know, companies can implement that strategy on a regular basis through contract provisions or by using insurance."

"Ah. You are right. Maybe I need to discuss basic strategies with them."

"Insurance bears more consideration than it usually gets" said Lee. "A true well thought out insurance plan goes a long way to help transfer legal risk in many situations. Consider the insurance aspects of the crisis you had."

"True" admitted Eunice.

"So, let's discuss insurance a little. Managing risk requires the identification, evaluation, qualification and mitigation or transfer of risk. Risk of course being primarily a loss. Some risks that are speculative, can result in a gain which is not insurable. Most risks however are pure or absolute risks that will result in losses and are insurable. So, insurance, if properly used, can be an effective tool to transfer risk or at least mitigate it."

"I see" said Eunice. "That's where risk evaluation and quantification come in. Insurance companies need to analyze the industry and historical losses a company has in order to properly forecast internal and external loss trends."

"Absolutely!" exclaimed Lee, knowing that Eunice was getting it. "In order for a company to have adequate insurance coverage, it has to look at the total cost of insurable risk. This means that an insurance provider or even insurance broker who puts out insurance coverage to bid needs to determine the most cost-effective way to retain and transfer risk. So, a company with property concerns must decide how much to insure property for while retaining a certain amount of risk. Companies who manufacture products have to decide how much to ensure products for while retaining some risk too. Maybe the companies retain some risk by self-insuring or just deciding how much deductible they should pay. You can only insure a certain amount of risk, but not all of it. And credit risk insurance may protect you from insolvent customers."

"So, in essence, to properly insure against risk or in our case legal risk, we go back to the old data integrity argument again. That determines the cost of insurance and applicability of coverage."

"That's right. You also have to look at the magnitude and complexity of risk that companies now face from cyber-crimes, terrorism, and even public pandemic diseases to see that risks are interconnected. So, companies now face a wide range of risks that must be properly managed. It is not only critical that a company manage risks to overcome crisis but that it manages risks to survive. That's where insurance comes in. So why don't you have a talk with your company's insurance department. Are all key risks identified and planned for? How does the company view insurance as a risk transfer tool?"

"You are right", admitted Eunice. "I can use insurance as a way to discuss risk at the management level."

Lee thought for a moment. "You should start by determining ten or so key risks your organization faced last year and whether the risks resulted in loss of income. Then determine what processes were used to identify the key risks and whether the Board or Management were aware of the risks. That way, it's possible to see whether or not Management and or the Board was in fact aware of the need for insurance."

Eunice pondered what Lee said. "That way, I can show the company the reasons why not only insurance was needed but why risk management is really necessary."

"Right. Remember, there is a link between risk management maturity and financial performance. Those companies that manage risk actively have a better return on equity than those who don't. Equity increases as risk management practices improves. In fact, stock price volatility decreases as risk management practices starts to improve. So, it really behooves the management of any organization to get behind risk management."

"I see."

"So, in the long run, an insurance program is a good way to jump start a risk management process. Consider that."

Eunice considered what Lee said. "I wonder if it could have helped us last week! One of our customers, the XYZ Company went belly up. It bought $10 Million worth of inventory from us 30 days net and failed to pay after 30 days. If I knew it was going insolvent, I would have called the shipping company and told them to turn the trucks around."

Lee chuckled. "Yea, I remember reading about XYZ in the paper. Well, it may not be too late, but remember, transferring risk is one of your goals. Credit risk insurance is a good tool to use if available. Why don't you call your broker and see if you can get a credit risk insurance policy on XYZ? It is probably too late but try."

17   Lee Discusses Checklists With Eunice

Lee was looking forward to seeing Eunice. It had been a month since he last saw her, but he wanted to meet her one last time over coffee to see how she was doing. As an excuse, he mentioned he had an important topic to discuss. So, he sat down at the lobby lounge near the window and waited for Eunice to come in. Seeing Eunice come in made Lee smile. Well he thought, she looks like she is doing well. Her clothes looked very expensive as did her newly acquired briefcase.

Eunice saw Lee sipping coffee and sat down across from him. "I thought we finished our discussions" she said laughing.

"Well, I thought we could do with one more. I had been going through the notes in my desk recently and stumbled across a note on checklists. I completely forgot about it. Checklists are one of the least appreciated but easy to use tools to help manage and control legal risks. I thought you might be interested in discussing them. Remember, when it comes to implementing a myriad of processes, you need to know all of them are being covered. Are the right questions being asked? What tools do you use for it? Checklists!"

Eunice's interest peaked. "Sure. Of course."

"Well, I like to use checklists on a regular basis for many departments as checklists bring to focus not only risks that have been encountered in the past but can be tailored for a particular industry or sector or business division and cover potential or future risks."

"What are checklists?" asked Eunice.

"Checklists are a list of topics, questions or items normally derived from the risks encountered previously that provide a convenient means to rapidly and easily identify possible risk. They take the form of either a series of questions or a list of topics or items or ideas that should be or need to be considered. Organizations may generate checklists for themselves or make use of standard checklists available from their particular industry or business sector. The nice part about checklists is that they are easy to create (once you know the right questions to ask) and use as a method of reducing risk. Surprisingly, departments in many organizations have failed to create checklists, probably because they are afraid to ask the really tough questions. But as a risk manager or in-house counsel, your job is to ask the tough questions!"

Lee continued. "For example, if you are in a manufacturing company which designs products, you should have a checklist about the safety steps that must be followed instead of trying to reinvent the wheel by figuring out what potential safety issues actually exists. Checklists can be used forever once the right questions are asked. In essence, once created for a certain line of business, the checklist or checklists can be used over and over again. It should be noted that checklists should be reviewed on a periodic basis and updated to reflect new standards or newly discovered risks and/or processes. Things do change, but still they are a great tool."

Eunice started to understand the implications of using checklists. Interested, she began asking questions. "What are the types of checklists that can be used?"

"Well, the kinds of checklists are endless. But some of the most common involve day to day processes."

Pulling out a sheet of paper Lee began to read off a list of checklists that can be used.

They included the following such as:

Checklists for Manufacturing Companies

- Do written procedures for the design program exist?
- Are there written procedures for the development of specifications?

- Are there procedures for construction and testing and prototypes?
- Have malfunctions been looked at?
- Can the product be manufactured in accordance with the specifications?
- Serviceability: Are the products too difficult to service or maintain correctly
- Is everyone in the design department familiar with all design procedures and processes?

Checklists for New Product Introduction

- Can your company show a concern for safety?
- What are your safety margins?
- What are your safety margins relative to material specifications?
- Do you have documentation of analyses and tests?
- Did your engineers test the lifecycle of the product?
- Have you conducted a failure and hazard analysis?
- Have you conducted a worst-case analysis?
- Does your design include a fail-safe design?
- What are the hazards (use and misuse) of your product?
- What are your warnings and instructions?
- What inspection and quality control steps did you take?
- Was the product evaluated by an independent laboratory?

"What if you are drafting the warning and labels for products your company is manufacturing?" asked Lee. "Wouldn't a checklist of questions help in the drafting of warnings?" Lee handed Eunice another list.

Typical warnings for a manufacturing company:

- Are warnings adequate?
- Do warnings address misuse of product?

- Do warnings cover inherent hazards?
- Are hazards properly covered?
- Do warnings warn users against obvious risks?
- Do warnings clearly state the consequences of improper use?
- Do warnings warn users against all risks?
- Do warnings reasonably communicate the seriousness of harm that may result from improper use?

Lee looked up from reading his list. "As you can see, checklists containing the right questions or many to do items can be easily used to mitigate risk. You need to know the right questions to ask which also means you need to understand the issues surrounding potential risks. This requires that you need to know your industry, business sector or organization in order to properly tailor the checklists to your needs. Especially in the pharmaceutical business."

Eunice nodded in agreement. Yes, checklists are a very important tool she thought. She could use them in any industry. "Well, it has been an honor to talk with you all of these months. "Our talks really helped FIVE STAR and of course me too. Thanks for everything. You turned me into a risk management convert."

Summary

LRM focuses on processes that control, manage, and mitigate an organization's legal exposure. The processes can be preventive in nature, such as training or implementation of insurance programs. An example of a preventive process would be the implementation of a compliance program. This can minimize fines, lawsuits, and investigations.

To be successful, LRM processes need to be properly applied in an organization's structure. If applied in a corporate setting, such processes should be controlled by the Law Department or Risk Management Department covering such areas as oversight of product safety issues, insurance coverage, and compliance. The RMD or Law Department must take an active role managing risk management functions and applying such programs.

The mandate to apply and manage LRM processes usually comes from executive management, including the board of directors. To be effective, the BOD must authorize and approve such programs. Hence, the BOD can only do so when fully informed on the necessity of such programs.

LRM processes take place in stages, normally prior to litigation (pre-litigation) or during lawsuits or investigations (the litigation stage) and claims. During pre-litigation, the company can take an "offensive" approach to prevent claims, such as the use of insurance or product risk management programs. Otherwise, LRM processes can be used during litigation in a more reactive manner, such as using tools to centralize and manage litigation in order to control costs.

Remember, legal missteps can lead to a major crisis. Therefore, the LRM process must be properly implemented in a corporation. Such implementation is discussed in a more detailed fashion in Part Two of this book.

To consider the implications of Part One of this book, review chapters 1-17 and then ask the following questions:

- What stage of risk management is my company presently operating in?
- What risk management concepts are being used?
- How can I assist my company to focus on legal risk management concepts?
- How can I best use risk management concepts at my business?
- What processes should I focus on to minimize the exposure of legal risk in my organization?
- What is the risk appetite of my company or organization?
- What tools should I consider using?

For more information on legal risk management and related topics please see my blog at www.Seoullegalriskmgmt.com

Part Two

Implementation of Legal Risk Management

18 Applying Legal Risk Management in a Corporate Setting

Legal risk management processes and procedures must be applied to provide risk management expertise and to prevent loss due to claims, litigation, and investigations and fines. LRM, when properly applied in a corporate setting, whether under the control of the company's law department or under the control of a separate division such as compliance or insurance, should cover general areas of responsibility or functions. This could involve such processes as:

- Periodic risk assessment of the company's operating divisions and departments, and reporting the results to management
- Developing solutions to risk management issues
- Advising the corporation on insurance coverage issues and potential alternatives for coverage
- Oversight of the company's defense of product safety litigation and claims and advise management and legal on a regular basis on product safety matters
- Monitoring of product safety issues and analyzing the need for governmental reporting and/or taking corrective action
- Oversight of the company's information and document retention program
- Compliance review
- Development of training programs
- Monitoring compliance issues

- Training the company's employees on risk management, product safety, and often various legal issues such as antitrust, product liability or intellectual property (IP) issues

In order to apply LRM in a company or corporate setting, legal and management must take an active role in applying the above areas of responsibility through processes or systems implemented within the company. Normally, a Risk Management Department (RMD) will be established separately or in Legal, Compliance, or other divisions that will have certain risk management functions, responsibilities, or mandates across the company or organization as a whole.

The issues facing many companies when dealing with legal risk management, whether through a stand-alone department—RMD—or within Legal or Compliance, is that divisions and/or departments within a corporation often fail to effectively partner with RMD or Compliance. This, in turn, leads to improper handling of major legal and sensitive issues, which can lead to legal claims, fines, and liabilities.

Effective use of the RMD or Compliance departments is important.

19 Legal Risk Management and Corporate Governance

19.1 US Obligations

Risk management as part of good corporate governance has become popular in many countries due to recent scandals such as WorldCom and Enron. Due to such scandals, the Sarbanes-Oxley Act (SOX) was introduced in the United States in 2002. SOX requires, among other things, that proper internal financial controls be established in publicly traded companies as well as whistleblower provisions and compliance policies. In fact, the U.S. laws and regulations regarding compliance requires that the board of directors are not only trained in compliance but also has compliance oversight. Similar measures have been passed in other jurisdictions as well.

The result of SOX and other laws in other jurisdictions was to force upon the board of directors (BOD or Board) the obligation of ensuring the proper financial controls are in place and that such controls would be properly followed and maintained.[1]

As such, risk management processes in general should be considered by the BOD in light of the board's fiduciary and legal responsibilities.

---

[1]   Paul M. Collier, *Fundamentals of Risk Management for Accountants and Managers*, (Elsevier, 2009), 15–19.

19.2 Fiduciary Oversight

Legal risk management not only plays an important part in the success or failure of a corporation, but it is so important that it must be elevated to the board of directors for such LRM processes to be effective. As the Board of a company owes a fiduciary duty and obligation to the corporation, such duty requires a Board of Directors that is fully informed and knowledgeable on major issues of risk. Whether it is ERISA issues, compliance issues, SOX, currency risk, antitrust, M&A issues, etc., the BOD must be fully informed to make the appropriate decisions involving the management of the company. Due to its very nature, the BOD cannot escape its fiduciary obligations with regard to understanding and approving LRM processes.

Obviously, to protect the board as well as officers from frivolous lawsuits, including shareholder actions, a company should purchase directors and officers insurance (D&O insurance). Whether to D&O insurance is a question that must be decided in the context of legal risk management. Good corporate governance requires the board to be fully informed as to the major risk issues facing the company. D&O insurance may be necessary to protect the BOD as well as executive management from lawsuits stemming from fiduciary responsibilities or lack thereof.

Failure to properly elevate risk issues to the board level is not only a failure of proper corporate governance but of LRM processes as well. Authority to implement many LRM processes must come from the BOD of a company, or its counterpart in other organizational forms. Therefore, failure to properly inform the BOD on LRM related issues can spell disaster.

19.3 Duty of Care in the US and Korea

Directors in many legal jurisdictions (whether civil or common law based) throughout the world owe their companies certain duties or obligations. Primarily, the duty of care and the duty of loyalty are front and center. In essence, directors fulfill the duty of care obligations by exercising a reasonable, objective standard of skill and care in discharge of their functions. In order to fulfill their duty of loyalty, they are required to act in good faith and in the best interest of the corporation.

In the United States, directors are shielded from legal liability according to the business judgment rule which provides that in making business decisions, they must act on an informed basis, in good faith and in the honest belief that the actions taken are in the best interests of the company. Therefore, as long as directors take reasonable steps to be informed about what they are expected to decide they won't be held liable.[2] Of course, directors are not shielded completely from their actions. Directors will not be protected if their conduct or decision making is utterly irrational, egregious or unwise as to fall outside the bounds of reasonableness.[3]

19.3.1 Duty of Care in Korea

Like directors in the US and elsewhere, directors in Korean companies have fiduciary related duties. Such duties are set forth in the Korean Commercial Code[4] and include:

- Duty of Care as a prudent manager
- Duty of Confidentiality
- Fiduciary Duty-the Duty of Loyalty

In Korea, if a director violates the duty of care as a good manager (including the duty to faithfully perform in the company's best interest) he or she may be held liable to the company or even to third parties and could be required to pay damages. Under Article 382-3 of the Korean

---

[2]   See Smith v Van Gorkom, 488 A 2nd. 282 (Del. 1985)
[3]   See Basri, Carole and Irving Kagan, Corporate Legal Departments, page 16-5, 3rd edition, New York, Practicing Law Institute, 2004. Note: The business judgment rule, in essence, provides that by following the duty of care and loyalty, directors are protected from liability.
[4]   See Article 382 (3) and 399 (1) of the Korean Commercial Code

Commercial Code a director's duty of care and good faith encompasses a number of duties including the:

- Duty to review the company's activities
- Duty to review corporate information and documents
- Duty to protect a company's assets
- Duty to supervise and oversee employees
- Duty to review all major filings with regulatory agencies

A director may even be subject to criminally liability as well as civil liability upon the negligent failure of fulfilling the obligation of care. Such liability may be found when the director fails to fulfill the duty of care and loyalty by:

- The intentional neglect or negligence in performing duties
- The failure to manage affairs as "an ordinary prudent person"
- Endangering company assets through gross negligence

Looking at the civil and common law aspects of the duty of care (Korean courts are trending towards the business judgment rule of the US) the following is true of directors in Korea today:

1. Directors may be liable to the company in providing a safe work space and work environment
2. Directors must use reasonable care in protecting the company's assets
3. Directors must use reasonable care in providing a safe work place and work environment

19.4 The Board's Risk Management Obligations

The corporate scandals in the US of the 1990's led to the Sarbanes-Oxley Act (SOX) of 2002 which helped to emphasize risk management as part of good corporate governance. Section 404 of SOX requires among other things that proper internal controls be established in publicly traded companies including compliance and risk management policies.[5] Now, US law and regulations regarding compliance, requires that the Board of Directors not only be trained in compliance but that it have compliance oversight. One of the most quoted court decisions involving compliance is the court in the Care Mark case.[6] The court in the Care Mark case discusses the Board of Director's responsibilities with regards to good faith and compliance and states:

"I am of the view that a director's obligation includes a duty to attempt in good faith to assure that corporate information and reporting system which the board concludes is adequate, exists, and that a failure to do so, under some circumstances, may in theory at least, render a director liable for losses caused by non-compliance with applicable legal standards."

As a result of the Care Mark case, as well as SOX and other laws and regulations in the US, corporate directors in the US now have an obligation (as part of the duty of care) to create compliance systems to detect corporate wrongdoing and protect them from liability. Of course, because of the scandals and court decisions requiring more focus on good corporate governance, international bodies such as the OECD, have included risk management policies as part of a board of directors' responsibilities.[7] This also extends to risk management processes as well when you realize that compliance is actually a part of risk management. In fact, the New York Stock Exchange Listed Company Manual provides that the Audit Committee (overseen by independent directors under SOX) has the following responsibilities:

- Discuss policies regarding risk assessment and risk management

----

[5]   15 USC Sec 72 (a)

[6]   Care Mark International, Inc. Derivative Litigation, 698 A.2nd 959 (Del. Ch 1996)

[7]   See James Lam, Enterprise Risk Management, Wiley 2nd Edition (2014), p 77 citing the Organization for Economic Cooperation and Development (OECD) Principles of Corporate Governance.

- Report directly to the Board of Directors
- Review independent auditor problems
- Engage Advisors
- Review internal auditing controls

20   Legal Risk Management-Pre-litigation and Litigation

20.1 Risk Management and Pre-Litigation

Minimizing legal risk or the exposure of legal risk takes place in several stages, basically, several stages prior to potential litigation or pre-litigation as it can be called. The last few stages would of course, take place during litigation and after or post litigation. Obviously, minimizing legal risk before litigation is a proactive or preventative stage in which risk management processes can be implemented to reduce the risk of lawsuits, government investigations, fines, or penalties.

This pre-litigation stage of LRM can be considered in essence a stage where the company can take a "proactive" approach to legal concerns and prevent potential exposure. This stage can cover areas such as:

- Prelaunch product review: What processes are in place to look at a product's historical data prior to its launch in the marketplace?
- Product safety: If a company produces products, what processes are in place to minimize claims, recalls, class action, CPSC settlements and potential fines.
- Product risk management: What processes are in place to encourage correct product use, increase customer satisfaction, and manage possible injury from its misuse? This also includes improving the ability of the company

to defend itself by substantiating defenses to liability, reducing exposure to liability, and assisting in regular compliance.

- Insurance: What processes are in place to review the company's insurance coverage? This includes assessments of availability/policy limits, relationships with insurance cost benefit analysis of premiums, and alternatives for coverage such as creating a captive insurance company.

- Information/document retention program: A major issue for companies dealing with the United States in any capacity is the creation and use of a document retention program. What processes are in place to implement a robust document retention policy, which minimizes fines, penalties, or sanctions during litigation? The program must be in place before litigation to adequately protect the company.

- Risk management assessments of critical departments within the corporation: What processes, if any, have been developed to assess the risk factors of major departments or divisions, such as Human Resources?

- Compliance: A properly implemented compliance program can have a great impact on corporate liability and exposure to legal risk. What processes, if any, have been put in place to develop a compliance program? Does one exist?

20.2 Legal Risk Management and Litigation

Legal risk management plays a vital role during litigation as well. LRM processes should drive a company's defense during litigation, especially litigation in the United States. Such processes should play a major role in coordinating a company's defenses against product safety litigation and claims, responding to government investigations, and product-related or service-related investigations.

- Establish e-discovery process controls.

From the above, it is apparent that the role legal risk management should play before litigation as well during litigation is important. Only a well-thought-out LRM program that considers all the above-mentioned issues and concerns will be successful.

21 Employment Law–Managing the Workplace

Making wrong decisions in the workplace can damage the company's reputation/brand and cost the company a lot of money. It is a major part of risk and needs to be dealt with seriously. As most companies in the U.S. face an increasing number of employment related claims, clear employment processes are vital. Legal exposure is now enormous. In fact, in the U.S. a number of large verdicts have been levied against companies that violated U.S. employment law, including:

- $190 million – Toyota (sexual harassment)
- $50 million – Abercrombie and Fitch (discriminatory hiring practices)
- Court-supervised recruiting for 5 years
- $2.2 million – International Brotherhood of Police Officers (retaliation)

In the U.S. and elsewhere, there are primarily 5 areas of Law Affecting a manager's decisions in the workplace. They are:

- Discrimination
- Retaliation
- Sexual Harassment
- Employee Leave/Reasonable Accommodation
- Wage and Hour

21.1 Discrimination

Basing any employment (including hiring) decision on a protected characteristic is discrimination and is Illegal.

What are protected characteristics in the U.S.?

- Age
- Race
- Sex/Pregnancy
- National Origin/ancestry
- Disability
- Religion
- Veteran Status
- Marital Status (NJ, CA)
- Sexual Orientation (NJ, CA)

What types of decisions can lead to discrimination claims?

- Hiring, disciplining and firing
- Promotions and pay increases
- Assignment of work
- What you say and how you act toward employees
- And many more

Illegal and Inappropriate Interview Questions

A number of questions have been found by U.S. courts to be illegal. Many foreign companies do not appreciate this. However, such questions can lead to discrimination claims.

ILLEGAL	LEGAL
ANCESTRY, PLACE OF BIRTH, PARENTS' PLACE OF BIRTH, 1ST LANGUAGE	Knowledge of foreign language, only if job-related
DATE OF BIRTH OR AGE	None

CHURCH AFFILIATION; RELIGION	None
MEDICAL CONDITIONS OR DISABILITIES	Whether can perform the requirements of job, i.e., travel, hours, etc.
MILITARY - TYPE OF DISCHARGE, SERVICE IN OTHER THAN U.S. ARMED FORCES	Military - Education, training, or experience in U.S. armed forces
ARRESTS	None
MARITAL STATUS (NJ, CA) - CHILD CARE ARRANGEMENTS	None

21.1.1 Practical Tips

Focus on qualifications/performance instead of characteristics. At the interview, ask questions about:

- The candidates' ability to do the job
  - Job description/duties
  - Resume
- The candidate's ability to work the hours required by the job
- The candidate's ability to travel

21.1.2 Interview Notes

Do not make notes based on a person's race, age, national origin, place of birth or any other "protected characteristic." You cannot base an employment decision on these "protected characteristics" so there is no reason to make note of them. Remember, in the US interview notes must be kept for 1 year and can be obtained in a lawsuit. Also remember, there could be severe penalties, including jail time for destroying documents that the Company is required to keep, including interview notes.

21.1.3 Discrimination Action Items

- Be alert! To hiring/promotion/salary decisions that result in an apparent preference of one group over another
- Be alert! To inconsistent discipline among employees
- Be alert! To deviations from policy when addressing behavior or performance issues
- Keep an open dialog with HR

21.2 Retaliation

Retaliation is a material adverse action taken against an individual that would dissuade a reasonable person from engaging in a "protected activity."

"Protected activities" include reporting a suspected violation of state or federal law or Company policy; participating in an investigation – internal or external; or asserting rights under the law

Retaliation is illegal. Retaliation takes many forms. Some obvious, others subtle. They include:

- Unwarranted discipline or termination
- Unsatisfactory performance evaluations
- Loss of opportunities for promotion
- Disproportionately low pay raises or bonuses
- Less desirable or more work assignments
- Excluding or shunning an individual

21.2.1 What should you do?

Work closely with HR whenever considering adverse employment actions, otherwise you may be acting without all of the facts and laying the foundation for a retaliation (or discrimination) claim. If in doubt, you should ask questions before acting.

Be alert to the timing of adverse employment actions (such as discipline or an unsatisfactory performance rating) in relation to a person's engaging in "protected activity." Sudden claims of behavior or performance issues become suspect when they arise in connection with or soon after a person engages in "protected activity."

21.3 Harassment

In the U.S., sexual harassment is defined as:

- Unwelcome sexual advances, requests for sexual favors, and other verbal or physical conduct of a sexual nature when submission to or rejection of this conduct explicitly or implicitly:
- Affects a person's employment
- Unreasonably interferes with a person's work performance
- Creates an intimidating, hostile or offensive working environment

Other forms of harassment in the U.S. include:

- Race, sex religion, national origin, disability, age, sexual orientation, marital status, veteran status, protected activity (defined as opposition to discrimination/harassment or participation in anti-discrimination/anti-harassment proceedings) or any other characteristic protected by federal, state or local law

Some examples of conduct that could be viewed as harassment include:

- Off-color, demeaning or abusive jokes or comments
- Display of offensive material
- Demands for sexual favors
- Touching/kissing/hugging
- Encroaching on an employees' physical space

- Comments about how a person looks or what he or she is wearing
- Viewing pornographic sites

21.3.1 Practical tips

- Lead by example – avoid off-color jokes/comments, etc.
- If you're not sure whether something is appropriate, best not to do or say it
- Be alert for serious infractions and repeated/persistent behaviors, i.e., inappropriate touching, name-calling, viewing of pornography, etc.
- Report to HR (briefly, but carefully, document it to HR)
  - Serious infractions and repeated/persistent behaviors
  - Incidents that were reported to you but that you did not observe
    - Documentation should
      - Be short and to the point
      - Contain facts, not opinions
      - Be accurate
- Resolve quickly – inappropriate (non-serious) infractions
- Maintain confidentiality

21.4 Employee Leave/Reasonable Accommodation

This is primarily and HR responsibility. Three reasons for discussing in this chapter:

- A manager may have or obtain information that is critical to the first stage of the process – identifying the need for leave
- A manager may have or obtain highly confidential medical information
- A manager's cooperation is essential to effectively administer the leave process and preserve the confidentiality of any medical information he or she receives.

21.4.1 Examples

Leave can be available under the federal and state family and medical leave laws, or as a reasonable accommodation under the Americans with Disabilities Act (ADA)

FAMILY AND MEDICAL LEAVE ACT (FMLA)	ADA
SERIOUS HEALTH CONDITION OF AN EMPLOYEE, CHILD SPOUSE OR PARENTS	As a reasonable accommodation for a disability – intermittent or in large blocks of time
BIRTH, ADOPTION OR PLACEMENT OF A CHILD	Unlike leave laws, there is no limitation on amount of leave available as a reasonable accommodation
LIMITED TO 12 WEEKS PER YEAR CALCULATED ON A ROLLING YEAR BASIS	ADA leave can piggyback on FMLA leave to extend the leave time well beyond 12 weeks
REINSTATEMENT TO THE SAME POSITION OR EQUIVALENT ONE WITH SAME PAY, BENEFITS, RESPONSIBILITIES AND OTHER TERMS AND CONDITIONS	Amount of time must be "reasonable" - Up to one year has been considered "reasonable" by some courts
	Reinstatement to same job (unless can demonstrate undue hardship)

21.4.2 What Should Be Done?

Management must be alert to patterns of absences. It should notify HR promptly. There may be a medical condition, disability or family circumstances legally justifying the absences (alcoholism is a "disability" in the U.S.). If a manager anticipates an employee to be out for a medical or family reason for 3 or more days, he or she should contact HR immediately.

- Do not elicit or disclose medical information.
- Managers may disclose to HR or the Company's attorneys handling any matters relating to this employee. Otherwise, in the U.S., disclosers of medical conditions is illegal.
- If an employee volunteers medical information
  - If possible, stop him or her and take them to HR or notify HR immediately
  - If not possible, notify HR immediately
    - DO NOT COMMUNCIATE TO OR DISCUSS MEDICAL INFORMATION WITH ANYONE ELSE – EXCEPT THE COMPANY'S ATTORNEYS IF REQUESTED
- Work with HR to determine and fill operational needs
- Follow direction from HR and Legal

21.5 Wages and Hours

Most employees who work more than 40 hours a week must be paid "Overtime Pay." Some countries may consider overtime pay justified before or after 40 hours.

Please note that some positions are "exempt" from these overtime pay requirements such as:

- Professional positions, i.e., attorneys, etc.
- Executive positions, i.e., management of a department with 2 or more employees
- Administrative positions, i.e., high level discretion and independent judgment

Recent settlements for alleged violations of overtime pay requirements (stemming from misclassifying positions as exempt)

- UBS - $89 Million

- IBM - $65 Million
- Morgan Stanley - $42.5 Million

21.5.1 Practical Tips

To avoid costly lawsuits and claims, it is advisable that managers at all times consider the followings:

- Work with Legal/HR to determine status of position
- Work with HR concerning salary, raises, performance, promotion – factor in status
- Control OT by controlling hours

21.6 Basic Employment Rule

In the U.S., most states follow the "Employment at Will" doctrine which states:

- An employer may discharge an employee for any reason or no reason but not for an unlawful reason; and
- And employee may leave at any time

However, the basic employment at will rule is usually not enforced. The real rule is that an employer:

- Needs a legitimate reason to terminate employment or an employee

Therefore, before terminating an employee, an employer should take steps to prevent employee lawsuits. Such steps are outlined below.

21.6.1 Steps to Take

- Performing a risk audit on company employment policies. Has Legal or HR looked at the current policies?
- Publishing or reviewing the company employee handbook. Is the employee handbook up to date?

- ADR – Is there an ADR in place to handle employee disputes?
- Training – Has Legal or HR provided management with training on sexual harassment, age discrimination, and hostile work environment issues?

21.7 Conclusion

Considering the seriousness of employment related litigation and the potential exposure to claims, managers should minimize the risk through the following:

- Follow the law and the Company's policies
- If you don't know or aren't sure, ask HR
- Issue-spot. Look at the BIG PICTURE
- Act quickly – DON'T WAIT UNTILL IT'S TOO LATE
- In resolving non-serious infractions of law or policy OR
- In reporting to HR persistent behaviors, serious infractions, or other important information that could create risk
- Take these responsibilities seriously

21.8 Hypothetical Case in Point

You hired and employee who is still within her probationary period. You're not satisfied with her performance, but you haven't mentioned it to anyone, and it's not documented anywhere. Now she's complained to you that she's getting all of the less appealing work assignments and that the two males are getting the challenging assignments. She's also complained about joking in the department. Apart from the performance issue, you're getting the feeling she doesn't fit in and she may be creating some conflict within your 4-person department

- What are the issues?
- What should you do/have done?

22 Trade Secrets and Unfair Competition

We live in a competitive world. The extent to which a company is able to protect its trade secrets is an important factor in its overall ability to survive and prosper. In the employment context, complicated legal issues arise when a departing employee is in a position to use and/or disclose confidential information to a competitor.

Complicated legal issues also exist when hiring the employee of a competitor. An important step in the LRM process is to implement processes to protect trade secrets and confidential information as well as protect itself from an unfair competition claims, as well as prevent raiding of its employees.

22.1 Understanding What Constitutes a Trade Secret

Prior to 1979, few states in the U.S. had trade secret statutes, and actions for theft of trade secrets were generally governed by the 1939 edition of the Restatement of Torts. The Restatement defined a trade secret as:

Any formula, pattern, device or compilation of information which is used in one's business, and which gives him an opportunity to obtain an advantage over competitors who do not know or use it. It may be a formula for a chemical compound, a process of manufacturing, treating or preserving material, a pattern for a machine or other device, or a list of customers. See Restatement of Torts section 757 (1939).

The National Conference of Commissioners on Uniform State Laws approved the Uniform Trade Secrets Act ("UTSA") in 1979. Since then 41 states (including California) and the District of Columbia have adopted the UTSA in some form. Texas and New Jersey have not adopted the UTSA. Under the UTSA, a trade secret is somewhat broader than the definition under the Restatement:

- "trade secret means information, including a formula, pattern, compilation, program, device, method, technique or process that:
- derives independent economic value, actual or potential, from not being generally known to, and not being readily ascertainable by proper means by other persons who can obtain economic value from its disclosure or use; and
- is the subject of efforts that are reasonable under the circumstances to maintain its secrecy.

22.1.1 Under the common law of the U.S. and other countries courts generally look at six factors for determining whether information is a trade secret. Those factors are:

- The extent to which the information in question is known outside the business;
- The extent to which the information is known by employees and others involved in the business;
- The extent of the measures to safeguard the secrecy of the information;
- The value of the information to the competitor;
- The amount of effort or expense required to develop or compile the information; and
- The ease of difficulty with which the information could be properly acquired or duplicated by others.

The determination of whether information constitutes a trade secret is extremely fact specific, and the courts have reached opposite conclusions on the same types of information depending on the facts presented. Two principal factors create the difference between cases that recognize information as a trade secret and cases that do not. First, courts determine whether the information is truly secret, i.e. not in the public domain or easily accessed. Second, courts determine whether the employer has taken reasonable steps to protect the secrecy of the information.

22.2 Steps a Company Can Take to Protect Its Trade Secrets

22.2.1 Physical Security Precautions

Failure to maintain appropriate physical security may doom a trade secrets claim. Companies should restrict access to its premises generally, and in particular, where trade secrets are located. Security services should enable the company t may be important to show that a disloyal employee entered or left a facility during unusual times. Smaller scale physical security within Departments is equally as important. Employees should be required to place confidential information in secured areas such as drawer, locked file cabinets. A security audit should be performed to determine its vulnerability to trade secret theft.

22.2.2 Communicating Confidentiality

A company or organization should communicate with employee's regarding its policies on confidentiality. Confidentiality policies should be included in employee handbooks and employees should receive periodic reminders regarding the confidentiality policy and any contractual obligations regarding confidentiality.

Document control is another essential means to communicate confidentiality. Document controls can be put in place that are simple and routine. Confidential documents may be marked "Confidential" or "Property of XXX." Automated headers and footers will increase the likelihood that the employees will follow the procedure. Upon termination of employment, exit interviews should be conducted to remind the employee of their obligations regarding confidentiality.

An effective exit interview should normally include the employee's supervisor and a human resources representative to serve as a witness. An effective exit interview also requires preparation. For example, the employee may be reluctant to provide information regarding his new position of employment. By checking with co-workers and doing some investigation beforehand, the employer may be able to gather important information for the exit.

1.1.3 During the exit interview, the company should remind the employee of his or her obligations regarding confidentiality of information. The interview should include a discussion regarding:

- The types of confidential information that the employee previously had access to during his/her employment;
- Any agreements with the employee regarding confidentiality or competition issues;
- The employee's obligation to return any confidential information (make sure you remind employees to return all electronic information stored in all locations, including personal laptops or home computers);
- The duties of the employee's new position;
- The employee's responsibility not to use or disclose confidential information

22.3 Contractual Protection

A properly drafted agreement which contains a restrictive covenant can be an effective tool for preventing trade secret disclosure. But what is meant by the term "restrictive covenant?" It can cover a wide array of devices including:

- A restriction upon use or disclosure of trade secret or other confidential information (a confidentiality agreement);
- Assignment of property rights (an invention assignment agreement)

- A restriction upon participation in competitive activities for a specified period of time (a non-compete agreement);
- A restriction upon soliciting the customers of the employer (a non-solicitation agreement); and
- A restriction upon soliciting or attempting to induce employees to leave the employer (a non-solicitation agreement).

All of these types of restrictive covenants have a potential role to play in an ongoing effort to protect trade secrets. For instance, a non-disclosure agreement can clarify that certain information is intended to be kept secret and if violated, may create a potential cause of action for breach of contract, supplementing statutory claims or common law claims for unfair competition, breach of the duty of loyalty and breach of fiduciary duty. Generally speaking, non-disclosure and invention assignment agreements must be signed by all employees at the inception of employment. Third parties given access to confidential information should also sign non-disclosure agreements.

- The employee's responsibility to contact the employer if there are any questions regarding confidential information.

The company should request that the employee sign an acknowledgement that he or she has been provided the above information. Such an acknowledgment can be persuasive evidence that the information treated was confidential and that the employee was aware of his or her obligations.

Practice Tip: Conduct an audit of the outstanding agreements to check whether appropriate restrictive covenants are properly used.

22.3.1 Non-compete Agreements

A more complicated analysis applies to non-solicitation and non-compete agreements. In the U.S. the applicable law involving the enforceability of such agreements is state specific, As such, it is imperative that counsel determine the state law which applies to the covenant being drafted and that it complies with the requirements of the law of the particular jurisdiction where it is sought to be enforced. For example, in California, the general rule is that covenants not to compete are unenforceable.

In California, due to the strong public policy against non-compete agreements, if the restriction too closely resembles a covenant not to compete, the employer can expose itself to potential liability. In contrast, in many states, there is no statutory prohibition against non-compete agreements. Unlike California, New Jersey's Supreme Court recently held that an employee's private dispute concerning a non-compete clause does not implicate a clear mandate of public policy under the Conscientious Employee Protection Act (CEPA).

Generally, in the U.S., it is recognized that an employer has an interest in protecting customer relationships, trade secrets and confidential business information. In order to prove that a restrictive covenant is enforceable, the employer must show that it is reasonable in light of all of the circumstances. It will generally be found to be reasonable where: (1) it protects the legitimate interests of the employer, (2) imposes no undue hardship, and (3) is not injurious to the public. Courts will apply a balancing test to all three prongs of the analysis, weighing the terms of the covenant based on considerations of what is reasonably necessary as to time and geographic area to protect the employer's legitimate interest.

22.3.2 Inevitable Disclosure

The doctrine of inevitable disclosure stands for the belief that a former employee due to his responsibilities will inevitably or unintentionally disclose to his new employer- trade secrets from his former employer. Most states recognize this doctrine and will enforce the doctrine and enforce Non-Compete Agreements based on the doctrine. The court looks at the factors such as:

- New employer's need for trade secret information, and

- Absence of a Non-Compete Agreement with former employer to make that determination

22.4 Marketing Materials

Frequently, the information that an employer asserts is confidential is contained in marketing material accessible on the Internet or given to a friendly journalist for use in a trade publication. Technical and scientific personnel are frequently publishing work in scientific journals or in association meetings. Accordingly, to avoid inadvertent disclosure of confidential information, a company should closely monitor its publications. Marketing materials should be closely scrutinized to avoid inadvertent dissemination of confidential information. A process should be implemented for monitoring publications.

22.5 Trade Secret Audits

Finally, a company should conduct regular trade secret audits to determine the effectiveness of its efforts to protect trade secrets. It should designate an individual or group of individuals to be familiar with internal secrecy and security standards at all times. To avoid potential legal pitfalls, this individual should routinely consult with in-house counsel to comply with pertinent jurisdictions.

22.6 How to Avoid Unfair Competition Lawsuits

22.6.1 Recognizing Potential Legal Pitfalls

The law of unfair competition encompasses a wide variety of unlawful business activities. Typically, unfair competition lawsuits will include claims for breach of contract, breach of the duty of loyalty, interference with contract and misappropriation of trade secrets. In furtherance of an organization's efforts to compete and protect its trade secrets, it has to be careful to avoid crossing the line into unfair competition. This section discusses some of the ways that a company can protect itself from unfair competition lawsuits.

22.6.2 Contract Claims

The starting point of any inquiry into any unfair competition claim is the existence of an express or implied agreement between the employee and his former employer imposing obligations during and after the employment relationship, such as the obligation not to use or disclose proprietary information. In some cases, the employee will be obligated to comply with the terms of a non-competition agreement and/or an agreement not to solicit employees or customers. Typically, as discussed above, the employee will enter into such an agreement at the inception of employment. In some cases, the employee may enter into a separation agreement that contains such terms. You need to know about these agreements and review the terms to avoid potential claims.

The competitor employer is not a party to such an agreement and therefore cannot be sued for breach. However, the competitor can be sued for interference with a contract or inducing the breach of contract.

22.6.3 Statutory and Tort Claims

The absence of an express or implied agreement between an employer and an employee competitor of potential liability. Business entities may have statutory obligations not to engage in unfair business practices. This is true throughout the U.S. and other countries.

Several states also recognize a fiduciary duty and a duty of loyalty by employees to former employers. In addition to the employee's own personal liability for breach of contract or breach of the duty of loyalty, the competitor can also be sued to aiding and abetting the breach.

22.7 Employee Raiding

No other area of unfair competition engenders more outrage than corporate raiding of a competitor's employees. To say the least, a thin line exists between the rights of employees to leave their employment and work for a competitor and rights of the former employer to prevent unfair competition. If a company orchestrates a departure of key employees of a competitor with an eye towards "crippling" the competitor or gaining access to confidential information, this may constitute unfair competition. Courts have been willing to grant injunctive relief, precluding the employees from working for the competitor.

22.7.1 Steps You Can Take to Avoid Unfair Competition Lawsuits

During the interview and recruitment process, care must be taken not to take action or make inquiries that could trigger an unfair competition lawsuit. For example, do not make inquiries regarding a competitor's confidential information, such as product plans, marketing plans, customers, etc. You should ask applicants to identify any sort of employment agreements with their existing/former employers which contain any provision providing for the protection of trade secrets and/or proprietary information;

To the extent an applicant has a contractual agreement with his/her former employer, care should be taken to analyze the terms (i.e. non-solicitation or non-compete provisions) with the assistance of counsel;

Applicants should be told during the interview process not to solicit or recruit any co-workers for employment. The applicant should be encouraged to view the recruitment and interview process as completely confidential. In the event that a company is interviewing more than one applicant from the same company, the interview and hiring process for each applicant should be kept completely separate. Offers of employment should be made on an individual basis and should not be made contingent upon another individual's acceptance of employment. Under no circumstances should employees be recruited as a team or a group.

Note: You should never contact one candidate for employment and induce and/or encourage him to recruit co-employees.

Even where no restrictive covenant exists, the new employer should advise applicants not to solicit their former employer's clients until they have resigned their employment and have physically left the premises.

Solicitation during employment can result in breach of fiduciary duty and breach of loyalty claims.

Under no circumstances should new hires bring to a company any items that contain or could be construed to contain the former employer's proprietary, confidential or trade secret information. This includes, but is not limited to, computer disks, customer lists, manuals, etc., that relate to or may be considered the property of the former employer. The applicant should be encouraged to conduct an extensive search for any such materials and should be in a position to warrant to his employer that he/she had returned all such materials and is bringing nothing from his former job that is proprietary in nature.

Once an applicant accepts employment, he should be encouraged to follow all of his former employer's policies concerning cessation of the employment relationship, such as return of any of the former employer's property.

If you do not have one already, it may be useful to consider implementing an acknowledgement form whereby the new employee is informed that the company prohibits new hires from bringing with them any property from their prior employer which was not given to them to keep. The acknowledgment should note that the company respects other employer's trade secret agreements, and that you expect all applicants and employees to honor all applicable restrictive covenants. When in doubt, always consult with a lawyer or risk manager.

Other Protections to Avoid Employee Raiding

A company can consider using various claims against former employees and their new employers based in relevant facts:

- Economic Espionage Act- can be used if it can prove employee or former employer has "misappropriated" trade secrets.
- Uniform Trade Secrets Act- it can obtain an injunction to prevent a former employee to work for another company if it can prove the employee will steal "trade secrets." California recognizes this statute.

- Tortious Interference with Contractual Rights
  - Recognized by many jurisdictions.
- Employee Piracy- Many courts will grant injunctions restraining companies from recruiting or attempting to recruit competitors' employees if it believes the companies' actions in recruiting employees reaches the level of "malicious interference" and infringes the employment relationship.

22.8 Steps to Prevent Employee Raiding

All new employees should be required to sign a confidentiality agreement which provides they will not solicit or assist their new employer in soliciting employees for one (1) year after they leave the company. All key employees (except those in California) should be required to sign non-compete agreements when they are hired.

Whenever employees leave to work for competitors, the law department legal should send letters to the new employer reminding it of the employee's contractual obligation. All current key employees should be required to sign non-compete agreements upon receipt of new consideration or value (i.e. monetary award). The company should initiate a process or procedure to protect all of its trade secrets. They should consider legal action against former employees or their new employers- if such conduct is "egregious" and it is clear employee piracy or trade secret misappropriation is about to take place.

22.9 South Korea's Trade Secret Laws

Like the states in the US which adopted the UTSA, South Korea has adopted its own trade secret law, the UCPA. [8] The UCPA covers..." Business or technical information including manufacturing methods, selling methods or information useful in the trade, which has an independent economic value and is maintained as a secret through

---

[8]   See Korea's Unfair Competition Prevention and Trade Secret Act (UCPA).

reasonable efforts of its owner".[9] According to Korea's UCPA, a trade secret exists only if the trade secret is actually secret. What does "secret" really mean? This means it is:

Secret (not generally known)

Secret (requiring reasonable efforts of its owner to maintain its secrecy); and

Secret (deriving economic value from the very fact that it is secret)

And of course, a trade secret must consist of information. There are numerous examples of information, many of which are apparent. Among the most common examples of business-related information is:

- Formulas for chemicals, drugs, cosmetics and food, etc.
- Industrial processes
- Blueprints and drawings
- Computer software
- Sources of supply, pricing information, customer lists, etc.

A simple compilation of customers 'names and addresses is normally public information and readily ascertainable. Therefore, it won't be considered a trade secret. On the other hand, Korean courts have interpreted the UCPA as requiring a trade secret to consist of information a competitor would have a hard time in obtaining. This could be customers' purchasing history, contracts information, preferences, etc.

22.9.1 Patents v Trade Secrets

In Korea, as elsewhere, it is important to realize what kinds of IP are protected and how they are protected. Patents are of course more protected than trade secrets. Under Korean patent law, a patent gives an exclusive right to the inventor or owner to exploit the invention. Therefore, a person other than the inventor or owner, who exploits the

---

[9]   Article 2 (2) of the UCPA

invention without a license from the owner, has in essence, infringed the patent and is subject to infringement proceedings by the owner. The patent owner, to obtain the patent had to make the patent filing public. So, unlike a trade secret, the patent is freely discoverable by the public and wrongful use of it is patent infringement. A trade secret of course can't be public to qualify as a trade secret.

A trade secret not only is not afforded the same protection as a patent, but the trade secret owner is not granted or even given an exclusive or unfettered right to the trade secret. Others are free to discover and use the trade secret as long as they do not wrongfully obtain the trade secret. In other words, misappropriation of a trade secret is wrong. But discovery of the trade secret by any fair means is acceptable.

22.9.2 Trade Secret (Theft) Misappropriation

In Korea, the majority of cases involving trade secret theft (misappropriation) usually involve employees. However, there are other cases not involving employees where trade secrets were obtained rightfully but used in breach of the agreement. [10] The major acts of misappropriation are:

- Employees learning trade secrets then jumping over to competitors
- Potential partners learning and then copying trade secrets
- Vendors or agents learning about the trade secrets then using them for other clients

What can be done to prevent, mitigate or stop unauthorized use of or misappropriation of trade secrets ion Korea? Options range from civil actions to criminal complaints. It depends of course on the situation.

---

[10] In Korea, from 2008-2013, 74% of all civil trade secret misappropriation cases involved employees, while 20% involved contractors and agents and 5% involved competitors.

22.9.2.1 Civil Actions

Like the US, civil based legal remedies normally stem from agreements such as restrictive covenants. Restrictive covenants in Korea usually comprise one of three covenants:

- Non-Compete Agreements
- Non-Disclosure Agreements
- Non-Solicitation Agreements

Remedies available in civil actions or claims include injunctions and damage claims. But in order to prevail in such actions, a plaintiff or trade secret owner has a heavy burden under Korean law. Korean courts require that the plaintiff must prove:

- The defendant has acquired or used the plaintiff's trade secrets; and
- The defendant acquired the plaintiff's trade secrets through improper means or by breach of confidence.

The degree of proof required by Korean courts is rather high- i.e. direct evidence. A mere suspicion or circumstantial evidence of trade secret misappropriation is insufficient to substantiate a trade secret claim. An example of direct evidence could be an email transmitting the trade secret from the *employee to the competitor, etc.*

22.9.2.2 Criminal Actions

In Korea, trade secret theft or misappropriation may also be deemed a criminal offense or violation.[11] To initiate a criminal investigation, the trade secret owner needs to file a complaint with the relevant investigating authority- normally the police. The problem in Korea is that though it is a crime, success depends on whether the police

---

[11]   In Korea, trade secret misappropriation may be deemed a crime punishable by up to 5 years in prison or a fine of up to 50 Million KRW.

conducts a search or seizure (as discovery is normally non-existent) that enables it to discover proof of the misappropriation. Therefore, it is imperative that the trade secret owner persuade the police to conduct a search or seizure, which the police are sometimes reluctant to do given the nature of the dispute.

22.9.3 Civil Remedies

In Korea, three kinds of restrictive covenants are generally used to enforce trade secrets:

- Confidentiality Agreements
- Non-solicitation Agreements
- Non-compete Agreements

The above restrictive covenants are usually enforceable and sometimes quite effective, depending on the circumstances and whether or not certain conditions are met. A closer look at the three agreements shows the following enforceability and usefulness to counter trade secrete misappropriation from employees or former employees:

(i)   Confidentiality Agreements
- Normally enforceable
- When used with employees jumping ship, not that effective

(ii) Non-solicitation Agreements
- Like confidentiality agreements, usually enforceable
- When used with employees jumping ship, sometimes effective

(iii) Non-compete agreements (see below)
- Usually enforceable if all elements are met
- When used with employees jumping ship, the most effective of the three agreements

22.9.3.1 Non-Compete Agreements

In Korea, courts began truly enforcing non-compete agreements in the early 2000s. These days courts will enforce non-compete agreements as long as the following elements are met:

- There is a legitimate business interest that needs protecting
- The individual being bound is a senior officer or is a long-term employee
- The circumstances surrounding the resignation include a voluntary change of employment
- The duration of the non-compete is not more than 2 yrs. Sometimes 3-5 years is acceptable but very limited.
- The geographical scope is limited

To enforce non-compete agreements, it is advised that the trade secret owner follow certain steps:

- Have employees sign non–compete agreements
- Tailor each non-compete agreement to a specific employee
- Renew non-compete agreements on a periodic basis if applicable
- If an employee hasn't signed a non-compete agreement get him to sign one during the exit interview.

22.9.4 Problems Facing Companies in Korea Facing Trade Secret Misappropriation

Though the UCPA does provide remedies against trade secret misappropriation, companies must realize there are still problems with enforcement and should tailor risk management processes and procedures to take such issues into consideration. Such problems include:

- It is difficult to obtain evidence for prosecution under the UCPA
- Electronics evidence is the best evidence, and access to such evidence is vital

- A criminal action may be necessary
- A warning letter is not usually helpful
- Postponing payment of a statutory owed severance payment due to the dispute is a violation of labor laws
- Non-competes work best

23 General Product Liability Considerations and Risk Management

Suggested forms and policies to implement appropriate product liability safeguards include:

Form: Claims Defense Policy
Form: Product Loss Control Policy
Form: Product Loss Control Committee
Form: Claims Investigation and Procedure

For more on loss control, see Appendix A.

23.1 Product Liability Concerns and Costs

Product liability claims, product recall cases, and related litigation, besides hurting the company's brand, image, and reputation, will entail many costs, expenses, and legal fees such as:

- Costs related to product incidents, including recall, retrofit, management and employee time, and lost profits
- Legal costs, including litigation costs
- Increased insurance costs
- Costs including those associated with a loss control program and other risk management–related processes

In order to implement a risk management program that covers all legal issues related to product liability in a specific jurisdiction or country, an analysis of the legal theories related to product liability in that jurisdiction or country should be reviewed. In the United States, such legal theories include:

23.1.1 *Typical Legal Theories on which a Plaintiff May Base a Product Liability Claim and/or Class Action*

- Breach of express warranty
  - Express warranty can be created by:
    - "Affirmation of fact or promise" made by the seller to the buyer, which relates to the product and becomes part of the basis of the bargain
    - Advertisements, labels, literature, samples or models, catalogues, and brochures
- Breach of implied warranty
  - Implied warranty of merchantability is implied by law in every contract with a merchant for the sale of goods—a guarantee that product will be merchantable (of commercially acceptable quality).
  - Implied warranty of fitness for particular purpose arises when the seller has reason to know that buyer wants goods for a particular purpose and buyer is relying on seller's skill to select suitable goods.
- Negligence

A manufacturer of goods or products has a duty to use reasonable care in the design of goods so as to protect those who will use them from an unreasonable risk of harm while the goods are being used. This includes using the goods for their intended purpose, or for any purpose, which could reasonably be expected. This duty extends to unintended yet reasonably foreseeable uses, as well as intended uses of the goods or products.

- Strict liability

In the United States, the Restatement of Torts Section 402 sets forth the special liability of the seller of a product in a defective condition resulting in physical harm to the consumer.

- 402A. Special Liability of Seller of Product in a defective condition unreasonably dangerous to the user or consumer or to his property is subject to liability for physical harm thereby caused to the ultimate user or consumer, or to his property, if the seller is engaged in the business of selling such a product, and it is expected to and does reach the user or consumer without substantial change in the condition in which it is sold.[12]
- Deceptive and unfair trade practices (DUTP)
  - In the United States, every state has a statue prohibiting deceptive trade practices.
  - DUTP claims are not based on contract; contractual limitations on liability, therefore, do not apply.
  - Claims are not based on warranty, so disclaimers of warranty do not apply.
  - DUTP can include:
    - Failure to disclose information
    - Oral and written misrepresentations
    - Ambiguous representations
    - Breach of warranty obligations
- U.S. consumer class actions against manufacturers

These class actions are normally brought in the United States on the following basis:

- DUTP claims
  - Aggregation of numerous small claims
  - Simplified compliance with states' procedural requirements

---

[12] Restatement of Torts (Second), Section 402, 1964.

- Proof of deceptive practices by defendant's documents (e.g., advertising literature)
- Common deceptive practice to all class numbers
- Common product defect

- Regulatory and general legal considerations
  - Consumer Product Safety Commission (CPSC)
    - CPSA Section 15(b) Reports: "Every manufacturer of a consumer product distributed in commerce, and every distributor and retailer of such product, who obtains information which reasonably supports the conclusion that such product ..._(2) contains a defect which could create a substantial product hazard described in Subsection (A)(2) or (3) creates an unreasonable risk of serious injury or death, shall immediately inform the commission unless the manufacturer ... has actual knowledge that the commission has been adequately informed of such defect, failure to comply, or such risk ..."[13]

23.2 Sources of Product Liability Risk

There are a number of areas that a company's Risk Management Department (RMD) or related divisions must consider when implementing a comprehensive legal risk management program to address product liability concerns. The main concerns are sources of risk, whether departmental or process oriented. Each step of the design, manufacturing, sales, and distribution chain contains numerous risks, including:

---

[13] CPSA, 15 U.S.C. Sec 2064(b).

23.2.1 Potential Sources of Product Liability

- Product design
    - Performance specifications
    - Safety analysis and features
    - Labeling
    - Instructions for use
    - Warnings and cautions
    - Detectability of malfunctions
    - Serviceability
    - Product warranty
- Manufacturing and distribution
    - Manufactured to specifications
    - Components meet design specification
    - Product testing
    - Product packaging
    - Record-keeping procedures
    - Suppliers
    - Contractors
    - "OEM" or "VAR" customers
    - Distributors
- Product promotion and service
    - Advertising copy
    - Product literature
    - Marketing and promotional material
    - Service and repair procedures

23.3 Possible Defenses to Product Liability Exposure

Though consumer warranties in the United States are governed for the most part under the Magnuson-Moss Act, the Uniform Commercial Code (UCC) addresses warranties when used in the sale of goods in the U.S. The proactive use of warranties can be seen as another tool to limit product liability exposure when dealing with the sale of goods in the United States. Such defenses include:

- Breach of express warranty
  - Possible defenses to a breach of express warranty claim include:
    - Lack of causation
    - Lack of damages
    - Disclaimers: UCC §2-316 provides that a disclaimer will be effective only to the extent that it can be read consistently with any express warranties made.
- Assumption of risk: UCC §2-715 indicates that when the plaintiff assumes the risk by using a product while aware of the breach of warranty, any resulting injuries are not proximately caused by the breach.
- Contributory negligence: Courts in contributory negligence jurisdictions have adopted an approach similar to that used in strict liability in tort—that unreasonable failure to discover the defect does not bar recovery, but that unreasonable conduct after discovery does bar recovery.
- Breach of implied warranty
  - Possible defenses to a breach of implied warranties claim:
    - Assumption of risk: UCC §2-715 indicates that when the plaintiff assumes the risk by using a product while aware of the breach of warranty, any resulting injuries are not proximately caused by the breach.
    - Contributory negligence: Courts in contributory negligence jurisdictions have adopted an approach similar to that used in strict liability in tort—that unreasonable failure to discover the defect does not bar recovery, but that unreasonable conduct after discovery does bar recovery.
    - Comparative negligence: Courts in comparative negligence jurisdictions use comparative fault

notions in warranty cases to reduce damage awards in the same way as in strict liability cases.

- Disclaimer: Disclaimers of liability for breach of implied warranty must be specific and are narrowly construed. See UCC §2-316.
- Notice of breach: UCC §2-607 requires the buyer to give the seller notice within a reasonable time after the buyer discovers or should have discovered the breach.
- Lack of (horizontal) privity: The implied warranties most likely will extend only to the immediate buyer and his or her family and not to third parties such as those parties which receive the products as gifts or buy them used.
- Statute of limitations.

23.4 Loss Control

Loss control is another tool a company or organization should use to minimize or reduce risk. If properly used, loss control can reduce losses and decrease exposure associated with such losses. Harrington and Niehaus define loss control simply as "efforts that reduce expected losses".[14] Loss control refers to those processes that can prevent, reduce, or mitigate losses. Loss control processes, in other words, if properly used, can mitigate and reduce risk. Normally, loss control processes can be very effective in reducing product liability costs and expenses.

23.4.1 Loss Control: Possible Defenses to Product Liability Exposure

Loss control processes are usually divided into two main categories—loss prevention and loss reduction. They are defined as follows:[15]

---

[14] Harrington and Niehaus, Risk Management and Insurance, 2nd edition, New York: McGraw Hill, 2003

[15] Id

- Loss prevention: activities that reduce expected losses of inventory or monies associated with inventory by proactively reducing the frequency of losses
- Loss reduction: activities that reduce expected losses of inventory or monies associated with inventory by decreasing the size of the loss, which is a reactive and not a proactive process

23.4.2 Loss Control Committee

Implementation of loss control processes, whether loss reduction or prevention, is best managed by oversight of a loss control committee or LCC. The loss control committee, consisting of members from Sales and Marketing, Legal, Risk Management, and Service (as well as others if needed) can review current practices, policies, and procedures to make informed decisions as to the viability of loss control policies. The loss control committee can review warranties, labels, literature, and related product literature to make recommendations that could prevent claims by preventing losses.

I found the loss control committee to be a very useful tool if used properly and on a regular basis. Though information provided to and considered by the loss control committee may be limited in scope, the reasonable judgment of people with various viewpoints from various departments within a company can often prove to be very valuable, especially when given as a group after careful consideration.

For a sample loss control policy and loss control committee form, see Appendix A.

23.4.3 Loss Control: Case in Point

Sarah Jones, the risk manager for XYZ Company, was excited about her new duties. Because of rising product claims and increasing reports of product malfunctions in the field, the VP of Service persuaded management to establish the Product Loss Control Committee (PLCC), with Sarah as the RLCC lead.

Sarah, however, was not exactly certain who should be on the committee and what the committee's mandate was. She decided to focus on product issues, thinking that product safety, R&D, quality control, and claims handling were all important aspects to be considered by the PLCC. Sarah knew, however, that before she could do anything she needed the express approval of executive management. She therefore decided to create a policy and procedures manual, which would be approved by the CEO and VP of Service.

Working with her internal Law Department, Sarah developed a policy and procedures manual setting forth the duties and responsibilities of the PLCC in detail. Under the PLCC policy and procedures manual, the company's various division VPs were responsible for the development and maintenance of the PLCC and had to appoint a representative of each division to sit on the PLCC. Furthermore, the PLCC policy and procedures manual set forth all processes and procedures regarding complaints and claim handling as well as claim processing.

While talking to XYZ's insurance company, Sarah mentioned the establishment of the PLCC to the lead insurance agent, Mr. Smith.

Mr. Smith was intrigued, stating a proper PLCC would hold decrease XYZ's insurance premiums, as a loss control process was considered a very valuable risk management tool and often led to processes that would help control product loss and claims and expenses associated with products. Mr. Smith asked for more details regarding the PLCC.

- What processes and procedures should Sarah consider for the PLCC?
- How should claims handling be addressed?
- Should the PLCC consider product warranty issues?
- Should the PLCC review product literature?
- Should the PLCC consider claims defense processes?
- Who should be on the PLCC for it to be an effective loss control process?

24   New Product Planning and Development Management

New product planning and development has the potential for great risk, but also for mitigation of risk if the right mechanisms can be used in a timely fashion. As stated previously, companies need to be very detailed to avoid product liability litigation and legal exposure. If implemented in a timely and correct manner, such processes can minimize legal risk, especially regarding class actions.

24.1 Stages

Product development and planning normally involves four distinct stages prior to mass production:

- Product planning
- Development planning
- Development (implementation)
- Production readiness

In each stage there is potential cause for risk, as each stage involves processes that can potentially expose a manufacturing company to great legal risk such as:

- Product planning
  - Product planning & review
  - Design
  - User interface development

- Development planning and standardization
  - Standardization of design
  - Development of machine parts
  - Development of electric parts
  - Software development
  - Tooling development
  - Engineering sample
  - Final parts development
- Development implementation
  - User manual and training manual developed
  - Regulations reviewed and approval obtained
  - Reliability assurance test performed
  - Final user interface developed
  - Product preparation for mass production
- Production readiness
  - Test reliability of mass production
  - Create manufacturing training material
  - Prepare JIGs and dyes

In each stage of product design, development, and production, many departments must share and coordinate information, tasks, roles and responsibilities, and communication with each other. Failure to do so in an effective manner in accordance with proper procedures and processes leads to not only failure but potential legal liability. For instance, let's look at the main stages of a product planning cycle in a new product development scenario.

24.2 Product Planning

A typical product planning life cycle would involve at least eight departments and look something like this:

- Product planning department
  - Conceptualize product development
  - Establish management plan for product

- Share information between related departments
- Marketing
  - Confirm long- and short-term marketing strategy of product
  - Suggest retail sales points
  - Project potential sales issues
  - Strategize marketing launch
  - Plan advertising for launch
- R&D
  - Suggest development of technology and parts
  - Suggest new features
  - Review development plan in accordance with product's features
- Design department
  - Review strategy
  - Suggest materials, design, and colors of parts and products
  - Research and analyze design trends
- Quality control
  - Provide appropriate standards and regulations
  - Review production liability laws
  - Supply quality checklist
  - Review field claims at product issue
- Technology planning
  - Analyze long- and short-term trend and forecast of future technologies
- Others
  - Collect information from end-user
  - Share service information
  - Review information from sellers, distributors, and dealers

24.3 Standardization

One of the key stages of new product development once product planning is finalized is development planning and standardization. This stage involves many processes that, if not handled properly, involve legal risk. A typical "standardization" stage would look something like this:

- R&D Department
  - Construct product structure
  - Covert product design into engineering sample
  - Standardize all parts
  - Confirm engineering samples
- Quality Department
  - Provide past failure examples and improvements
  - Provide quality control information
  - Review designs
- Production Technology Department
  - Establish pre-mass-production line
  - Create concept design for production line
  - Provide advice on improvements
- Design Department
  - Materialize design concept through 3D modeling or mock-up
  - Cooperate with Marketing Department
- Product Planning Department
  - Review design in regard to product planning
- Marketing Department
  - Review designs in regard to marketing
- Legal Department
  - Research existing patents
  - Apply for patents
  - Review designs

24.4 Development Implementation (Including Design Verification and Production Validation)

- R&D
  - Product evaluation review
  - Preparation of parts development

- Provide parts for working sample
- Production technology
  - Design manufacturing process
- Quality control
  - Establish quality standards
    - Testing of parts
    - Testing of specs
- Design
  - Check structural specs
- Marketing
  - Review marketing and promotional material

24.5 Production Readiness

The last stage before mass production involves the same of the most important processes as regarding legal risk. This is the last stage prior to putting a product into the stream of commerce.

- Production technology
  - Lead mass production line
  - Optimize manufacturing
  - Design mass production flow structure
- Quality control
  - Test reliability of mass production
  - Review mass production product quality
- Product planning
  - Check on product feature charges
  - Check on design feature charges
- Marketing
  - Check on product launch
  - Review production quality
  - Provide market info
- Other departments
  - Provide end-user manual
  - Provide service training manual

- Provide quality check manual

24.6 Mitigating Legal Risk in New Product Development and Planning

When it comes to legal risk, a company must take the production of new products seriously. A company faces various threats, especially class action exposure in the United States. Such exposure comes from claims involving:

- Breach of warranty
- Deceptive and unfair trade laws (DUPTA)
- Product defect claims

LRM processes can be used to minimize legal risk, especially those involving class action claims, if properly implemented. They include the following processes:

24.6.1 Limitation of Remedies

A company may limit remedies that end users have through properly drafted warranties. In the United States, the Magnuson-Moss Warranty Act limits remedies to whichever the warrantor elects:

- Refund
- Repair
- Replacement

A properly drafted warranty can limit the end users' remedy. Also, it can limit the liability from a buyer or consumer's failure to comply with conditions for warranty coverage. By using the buyer's own conduct as a basis of an affirmative defense, manufacturers can limit their liability.

So, the first step in minimizing your liability or minimizing legal exposure from the sale of goods or products is the use of an appropriate warranty, which limits remedies and limits or eliminates warranties based on the buyer's failure to comply with conditions of warranty coverage.

24.6.2 Warnings

Another useful LRM tool to minimize liability is to develop appropriate warnings in product literature.

Such warnings should:

- Describe product's limitation.
- Describe product risks.
- Stress dangers of not following the instructions.
- Warn of misuse and hazards to the user.
- Specify maintenance procedures of the product.
- Ensure that labels and warnings comply with federal and industry regulations and standards.

24.6.3 Sales and Marketing Literature

In order to protect itself from class actions involving the sale of products, a company should also review its sales and marketing literature.

- Do all sales and advertising manuals accurately describe the product?
- Are all disclaimers and limitations of warranties adequately reflected in the sales literature?
- Does the sales literature contain misleading statements?

24.6.4 Other Ways to Limit Liability

There are other processes and procedures and LRM tools to use to limit liability. Some will be described elsewhere in this book. However, some of the more common ones depend on following detailed product planning processes set forth in this chapter, including:

- Early detection of defective products
- Use of processes to carefully select vendors involved in manufacturing
    - Do they have insurance?

- Can they indemnify you?
- Implementation of a loss control policy procedure
- Use of insurance coverage

The LRM processes outlined in this chapter involve design, warnings, warranties, labels, and service procedures that can effectively limit or mitigate legal liability. They are set forth in more detail in the next chapter.

25 Design Risk Management

When designing products, manufacturing companies need to be very detailed to avoid product liability litigation in the United States. Product planning is a very detailed process involving many departments, as we have seen. As part of an overall plan to reduce risks of product liability litigation as well as class actions and government investigations raised by CPSC or FTC concerns, it is recommended manufacturing companies develop a detailed design risk program or "DRP." Such processes can minimize, reduce, or prevent liability when claims are brought. A checklist should be developed to cover such issues. Checklists are another handy tool to use when looking at processes and procedures to minimize legal liability. Product planning and design process considerations of an effective DRP should normally include the following:

25.1 Product Design Issues and Considerations[16]

- Written procedures for the design program, including:
    - Design choices—consideration of alternative designs
    - Specifications—definition of specifications used in designing the product

---

[16] For a discussion see Kenneth Ross, Martin Foley and Barbara Wrubel, Product Liability of Manufacturers, Preventions and Defense, NY: Practicing Law Institute, 1988

- Establishment of a design review committee
- Establishment of written procedures for the development of specifications, which verify that specifications are accurately reflected in the designs.
- Establishment of procedures for construction and testing and prototypes.
- During the design: Evaluation and consideration of:
  - Determine types of people likely to be exposed to the product, consider unique risks to these groups
  - Tailor labeling and develop safety features to address the unique risks to the intended users
  - Risks of intended use—test and evaluate to determine what risks are presented if the product is used as intended; reduce these risks through design changes, safety features, and/or labeling.
- Assess the likelihood that products will be misused; identify and reduce the probability of misuse through design features, safety features, and/or labeling.
- Malfunction: Incorporate features that prevent critical failure or malfunction. Is it safe to use? If not, what features can render it safe?
- Design manufacturing considerations: Can the product be manufactured in accordance with the specifications?
- Serviceability: Are the products difficult to service or maintain correctly?
- Consider the materials, components, equipment, and software that should be used in manufacturing the device.
- Assure that designs comply with applicable code certifications and standards. Are they appropriate? Do they comply with governmental and industry standards?
- If using an outside company to develop or provide product designs, review and evaluate the designs.
- Monitoring of designs, including continued research and testing and review of new information respecting the products.

- Record-keeping of all product designs and processes to show all the above processes were considered.
- Is everyone in the design department familiar with all design procedures and processes?

24.2 Labeling

Proper labeling is also mandatory to avoid or mitigate legal risk or exposure. Numerous class actions have and are continuing to be brought on the basis that product labels were misleading, false, or failed to adequately warn of the danger posed by the product. Such labels need not only to warn the users against all risks, including those risks that are obvious, but the labels must clearly state hazards and warn anyone about the potential or likely consequences of using the product improperly. Failure to do so will result in litigation. Of course, labels need to follow the requisite local standards.

It is recommended that significant time be spent on labels, as improper use of a product resulting in injury may very well end up in litigation. Labels may not play a big role in determining potential liability but inadequate labels or labels that fail to follow local rules and regulations can result in governmental fines, penalties or worse.

The following checklist summarizes what companies need to do when considering labels.

24.2.1 Labels, Labels, Labels

- It is important to establish a labeling review committee. Manufacturers need to review and modify labels on a regular basis, so it is advised that a committee be formed to handle it. Or, in fact, the loss control committee can help in this regard. I have used the loss control committee to review labels as well as using a labeling review committee. A regular review is necessary to keep the labels updated which is quite important to prevent and minimize product liability.

- Consider the intended users of the product. How should the label or labels be drafted?
  - If general consumers will be using the product, develop labeling that is easy to read and understand, warn against all risks, including all obvious risks, and warn about the consequences of improper use.
  - If professional operators will be using the product, you should specify on the labeling that only qualified personnel may use/operate the device and warn against unapproved uses.
- Provide users with clear and concise directions, information, and precaution for use on labels, if possible. Of course, it should also be reflected in the manuals and instructions.
  - Ensure that the label is accurate, complete, visible, and easily understood by the intended users.
  - Provide information on labels affixed to the product or through inserts or packaging.
  - When it is not feasible to provide full information on a label affixed to the product, affix a label that refers users to inserts or handbooks that will provide full information.
  - Warnings and information on the label should be consistent with warnings and information used elsewhere, such as in packaging or inserts. You do not want the label to contradict or modify warnings made elsewhere.
  - Include information on where and how to obtain service and warn against improper or unauthorized service.
  - Include information on where users should send complaints about the products; encourage users and distributors to report adverse information.
  - Include adequate warnings in labeling, including warnings as to:
    - Risks of customary use
    - Risks of misuse and unapproved uses

- Risks of improper maintenance
- Include information in labeling on:
    - Maintenance
    - Service
    - Alterations
    - Where to send complaints or questions
- Review all inserts and information on packaging for accuracy and to assure that they are consistent with other labeling elsewhere.
- Comply with all appropriate governmental requirements or regulations. If selling products in other countries, your labels should also comply with the labeling requirements of those countries or local jurisdictions in which your products are sold. This is another process that is quite important and must be followed.

24.2.2 Post-sale Monitoring of Labels

Once the product is sold in the marketplace, it is best to follow up on the adequacy of labels. Reports from Service might provide some insight, as the Service Department usually hears about defects, misuse, and other performance related problems first.

- A company should monitor the adequacy and accuracy of labels.
- A company should establish a field service reporting mechanism to a committee such as the loss control committee on how devices are used in the field and to give information on service and maintenance problems caused by users who misunderstand the labels.
- A company should evaluate complaints, failures, and malfunctions as it relates to labels.
- It is advised that a company evaluate all failures and malfunctions to determine whether they were caused by poor labeling or by user misunderstanding of the labeling.

- It is important to monitor labeling practices in the industry. What are they?
- A company should also monitor legal and regulatory developments related to labeling.
- A manufacturer should also keep labeling-history files, including test results and records of post market surveillance, as well as loss-prevention procedures. These files will be necessary in the event of a product liability lawsuit to show the requisite steps were taken to prevent injury or that the manufacturer took all possible steps to prevent injury.

24.3 Marketing Literature and Review of Manuals

Not only does product design and labels play a part in a good legal risk management program or LRM program, but a good LRM program requires manufacturers and distributors to review all marketing literature as well. Often companies fail to adequately review marketing literature even though poorly drafted marketing literature results in claims, litigation, and class actions, especially if a user is injured when allegedly following or relying on statements made in product literature. Plaintiff lawyers often cite misleading marketing literature as a major reason for filing DUTP claims. It is extremely important that a company invests time and resources to ensure its marketing literature is correct. This process may determine if a company or organization is exposed to class actions or not. Therefore, it is advised that a company should take the following important steps when drafting and reviewing marketing literature.

24.3.1 Marketing and Advertising Literature

- Review all published statements about the products, including marketing, advertising, product listings, and catalogues to ensure that they do not mislead users or encourage users to disregard directions and warnings contained in the labeling.

- Include provisions in distribution and purchasing agreements so that distributors and/or end users will:
    - Notify the company of any product failures or malfunctions or potential or alleged malfunctions.
    - Use the products strictly in accordance with the instructions provided.
    - Refrain from using the product after failure of the product or after a product malfunction.
    - Use the product only with compatible systems, components, or parts. Many products these days are used in conjunction with other products or systems, such as those sold by VARs.
    - Have the product serviced only by company service personnel or entities approved or certified by the company and avoid using unauthorized service providers.
    - Keep and provide the company with records of product sales for traceability purposes, especially if the product is manufactured in lots or batches. This will be important in the event of a product recall.
- Traceability: Provide for the tracing of products and important components to the point of origin by identifying and marking products during manufacture. Keep and maintain records of product lot and serial numbers, product release information, and identity of product users. This is vital in case of defective products that can be traced to a specific lot, which is necessary during a product recall.
- Warn against combining your products with incompatible systems. You never know what buyers or end users will do regarding your product. Even VARS or distributors may try and combine your products with incompatible systems. You should also prohibit VARS and distributors from combining your products with incompatible systems in your contract with them.

24.3.2 *Establish a Review Committee to Review Manuals, Labels, and Warnings*

I established a review committee to draft and review manuals, warnings, and labels. This was very effective, as not only the Sales and Marketing Departments had input but obviously Service, Legal, and Risk, as well. In fact, the loss control committee can provide this function or can provide assistance in forming a review committee. The more input from the various relevant departments the better.

- Instruction manuals[17]
  - In general, instruction manuals or guidebooks should contain detailed information not only about the product in question but also about publication of the manual and a disclaimer of relevant warranties, if applicable, including
    - the date of publication and a description of the manual(s);
    - appropriate disclaimers of express or implied warranties, if needed;
    - the name and description of the product and its overall function and other relevant product information, such as its model, lot, or serial number;
    - a summary at the front of the manual, directing attention to any known product hazards, if any;
    - consistent restatements of all warnings that appear on the products and additional safety information;

---

[17] For a good discussion on drafting instruction manuals and warnings see Kenneth Ross, Martin Foley and Barbara Wrubel, *Product Liability of Manufacturers, Preventions and Defense,* New York: Practicing Law Institute,1988

- a statement of the recommended operational limits of the product, accompanied by warnings against foreseeable misuses or mistreatment of the product(s);
- a listing of the relevant codes or standards or service classifications that it complies with;
- a detailed listing of the location and function of all components, parts, and accessories;
- instructions for assembly (especially complex products that may require separate manuals for each product-related task—installation, maintenance, repair, etc.);
- installation instructions;
- directions for operation if needed;
- directions for inspection, maintenance, and adjustment of the product(s);
- instruction for overhaul and repair of the product(s) if needed;
- instructions as to when special training or other qualifications may be required to perform a given task or operation with regards to the operation of the product(s);
- instruction for safe disposal of the product(s) or components thereof;
- Information on how to obtain additional or replacement manuals; and
- information on reordering parts, emphasizing safety-critical items, as well as information on obtaining replacements for warning labels.

24.3.3 Review Warnings[18]

A great deal of time should be spent to ensure warnings are appropriate for the product being sold. It is very important. Therefore, the following steps are recommended:

- The warning must adequately indicate the scope of the danger.
- The warning must reasonably communicate the extent of seriousness of the harm that could result from misuse of the product.
- The physical aspects of the warning must be adequate to alert a reasonably prudent person to the danger.
- The warning must indicate the consequences that might result from failure to follow it.
- The means to convey the warning must be adequate to bring the warning home to the user.
- The specific nature of the hazard and the gravity of the risk to which users may be exposed must be clearly stated in a warning.
- Indicate the level of hazard seriousness.
- Indicate the likelihood of the hazard resulting in harm.
- Note: Inadequate warnings have been the subject of much litigation in the United States. It is vital to have correct warnings on your product as well as in the instruction manual. Also, other countries besides the U.S. may take warnings seriously. It is advisable to discuss warnings with local legal counsel and check what local regulations exist, if any, that will impact the warnings you use.

24.4 Manufacturing and Distribution Issues

Obviously, when manufacturing a product, a company complies with local manufacturing standards. But, if it decides to sell and distribute products internationally, or if in the United States it decides

---

[18] Id

to distribute such products interstate, what are its concerns? Companies selling interstate or internationally need to comply with all applicable manufacturing standards, including international standards that are applicable to the relevant industry. Such standards may call for testing, certification, even certification of third-party service providers. You should make certain that your manufacturing processes are conducted in light of all regulatory requirements and that they address all legal issues. Therefore, applicable LRM processes regarding manufacturing should include the following consideration of manufacturing issues and warnings.

24.4.1 Manufacturing Issues

- Comply with all required manufacturing standards.
- Provide for different types of testing of devices, components, and material at different stages of the manufacturing process.
- Assure through testing that the manufactured device meets design and performance specifications.
- Conduct testing that accounts for the following:
  - Reliability
  - Environmental factors
  - System interface
  - Safety features
  - Serviceability
  - Shelf life and storage conditions

- Conduct validation of testing processes in accordance with applicable federal or international regulatory guidelines.
- Address quality of equipment used in manufacturing.
- Address quality of software.
- Address quality and suitability of buildings and facilities in which items are stored or manufactured.

- Procedures for testing of components and materials obtained from suppliers, and procedures for auditing suppliers and contractors.
- Agreements with suppliers and contractors, which include provisions that will help you address loss prevention concerns, including provisions for the following:
  - Periodic audits of suppliers
  - Notice to you of any significant malfunctions in the product supplied or manufactured

24.4.2 Service Issues and Procedures

Service processes and procedures, if correctly implemented, will not only mitigate legal risk and exposure but will actually first alert a company to any potential design or manufacturing defects as well as label, product manual, or literature issues. Service is usually the first division or department in contact with the end user or consumer. It is, in other words, the front line of a company's defense. It is the first to know if there is a problem. Therefore, it is recommended the following processes be strictly implemented and followed by the Service Department:

24.4.3 Service

- Investigations: It is vital that Service evaluate all service-related complaints according to written procedures that set forth valid and uniform criteria to determine validity, seriousness, fault, and repeatability, and determine whether the complaint falls within government regulatory requirements.
- Provide new information on proper use of risks associated with use.
- Warn against further use of an obsolete or hazardous product.
- Warn against misuse or unapproved use and supply information on the risks of such use.
- Advise when the product should be repaired or replaced.

- Provide information about obtaining product service from the manufacturer.
- Provide information about where to obtain service from third parties if necessary.
- Train field-service personnel in loss-prevention concerns, including the potential liability impact of their statements to users. Service personnel are often the first people users come into contract with and misstatements can lead to litigation or claims.
- Require field-service personnel to submit standard forms giving information on product problems and contacts with users.
- Instruct field-service personnel who also service other companies' products to:
  - Repair only products about which they have sufficient information.
  - Disclaim responsibility for the inherent quality of other companies' products.
  - Notify other companies of any problems relating to their products.
- Warn users to have products only serviced and repaired by authorized personnel.
- Document product-service loss-prevention measures and keep records of employee training and relevant agreements with users and service companies.

24.4.4 *Third-Party Service Providers*

It is common for manufacturers, especially in the consumer products industry, to use third-party service providers to provide service, especially product repair. Many foreign manufacturers do not have the resources or facilities in all countries to provide direct service without using third-party service providers. This is especially true in the consumer electronic industry. The use of third-party service providers, of course, inserts a third party in between the manufacturer, distributor or dealer, and the end user or consumer. It can be another source of legal risk! Therefore, the following processes should be required of third-party service providers:

- A report from the third-party service provider should include information such as:
    - Information on the product repaired
    - The nature of the work performed
    - The equipment and materials used to repair the product, if any
    - The identity of user and service
    - The place and date of repair
    - The condition of the product as received
    - The testing performed
    - Information about their procedures, employee training, and quality assurance
    - Indemnification for liability created by improper servicing of the service-provider
- Written procedures for the certification of third-party service provider should be required. The company should audit the third-party service provider to determine compliance with procedures on a regular basis.

26 Risk Insurance

Insurance, if used properly, is a great tool to shift legal risk or exposure to another entity (i.e., the insurance provider). Many companies fail to adequately consider insurance options, cover risk, or consider appropriate insurance tools that can shift or transfer risk of loss, litigation, or claims. A proper legal risk management program needs to adequately address these issues and to consider the insurability of risk. Insurance, if properly used, can be a great LRM tool. It all starts with a risk assessment such as set forth below.

25.1 Insurance Considerations: Risk Assessment

- Conduct a risk assessment to create a business risk profile to identify factors that have the greatest financial impact, then integrate appropriate risk transfer strategies to
    - stabilize insurance costs,
    - mitigate extraordinary financial impact,
    - ensure cost effective protection against catastrophic losses,
    - leverage risk bearing capital, and
    - optimize tax and accounting issues.
- Conduct an analysis of current coverage, amounts, deductibles, and excess.

- Consider custom-designed protection programs by product line (e.g., televisions, automobiles, or microwave ovens).
- Evaluate product recall insurance. Is it necessary?
- Investigate establishment of a captive insurance company.

25.1.1 Historical Data

It should be noted that companies use insurance as a risk mitigation or transfer tool and that they manage insurance programs differently than the average consumer. When developing a risk assessment of insurance considerations, data is extremely important when considering a probability or a risk-related event. The collection of relevant data will determine what kind of insurance policies can be obtained, the price, and even the availability of certain insurance programs. How far back a company can go historically to obtain data determines the potential risks a company faces and, therefore, what insurance program and provider is available as well as the costs involved.

When looking at risk insurance programs, the first question that should be asked by the company is whether it has accurate data. Does it have a good risk management information system in place? If not, does its insurance broker or provider have one? Or maybe the insurance broker or provider can help develop one.

Accurate data leads to the right risk management strategy and the right insurance program. Lack of data makes it harder to have an accurate picture as to the risks involved and, therefore, harder to develop the appropriate insurance strategy and program. It is necessary to obtain accurate historical data if at all possible.

25.2 Coverage

The main reason that companies make extensive use of insurance coverage is to diversify and shift risk through use of business-related insurance. Remember, insurance, if properly used and maintained, can be a major risk management tool.

A major issue facing companies when trying to insure legal risk is the insurability of the risk. In essence, the cost of insuring the risk may be too great to justify the particular form of risk insurance. So when a risk assessment identifies a business risk, not only does the company need to determine if insurance coverage exists to cover the risk, but whether the cost of such insurance justifies its acquisition. Many manufacturing companies will not purchase product recall insurance or similar insurance because of its expense. Some manufacturing companies or organizations will not even purchase credit insurance because of its expense. Therefore, a company or corporation must pay attention to costs and consider methods to reduce the cost of insurance.

25.3 Costs

There are numerous factors in determining the cost and the desirability and practicality of various forms of risk insurance. However, the most important factors in determining cost of the insurance product normally include:

- The cost of the insurance policy or risk insurance product.
- Insurance premiums, if any.
- Whether coinsurance is required. Note: coinsurance is a specific portion of the loss (i.e., 10 percent, etc.) the insured is required to pay.
- Deductibles: this eliminates use of insurance for small claims as deductibles maybe too expensive or burdensome to pay in case a loss is a minor one.
- Contractual provisions placing specific burdens on the insured, such as exclusions to coverage.
- Policy limits: insurance policies usually limit the amount of coverage by placing a limit on the coverage. Perhaps the product liability coverage covers only $ 1 million per occurrence. The greater the policy limit, the more desirable the insurance policy is. However, it is always a function of cost.
- The claims history of the insured.

25.4 Insurance Analysis

A company, when deciding to shift its risk to an insurance company, must conduct a detailed analysis on potential insurance coverage as well as its own claims history or the potential claims in its industry, if it has no claims history. Only with an analysis of insurance coverage, deductibles, excess premiums, and coinsurance is it able to make a reasonable risk assessment as to the cost and desirability of the coverage. It is possible that such analysis may lend to customization of the insurance coverage (certain insurance programs may get different coverage) or certain forms of insurance coverage may not be purchased (i.e., product recall insurance) at all.

25.5 Evaluation of Insurance Providers

In determining which insurance provider to use for specific risks, a company needs to sit down with its insurance broker. Some companies opt to purchase insurance directly online or through agents or insurance company employees. However, it must be remembered that an insurance broker is an independent organization or entity that represents the purchaser of insurance, while an agent normally represents the insurance company.

Insurance brokers, which are usually brokers of record, normally have relationships with multiple insurers. As the broker of record, insurance brokers are normally able to obtain coverage quotes from numerous insurance companies. If a company seriously considers shifting risk through insurance, it needs to seriously consider those brokers that are able to provide risk management services and insurance products across a wide range of product lines and product categories. The large international brokers are often able to provide companies products and services that small or regional brokers are usually not able to provide. A company should take into consideration what insurance products and services it needs prior to sitting down with insurance brokers.

Though most companies use one broker of record, it is common for companies to contract with multiple insurers, as certain types of insurance coverage is very business specific. Thus, brokers tend to match the needs of the company to certain specific insurers, according to the industry or product line. For example, a company could have one insurance company handle EPL insurance, one handle credit insurance, one handle transportation or carrier related insurance, and another one handle product liability insurance.

It is advised, therefore, in order to develop a strong insurance program that adequately addresses the legal risks a company faces, the company must sit down with its broker after conducting a detailed risk assessment and analysis of current insurance coverage, amounts, deductibles, and excess. At a certain point a company may want to consider establishing a captive insurance company if the cost of insurance becomes too onerous.

25.6 Creating a Captive Insurance Company

What is a captive insurance company and why should it be considered? A captive insurance company is defined as: A closely held insurance company whose insurance business is primarily supplied and controlled by its owners. As the owners are the principal beneficiaries as the insured, they have direct involvement and influence over a captive's major operations.

Many companies, especially those who have subsidiaries, have opted to create a captive insurance company. Single parent captives, as they are sometimes called, are: (1) owned by a single entity, (2) exist primarily to underwrite risks of the parent and affiliated companies, (3) may also underwrite risks of unrelated parties, and (4) the financial results are normally consolidated with the parent's for financial reporting.

Besides single parent captives that underwrite the risks of the parent and its subsidiaries, there is also the group captive insurance company. Group captives (1) have multiple owners, (2) the owners are usually homogenous (they are in similar industries with similar risks), and (3) they engage in risk sharing, which is spelled out in corporate governance documents.

25.7 What Are the Primary Reasons to Consider a Captive Insurance Company?

- Primary reasons:
  - Cost
  - Coverage
  - Control

- Cost
  - Premiums that would ordinarily be paid to commercial insurers can be invested for the benefit of the captive, and the parent companies, until claims are paid.
  - Captives would expect lower "frictional" costs of providing coverage (i.e., lower acquisition cost and no imbedded shareholder profit to consider.

- Coverage
  - Greater flexibility: obviously the captive can provide greater coverage for the cost.
  - There are fewer limitations on ability to offer specific policy terms and conditions.
  - The insured can dictate terms as needed.
  - Result: better matches of needs and coverage.

- Control
  Owners of a captive insurance company can exercise extensive direct control over all phases of the insurance process:
  - Underwriting
  - Claims adjusting and philosophy
  - Claims defense
  - Selection of counsel and philosophy
  - Selection of all vendors

- When should a captive insurance company be considered? Normally, when the company has:
    - Consistently high insurance premiums in the commercial market,
    - Uninsurable or difficult-to-place coverage,
    - Decentralized business units with different insurance programs, and
    - A chance to take advantage of an arbitrage opportunity when reinsurance rates are considerably below rates of the commercial market.

- Risks
    Like any insurance strategy, there are risks to consider. Such risks include:
    - Laws governing captive insurance companies continue to evolve.
    - Tax laws are transient and may change, affecting financial issued tied to taxation.
    - Reinsurance market viability to the extent that reinsurance is used.
    - Need for effective counseling on expected loss predictions, especially in early years.
    - Exit issues—if members decide to return to commercial insurance, the captive may have created obligations that extend for several years.

- Other issues include:
    - Tax issues
    - Domicile—where to form the captive
        - Domestic
        - Offshore
    - Structure and loss sharing among owners
    - Financial statement analysis
    - Loss history analysis
    - Comparison with alternatives

- Management: who will run the captive?

Note: the above issues should be considered during a feasibility study.

- So why is a captive insurance company worth considering?
  There are many reasons to consider a captive insurance company, including:
    - Problems with availability of commercial insurance.
    - Financial opportunities to invest significant premium dollars for the company's benefit.
    - When the company will benefit from lower-than-expected losses in given policy years that will create a true incentive to produce safe and effective products and facilities.
    - It could open greater reinsurance opportunities for the company.

- What should a company do when considering the captive insurance alternative?
    - Conduct a feasibility analysis
    - Review results of the analysis
    - Agree on the data points involving the analysis
    - Answer the above-mentioned issues

27 Credit Risk Management

Forms that may be useful in managing credit insurance and credit risk may include:

Form: Credit Risk Insurance
Form: Put Agreement

27.1 Credit Risk

Many companies that sell products to distributors, dealers, and retailers are exposed to credit risk when their customers don't pay for the product prior to or upon taking delivery of the product. This is often seen in purchase or sales contracts in which payment terms are net thirty, net forty-five, or net ninety. Of course, if the parties enter into a consignment arrangement, this is not the case.

Credit risk covers many loss scenarios in which a borrower (normally a buyer or customer) fails to fulfill its payment obligations. Such scenarios involve borrowers regardless of size or scope, including small companies, midsize, or even large companies, and sometimes even governments. Credit risk management is an extremely important piece in the LRM process. However, one of the most important forms of credit risk involves trade credit risk (i.e., the credit risk a company faces when its buyers or customers fail to pay on time or, in some situations, at all). How can a company handle its receivables credit risk or trade credit risk problems?

A company, when calculating the risk of nonpayment, needs to consider ways in which it can transfer or mitigate the risk.

27.2 Credit Risk Processes

Companies that experience credit risks on a regular basis should create a Credit Risk Department. The Credit Risk Department can implement a number of LRM processes or risk management tools and procedures that can mitigate or minimize the impact of credit risk. It is essential that a department or individual continuously monitors the credit risk of customers, as financial circumstances can change very quickly.

Normally, procedures and processes used by a Credit Risk Department in conjunction with Legal, Finance or Risk Management would include the following steps:

- Implementation of credit risk procedures: Normally standardized credit processes including credit terms and conditions of using the terms. The Credit Risk Department should run all terms by Legal. In fact the right terms on a credit application may in fact mitigate or minimize legal exposure that results from a customer's breach or default.
- Credit acceptance: Usually the first step in the process for credit approval where the company decides whether customers or buyers qualify for extended credit terms and if so under what terms. It is up to the Credit Risk Department in conjunction with Finance to decide what the payment terms would be, such as net thirty, net forty-five, or net sixty.
- Credit collection: Implementation of credit collection processes, including use of credit collection agencies.
- Use of credit risk insurance: Establishment and implementation of a credit risk insurance program to cover all or most customers on extended credit.

It should be noted that credit acceptance decisions are normally based on a number of factors, including:

- A company's credit history, if any
- The credit application form, if any
- A company's credit report or evidence of credit worthiness
- Financial statements of the company
- Corporate guarantees or cross corporate guarantees in case a company has subsidiaries or affiliates
- Standby letter of credit or some form of an L/C
- Personal guarantees of the principle shareholders if the organization or corporate entity is small
- Personal financial statements of partners or shareholders of the firm if it is small or medium size

27.3 Credit Risk Insurance

Commercial credit risk insurance, sometimes called "trade" credit risk insurance, can help a company protect its account receivables (A/R) from unexpected losses due to nonpayment or slow payment by the company's buyers. It usually covers nonpayment because of a buyer's insolvency but may also cover nonpayment due to political events that hinder payment or distributors on credit. A/R is the money owed to a company by its customer for products and services sold on credit. Normally, a sale is only treated as an account receivable after the customer has been invoiced for the product or service.

Depending on the industry and size of the company, it may or may not sell many or all of its products via credit. The risk, therefore, of nonpayment or slow payment (90 or 180 days after invoice, etc.) can be quite serious and expose the company to a potential crisis if the A/R is not paid. This is a major concern for any company selling product on credit.

27.3.1 Types of Credit Risks

Credit risk insurance normally covers two kinds of risk: commercial risk and political risk.

- Commercial risk
  - Insolvency or bankruptcy
  - Protracted nonpayment
  - Default of customer

Note: Credit risk insurance will not usually cover nonpayment due to contractual or legal disputes between the company and customer.

- Political risk
  - War, strikes or other potential civil disturbances
  - Repatriation concerns: decision by the government not to allow repatriation or release of the funds
  - Transfer risk: political events including wars or political disputes preventing transfer of payment

27.3.2 Benefits of Credit Insurance

There are numerous benefits for using credit insurance, if applicable. The most obvious benefits are:

- Transfer or mitigation of risk. Credit insurance assures a company that its A/R will be paid if one of its customers declares bankruptcy or is unable to pay. This is subject to the terms and conditions of the insurance policy.
- Improved cash flow. A timely collection of A/R provides much-needed operating cash flow.
- Sales. By using credit insurance, a company is able to extend more credit to its primary customers, promoting increased sales. This can be cyclical, allowing increased turnover of products and, therefore, increased sales.

27.3.3 Types of Coverage

Credit risk insurance normally consists of two kinds:

- Traditional coverage
- Excess-of-loss coverage

- Traditional coverage
    - It is cancelable by the insurer.
    - The insurer assigns credit limits and monitors specific credits.
    - Low deductibles.

- Excess-of-loss coverage
    - Non-cancelable by insurer.
    - Policies usually provide a large discretionary credit limit.
    - Insured are able to set the majority of its credit limits on its customers.
    - Policy will include an annual aggregate deductible, above which losses are covered.

27.3.4 Insurance Provider

Credit insurance is a very specific insurance product. Usually, only international or specific insurance companies offer such insurance.

It should be noted that as credit risk covers many loss scenarios due to the failure of the borrower to fulfill payment obligations, trade credit risk encompasses the potential loss of a company's A/R due to nonpayment of a customer. Obviously, other credit risk scenarios exist, including project finance risks, but in this chapter, we have concentrated on trade credit risk and trade credit risk insurance.

27.4 Put Agreements

Besides shifting or minimizing credit risk through insurance, companies are able sometimes to shift the risk of a buyer's nonpayment contractually. Put agreements, as they are called, may also protect a company's A/R when a purchaser fails to pay or is slow in paying its obligations. The terms of put agreements vary depending on which insurance provider, financial institution, or flooring company is willing to provide the put agreement. Normally, put agreements do not cover all receivables but will cover most of them. The put agreement can be used in conjunction with credit risk insurance if the credit risk insurance does not cover 100 percent of the risk.

12.5 Factoring

Another method of shifting or mitigating legal risk through insurance is through a factoring agreement. Basically, a company sells its A/R that is under a particular agreement to a financial institution or financial company that specializes in factoring agreements for a percentage of the A/R value. This works well if the company has a low-risk customer with poor cash flow. However, unlike put agreements, the factoring company will hold the company liable if the trade debt or outstanding A/R remains unpaid, such as in the case of bankruptcy of the debtor.[19]

---

[19]   See Paul M Collier, *Fundamentals of Risk Management for Accountants and Managers*, Oxford, UK: Butterworth-Heinemann, Elsevier, 2009 p 181

28 Data Privacy and Risk Management

An often-overlooked area of risk management is data privacy or data protection. Many companies do not even associate data privacy with risk. However, as more and more countries begin to regulate the use of data by companies, data privacy has emerged as one of the hot topics of legal risk management. There are five main reasons why data privacy has become a major area of risk requiring attention of a company's Law Department, Risk Management Department and, ultimately, management itself.[20]

- Knowledge economy: Many businesses, through the use of the Internet and computers, compile and use large batches of data.
- Penalties: The European Union, Canada, and other countries, such as South Korea, have strict data privacy laws, which can levy significant penalties and fines for data privacy law violations.
- Publicity: As more and more people begin to jealously guard their personal data, a company's violation of data privacy laws can create a publicity nightmare, creating in effect a crisis of potential epic proportions. This has to be managed or contained.

---

[20] See the data privacy discussion set forth in chapter 24 of *International Corporate Practice*, edited by Carol Basri, New York: PLI, 2011, 24–2 – 24–3.

- Extraterritorial reach: More and more data privacy laws restrict the transmission of data abroad, creating cross-border risks.
- Tougher regulations: More and more countries or jurisdictions, such as the European Union, are enacting tougher and tougher regulations on the use of personal data.

28.1 Personal Data

Though there are many kinds of data, data privacy issues normally concern "personal data." The European Union, for instance, considers personal data as any information that relates to an identifiable natural person. Such personal data can include an identification number, an employee's position, a person's e-mail address, phone number, etc. Basically, any information that relates to a natural person (not a corporation) regardless of whether the data relates to an employee or a customer, etc.[21] This interpretation has been carried forward into the EU's recent data privacy law called the General Data Protection Regulation (GDPR) that went into effect on May 25, 2018.

The EU Data Directive, which was the European Union's comprehensive data privacy law, not only covers computerized data, but also covers written, Internet, and oral communications. Thus, any company doing business in Europe or interfacing with European companies that may result in the use of personal data from Europe could be exposed to a comprehensive data privacy law that is extraterritorial in reach.[22] The GDPR, replacing the EU Data Directive, still covers all data that the Data Directive covered but with more teeth.

The GDPR which is now the EU's current data privacy law or main regulation, not only tightened the EU's already strong data privacy laws but has resulted in the creation of the European Data Protection Board

---

[21]   See Rebecca S Eisner, *European Union Data Privacy Requirements, A US Perspective, Tenth Annual Institute on Privacy and Data Security*, New York: PLI (2009) p 662

[22]   See https://ec.europa.eu/info/law/law-topic/data-protection/reform/what-personal-data.eu

(EDPB) which groups all 28 of the EU's data protection authorities together into one body. The EDPB has the authority to adopt binding decision as well as impose fines. The fines the EDPB may impose on businesses are quite draconian in nature- up to 4% of a company's worldwide turnover.[23]

Other countries may not have privacy laws as onerous as the European Union, such as the United States, but more and more countries are beginning to aggressively enforce their data privacy laws. This will only continue, especially as more lawsuits involving the privacy rights of corporate whistleblowers and potential wrongdoers are filed.

28.2 Data Processing

Obviously, companies must be concerned about personal data, but it is the processing of data that normally gets a company in trouble. What is processing? How is it defined? What does it involve?

The European Union considers processing of data as any operation or set of operations performed upon personal data. From a legal perspective, almost any data-related operation involves processing. If you are in the United States, and you are reviewing personal data from an employee situated in the European Union, or your servers in the European Union transfers such information to your server in the United States, you may have violated EU data privacy laws. As Canada's privacy laws are also based on the EU's laws and regulations you also should be concerned if your servers in Canada share personal data with your servers in the U.S. Be careful!

28.3 Other Data

Besides personal data, a company must also consider the risks of unauthorized access or dissemination of other kinds of data. Such data could include various kinds, such as:

---

[23]   See europa.eu/dataprotection

- Financial data
- Medical data
- R&D data
- Marketing strategy data
- Technology-related data

Therefore, a company or organization must consider regulatory requirements, global data protection laws, US state laws, and its own compliance policies and corporate regulations when considering how to handle and protect data, as well as the risks surrounding unauthorized access or use of such data. Not only is a company's violation of data privacy laws looked upon seriously, but data theft or lack of appropriate data security systems likewise are frowned upon by society in general but looked upon as inexcusable by an organization's stakeholders. Failure to properly handle and protect data can lead to headaches for everyone concerned. This is a major issue as more and more countries and legal jurisdictions are implementing tougher and tougher data protection laws. Of special note is South Korea.

28.3.1 South Korea

South Korea has taken data protection very seriously and has implemented a general data protection law- the Personal Information Protection Act or "PIPA". Amended in 2016, PIPA places strict requirements on data privacy in other sectors such as IT Networks, credit card information, cloud computing and online advertising.

The 2016 updates were in response to the credit card scandal of 2014 in which 3 major credit card companies faced a massive data breach. Korean data privacy laws as well as its regulations and guidelines have all been tightened in an attempt to prevent a reoccurrence of such a scandal. There will always be a risk of unauthorized access to data unless companies and governmental agencies implement and continuously update risk management processes in dealing with the protection of personal data. There have been many changes to Korea's main data privacy law – PIPA as well as specific industry related data privacy laws and regulations over the last few years. Some are listed below:

A. PIPA

1. Collection of information on privacy- ICSPs are limited from collecting more than the absolute minimum level of privacy related information from users, regardless of whether they obtain the user's consent or not.
2. Report of Data Breach- there is a 24-hour deadline in reporting a data breach to the Korea Communications Commission ("KCC").
3. Increased Administrative Penalties- Administrative penalties have increased in the case of ICSPs who collect or process personal information without the user's consent. The penalty has now increased to 3% of annual turnover.
4. Chief Privacy Officer- ICSPs who meet certain criteria are required to designate a Chief Privacy Officer (CPO) and report such designation to the Minister of the Ministry of Science, ICT & Future Planning.

B. Cloud Computing

1. The Cloud Computing Act which took place in 2015 specifically identifies personal data and seeks to protect the personal data of users. The Cloud Computing Act stipulates that PIPA applies with respect to protecting data of users of cloud computing services that have been stored in the cloud.
2. Cloud computing service providers (CCSPs) are required to notify users of any cyber security incident, cloud data leakages and service interruptions. They must also notify the Minister of Science, ICT and Future Planning in the event cloud data is leaked.

C. Act on Promotion and Communications Network Utilization and Information Protection

1. The Network Act was amended to provide that from March 23, 2017, in the event any information and communications service provider (ICSP) needs to access certain data stored on a user's smartphone, it must obtain prior informed consent from the user.

2. Furthermore, the ISCP may not refuse to provide smartphone services to the user based on the user's refusal to provide consent to the ISCP to access its data.

3. If the CPO of an ICSP becomes aware of a violation of the data protection /privacy laws or regulations, the CPO must take steps to remedy the situation and also report the violation.

D. Online Behavioral Advertising Guidelines

1. On February 7, 2017 the Korean Communications Commission (KCC) set forth guidelines on privacy and online behavioral advertising ("Guidelines") to promote a healthy advertising ecosystem by minimizing the risk of privacy invasion users might experience as a result of being targeted by online advertisers. The Guidelines take effect in July of 2017.

2. The Guidelines contain a number of requirements including: (i) transparency in the collection and use of online behavioral data of the users, (ii) the users are guaranteed the right to control exposure to online targeted ads, (iii) the online advertisers must guarantee the security of online behavioral data and (iv) mechanisms giving users the right of redress must be strengthened.

3. Online behavioral advertising businesses must retain personal data for only the minimum period necessary to provided online targeted ads and must take measures to destroy the information once the purpose for retaining the information has been achieved.

It is clear that the regulatory trend for data protection in Korea is for the increased accountability for the collection, storage and use of personal information and data. Basically, stricter requirements have been placed on financial institutions and credit card companies. Compliance with PIPA and other regulations will become very important as more and more penalties and fines are levied against those who fail to comply.[24]

28.3.2 *Data Privacy Laws in Asia*

Besides South Korea, there is no doubt that privacy laws in Asia have become very important to businesses operating in the Asia Pacific region. Here is a brief summary of the privacy laws of several jurisdictions in Asia such as:[25]

1. Australia- Australia's privacy law was first enacted in 1988. It has been modified twice since then, most recently in 2012. There is no provision for a data protection officer. However, under the Privacy Act, there is an obligation to follow or comply with the procedures set forth in the Privacy Principles, a set of privacy principles enacted with the 2012 amendments. One of the most significant changes in the Australian Privacy Act was a provision extending the applicability of the privacy laws to cover overseas handling of personal information.

2. Hong Kong- Hong Kong was one of the first jurisdictions in Asia to adopt a comprehensive data privacy law. The law, called the Hong Kong Privacy Ordinance, was enacted in 1995. The Privacy Ordinance applies to both public and private sectors and protects private information of natural persons. Amended in 2012, the Privacy Ordinance regulates the use of personal information in marketing activities. Like Australia, the Hong

---

[24] See my blog "Data Privacy Laws in Korea- An Update" at https://seoullegalriskmgmt.com. April 28, 2017

[25] See Privacy Laws in Asia by Cynthia Rich, BNA Insights, Vol. 14, No. 20 (2015)

Kong privacy law does not require the appointment of a DPO, but it is recommended that companies appoint one.

3. India- India issued regulations in 2011 that implemented parts of the original 2008 Information Technology Act. The 2011 regulations cover the protection of personal information. The regulations set forth how personal information may be used and collected by all organizations in India. Like Australia, the Indian privacy rules do not require the appointment of a DPO. There are however, limitations on cross-border transfer of private information but such limitations apply only to sensitive personal information.

4. Singapore- Singapore's set of comprehensive data privacy laws known as the Personal Data Protection Act 2012 was implemented in 2013. The law governs the use, collection and disclosure of personal information by organizations in the private sector. Unlike, Hong Kong, Singapore's privacy law requires appointment of a DPO and restricts cross-border transfers of personal information.

Asia is clearly taking data privacy seriously. Any company doing business in Asia must carefully consider any and all risks stemming from data privacy concerns.[26]

28.4 Data Processes and Related Risks

When an organization confronts the risk inherent in unauthorized use of its data, it must keep in mind three basic risks involved with data processes before implementing risk management solutions.

---

[26] For an in-depth discussion see my blog "For Asian Companies the New EU Privacy Laws Can be a Headache" at https://seoullegalriskmgmt. com, - April 24,2017

- Financial risk: Fines and penalties resulting from privacy laws, EU directive, litigation, litigation costs, U.S. data protection laws, and U.S. state data protection laws
- Intellectual property risks: Loss of competitiveness in the marketplace due to loss of trade secrets or other forms of IP to competitors wherever situated
- Brand risks: Loss of reputation, customer loss, negative publicity, negative reaction of stakeholders, and increased scrutiny of regulators

The above-mentioned risks can be catastrophic when dealing with data and data processes. An organization must confront the three major risks in light of regular corporate data processes, primarily:

- Data usage: Data processes involved with data usage, such as data accessed by specific users
- Data storage: Data stored in servers
- Data transfer: Data transferred to third parties from specific points in a computer network

Each data process or stage of data usage poses specific risks that can harm an organization. In determining the risks a company faces prior to developing an LRM solution, an organization must answer a series of questions such as:

- What data does the organization have and where is it located?
- What kind of data does the company have and how sensitive or confidential is it?
- What processes, if any, are currently in place to protect the data?
- What company policies, if any, currently exists that control data and access to the data?
- What company process or procedures exist, if any, that control access of sensitive data by third parties?

- What company policies or procedures exist, if any, when dealing with personal data, especially personal data from EU countries or jurisdictions with rigorous data privacy laws?

Based on the answers to the questions above, a company can implement LRM solutions that can address and minimize the major risks a company faces when dealing with data, whether personal, financial, or IP related.

28.5 LRM Solutions to the Data Problem

After an organization conducts a risk assessment on data and data usage, it is in a better situation to appreciate the risks it faces regarding its data and can then take steps to implement an LRM solution.

When it comes to the unauthorized access or dissemination of data, a company should consider a solution based upon three key areas using a set of tools to implement the strategy:

- Technology: A policy-based approach using technology to discover and monitor potential data leaks or unauthorized data transmission over networks or mobile devices, such as PDAs, systems, and data repositories.
- Training: A company must develop a process covering unauthorized data transmission to third parties or nonessential personnel. Such processes should be reinforced and implemented by appropriate training programs.
- Management: Management must implement and oversee operational requirements that implement the solutions needed to prevent data leakage.

Regarding data privacy laws, most companies that must deal with the EU directive or similar data privacy regulations can minimize data privacy risks through a combination of the following processes:

- Contractually: use of binding standard contractual clauses that deal with privacy data.

- Binding corporate rules (BCR): codes of conduct accepted by the EU that binds the company to a specific code of practice when dealing personal data. The BCR requires a company to implement adequate safeguards required by the EU.
- Safe Harbor: a voluntary self-certification program available to US companies under certain circumstances.

However, to qualify, companies must adhere to the safe harbor rules, called the Safe Harbor Principles. To qualify, companies must:

- Bring the company's data protection rules into compliance with the Safe Harbor Principles.
- Verify the company is in compliance with the Safe Harbor Principles.
- Complete the certification process.

28.6 Real Case in Point – TJX

Data privacy has become increasingly important over the last few years. Recently retailers like Target and Michaels in the U.S. had their systems hacked and millions of credit card information stolen. However, one of the most famous cases involving a lack of data security involves the TJX companies.

TJX companies (T.J. Maxx, Marshalls, Home goods and A. J. Wright) experienced a hacking scandal of massive proportions. Starting in 2006 and continuing for 2 years therefore, hackers broke into TJX's central database and stole information about customers[27].

What was eventually discovered was that TJX had less data security processes in place than many people had on their home computer networks. It was reported that for at least one and a half years, TJX had no idea its computer systems had been hacked.

---

[27] *Buchholts and Carroll, Business and Society, 7ʰ Ed, South-Western (2006), p 303*

As a result of an investigation, it was concluded the hackers stole 45.7 million credit card and debit card numbers and may have made off with up to 200 million card numbers.

Besides that, TJX hackers got personal information such as driver's license numbers, social security numbers and other ID numbers of approx. 451,000 customers[28].

Though TJX apologized for its inept security policies, the damage had already been done. It was clear TJX had to upgrade its data security systems.

- Does your company have strong data security systems?
- Is your company compliant with local and international data security standards?
- Are you able to detect hacking from the inside as well as outside?

[28] *Id*

29   Contract Management

Suggested Form: Contract Management Process

29.1   Contract Risk Management

A major area of legal risk for any company is the negotiation, execution, and performance of contracts. Many companies have spent much money creating and/or improving the contract management process. Some companies simply rely on outside counsel to handle its contracts, blissfully unaware that the lack of internal contract risk management controls exposes it in the long run to major legal and business liability—a lawsuit waiting to happen!

A company needs to address many contractual areas prior to drafting contracts as well as managing them. Not only must a company negotiate agreements, but it must also manage and comply with the agreements once they have been negotiated and executed. Companies cannot rely on outside legal counsel to do this for them.

Some of the areas that need to be addressed include:

- IP
- Warranties
- Indemnities
- Tax
- Sales and marketing issues
- Responsibilities and obligations

- Deliverables
- Payment obligations
- Industry terms and conditions
- Insurance

Obviously, if a proper contract management system is not in place, some or all the issues above may be affected, causing great harm to the company. Pricing could be impacted, or missed contractual obligations could result in the company's indemnity obligations to cover more than expected. Contractual defenses as well may not be implemented due to the lack of appropriate contracts or contractual terms.

29.1.1 Contract Management Issues

In order for a company's contracts to be negotiated, performed, and executed properly, a number of organizations within a company must work together and coordinate efforts. Depending on the kind of contract, its size, and scope, not only should divisions or business units work together, but appropriate policies and processes must be implemented and followed.

For instance, decision makers within a company need to make informed and timely business decisions prior to execution of a contract but can only do so based on input from internal stakeholders or division heads. A process needs to be in place to ensure timely advice is provided. Depending on the nature of the risks and issues involved (i.e., billing, tax, etc.) appropriate departments will need to be involved.

A proper LRM audit needs to be conducted to ensure the proper contract management process is in place. Such an audit should cover roles and responsibilities of departments within an organization, the kinds of contracts used by the business units, the major legal and business term that must be addressed, the process for informing the relevant decision makers as to the risks faced, and the process for ensuring the contracts are not only signed but also performed. A contract management process can be very detailed, which is why some companies have failed to adopt the process. Of course, when a company fails to implement a contract management process, it opens itself up to potential legal and financial exposure.

A company's contract management process must allow for negotiation and resolution of major business and legal issues while its customers or vendors are satisfied with the process. Therefore, a company's contract management process must not only allow for proper negotiation and resolution of contractual issues, but must also ensure the company is not exposed to undue risk. Though a company may be willing to assume a moderate level of risk, it may not be willing to accept a greater degree of risk without pricing the risk or cost of risk into its pricing calculations. From an accounting standpoint, a company may wish to increase its reserves as well.

29.1.2 *Roles and Responsibilities*

A company's various business units as well as Legal, Sales, Risk, Finance, Human Resources, Contract Management (if it exists), and other impacted corporate departments or groups must work together to minimize undue risk to the company and ensure how the risk should be managed.

Roles and responsibilities of certain organizations within a company or corporation normally include:

- Corporate Risk Management: The division head or department head responsible for identifying risk and facilitating mitigation by working with Legal, Business Units, and decision makers. Corporate risk management implements policies and procedures to ensure risk mitigation strategies are pursued throughout the life of the contract.
- Legal: The department responsible for identifying legal risks and available legal options and preparation and maintenance of contracts and contract templates. Also responsible for negotiating legal terms.

- Contract Management: The department responsible for identifying and documenting legal and business issues raised during negotiation of contract terms (if not done by Legal) and escalation of legal and business terms to the correct decision makers within the company. Usually has to notify Legal of complex legal issues.
- Finance: The department responsible for issues including cash flow, time value of money, and reserve calculations.
- Sales: The division or department responsible for communicating with and maintenance of the customer relationship while helping to mitigate risk to the company. Needs to understand basic risk issues.
- Business Units: The division or various departments responsible for identifying the strategic value of the contract. May want contract managers to stay in their unit.
- Human Resources: The department responsible for issues involving personnel management and secondment if needed, noncompetition issues, and other matters having a direct effect on employees.

Other decision makers or internal stakeholders may also be involved besides the groups listed above. The board of directors (BOD), executive committee, CEO, CFO, or controller, etc., may get involved to discuss risk mitigation strategies as is necessary.

29.2 Contract Management Processes

The contract management process, to be effective, must include processes and procedures that identify and resolve certain legal and business issues.

Among those processes and procedure are:

29.2.1 The Escalations Process

This is the process in which certain important legal and business risks get escalated to the proper organization for resolution. Such a process should include:

- Identification of the issues
- Communication to relevant stakeholders
- Business impact analysis
- Resolution of issue
- Communication of resolution and documentation of the resolution

29.2.2 *Contract Approvers and Processes*

A process has to be implemented to ensure that:

- All Contract Management/Legal comments have been incorporated into the contract or at least properly considered.
- The contract is ready for execution or for the signature of the other party.
- The most current version of the contract is ready to be uploaded into the database.
- The correct contact names and billing addresses are in the final version of the contract.
- All payment terms are final and correct.

29.2.3 *Standard Billing and Payment Terms*

A company normally has certain standard billing and payment terms in its contracts. Such terms need to be included in the proper agreements. Depending on the kind of contract in question, such terms could include various payment models such as:

- Fixed fee payment
- Time and materials
- Milestone payments
- Maintenance payments
- Payment based on credit

The process should ensure, absent escalation that the standard billing and payment terms are in the contract as required.

29.2.4 *Ownership of Intellectual Property (IP)*

One of the most important assets of any company is of course its IP. It, therefore, stands to reason that IP concerns and considerations must be properly reflected in the contract management process. IP concerns include:

- Ownership of IP rights
  - Does the company retain or receive IP rights?
  - Does the other contracting party receive right and title to the IP?
- Retention of IP rights
  - When does the company retain all right, title, and interest in any and all IP?
  - When does the other contracting party retain all right, title, and interest in any and all of the IP?
- Ownership of newly created IP
  - What happens when the company or contracting party creates IP during performance of the contract? This could be in the form of manuals, software, training materials, and other media and information
- Similar works
  - What happens when the company performs similar services for third-party customers?

29.2.5 *Typical Customer or Vendor Requests*

A company's customers or vendors may typically ask for certain terms in a contract. Such terms could impose undue risk on the company or negatively affect its contractual relations with third parties. The contract management process must address and resolve the issues caused by such requests. Terms typically asked for may include:

- Customer retention of IP rights
- Noncompetition provisions

- Customer ownership of deliverables
- Nonstandard payment terms
- Staffing changes
- Broad indemnity provisions
- Limitation of liability

A company's contracts would or should normally address all of the above-mentioned issues. The contract management process must ensure that the issues are escalated to and resolved by the appropriate stakeholders and that all appropriate terms have been negotiated and addressed in a timely manner.

29.2.6 Preliminary Agreements

A well-thought-out contract management process will contain certain company guidelines and preliminary agreement templates to facilitate the deal. A LRM audit should review any and all preliminary guidelines and document templates to ensure the needs of the company are being met and potential legal and business risks are mitigated. Preliminary agreements include:

- Letter of intent (LOI): Normally a document reflecting the understanding between the company and customer or vendor without creating a binding contractual obligation.

  A corporation's LOI usage guidelines should address subject matter of the LOI, the fact that the parties do not wish to be bound, when a nondisclosure agreement is needed, and under what terms the parties expect to be bound at a later date.

- Memorandum of understanding (MOU): Normally a document for establishing an agreement of critical or major terms between the parties before a full and final contract is negotiated and executed. May have binding terms and conditions.

A corporation's MOU usage guidelines should address what obligations the company is willing to commit to before negotiating a complete contract, as well as a definition of the framework for negotiation of such as the price, milestones, deliverables, etc.

- Letter of authorization (LOA): Normally a document containing a minimum set of key terms and conditions that the parties must agree upon in order to begin work during contract negotiations. Not always used.

  A corporation's LOA usage guidelines should deal with issues such as IP, liability, price, etc. that may be hard to negotiate after the work has started.

Note: A process must be in place requiring the signature and/or sign-off of the appropriate corporate officer or officers prior to execution of any of the preliminary agreements. It is best to get the appropriate sign off in writing.

29.3 Miscellaneous Issues

A contract management process must take into account other issues besides the basic contract issues of escalation, contract templates, indemnity clauses, sign-off authority, etc. Several of them are set forth below.

- Sales and marketing practices
  In order for the proper management of contracts, Sales must determine how annual sales, revenue, and profit will be achieved across the various business units. This should be reflected either in a sales and marketing plan or manual involving the account manager, product specialist (if any), credit manager, marketing manager, and business unit manager.
- Business processes

As the company's IP and other assets are very important, the contract management process should include business processes that protect the company's assets or mitigate risk. Such business processes should include:

- Computer safeguards
- IP safeguards
- Data privacy controls and safeguards
- Information controls and safeguards
- Competition-antitrust

  One of the most important legal and regulatory areas affecting a company and its business practices involves competition, or antitrust. The world's major economic regimes are enthusiastically enforcing antitrust/competition laws and regulations requiring competition guidelines to be not only enforced by a compliance program but implemented in a contract management process. The contract management process should address antitrust issues and enforce antitrust/competition guidelines by implementing processes and procedures that address major antitrust issues such as:

  - Exclusive dealing agreements
  - Discrimination among vendors or customers
  - Benchmarking with competitors on business practices and costs
  - Tying agreements

The contract management process contains many potential legal and business risks if not performed correctly. An LRM program should cover an audit of the contract management process and ensure that it reduces, mitigates, or prevents legal and business risk. It requires the active participation of all major organizations within a company, including Legal, Finance, Sales, HR, and Risk Management. If a company does not have contract management systems in place it needs to either design them or use off-the-shelf contract management software to implement the processes. A number of good off-the-shelf programs are available. However, it is advised that if a company uses an off-the-shelf program that it customizes the program to ensure the company's processes and unique concerns are adequately addressed by the software.

30   Antitrust and Competition Concerns

Antitrust or competition issues are among the most serious issues that in-house counsel or compliance managers will encounter almost anywhere in the world. Originally established by the US in the 1890s, antitrust laws have been adopted in certain forms or formats depending on the legal regime of the relevant jurisdiction (civil, common law, etc.). All antitrust laws of the various jurisdictions have one overriding theme- they are designed to promote fair trade. Perhaps, antitrust laws are the most important set of laws an in-house counsel or risk manager (or Compliance Officer) will face. I would therefore be remiss if I did not discuss antitrust (competition) laws and regulations in this book. So, a discussion of basic antitrust laws and what steps an in-house counsel or risk manager should take to comply with such laws is outlined below along with a case study.

30.1 The United States

The main antitrust laws in the US are federal laws which provide the basis statutory framework. These laws were promulgated over 100 years ago. The antitrust laws have an impact on many business activities such as pricing, licensing, M&A, marketing, etc. The main US antitrust laws are as follows: (1) The Sherman Act (Sec. 1 & 2) which covers conspiracy and collusion as well as monopolization; (2) The Clayton Act which covers tying, price and promotional discrimination, and anti-competitive mergers and acquisitions; and (3) The FTC Act which created an independent enforcement agency empowered to prevent "unfair methods of competition". [29] The Clayton Act was amended by the Robinson Patman Act in 1936 to prevent price and promotional discrimination between companies. It was also amended by the Hart Scott Rodino Act 9 HSR) in 1978 to cover pre-merger notification.

1. Sherman Act (1890)

Section 1 of the Sherman Act is the most well-known and important antitrust law in the United States. It is primarily used these days to prevent cartels and therefore should be reviewed in detail by in-house counsel. It states in part:

"Every contract, combination in the form of trust or otherwise, or conspiracy, in restraint of trade or commerce among the several States, or with foreign nations, is hereby declared to be illegal. Every person who shall make any contract or engage in any combination or conspiracy hereby declared....to be illegal shall be deemed guilty of a felony."

Section 2 of the Sherman Act is designed to prevent or discourage the creation of monopolies. It states:

"Every person who shall monopolize, or attempt to monopolize, or combine or conspire with any other person or persons, to monopole any part of the trade or commerce among the several States, or with foreign nations, shall be deemed guilty of a felony..."

2. Clayton Act (1914)[30]

Section 3 of the Clayton Act was promulgated to prevent tying. It states in part:

---

[29]   See 15 USC 1-2

[30]   Clayton Act (1914)

"...to lease or make a sale or contract for sale or fix a price charged therefore on the condition that the lessee or purchaser thereof shall not use or deal in the goods of a competitor ..of the lessor or seller where the effect...may be to substantially lessen competition...".

The Robinson Patman Act of 1936 was implemented to amend Sec 2 of the Clayton Act. It prohibits a seller of goods from charging different prices in reasonably contemporaneous sales to different purchasers of the goods if the goods are of "like grade and quality".[31]

In essence, a number of actions are in violation of US antitrust laws and not only violate antitrust laws but can lead to criminal prosecution, penalties, fines and imprisonment. In-house counsel and compliance related professionals need to establish programs and processes that prevent such actions from taking place. Actions that violate US antitrust laws and should therefore be prohibited include:

- Agreements between competitors
  - Any agreement to fix prices, rig bids, restrict or divide sales territories or limit supply

- Agreements between customers and suppliers
  - Any agreement about the minimum resale price the customer may charge

- Sales practices (tying arrangements)
  - Any situation where a seller coerces a purchaser to buy a product he doesn't want long with a product de does want

30.1.1 Potential Fines and Damages

In the US, violation of US Federal antitrust las can lead to not only criminal penalties but companies or individuals injured by antitrust

---

[31]   15 USC Sec. 13(a)

violations are entitled to recover civil penalties up to 3 times the amount of actual damages. They may also be entitled to litigation costs and attorneys' fees. Companies that violated antitrust laws may also be subject to injunctions that restrict their freedom to do business.

30.1.2 Antitrust Issues Involving Distributors and Dealers

In the US, the relationship between a supplier or manufacturer and its distributor is governed by a number of federal and state laws, which are often confusing. Because of state issues, federal issues and common law distribution laws, numerous lawsuits have resulted. The main cause of litigation in the US facing suppliers is distributor/dealer related. In fact, much of the litigation between suppliers and distributors centers on antitrust concerns.

Antitrust based litigation between dealers and suppliers covers the following laws:

1. Federal Antitrust Laws
   - Restrictions on suppliers who engage in dual distribution
   - Ability to "tie" to a distributor's purchase of one product to the purchase of a second
   - Robinson-Patman Act issues

2. FTC Regulations
   - Unfair or deceptive methods of competition
   - Franchises

3. State antitrust laws. mini FTC Acts
   - Dealer protections acts
   - Sales representative acts
   - State unfair trade practices

Most legislation between a distributor and supplier occurs when the supplier terminates or fails to renew the relationship. So, though there are numerous reasons to consider termination of the distributor relationship[32], remember antitrust concerns must be addressed. Careful consideration must be given to reasons for termination, as distributors will raise such claims as:

- Refusal to deal
- Price discrimination
- Resale price maintenance
- Conspiracy with a competitive distributor

It is advised therefore, that careful consideration be given to a distributor relationship and of course the contract. Oral communications should be kept to a minimum to prevent oral promises becoming contracts. Written agreements should address antitrust concerns including:

- Exclusivity
- Pricing and payment terms
- Returns
- Termination
  - When dealing with a distributor, remember when the relationship is in trouble, the distributor will litigate over:
- Antitrust issues
- Good faith and fair dealing
- State laws
- Pricing
- Contract issues

30.2 South Korea

The Korean antitrust regime is governed by the Monopoly Regulations and Fair Trade Act (MRFTA) of 1981. Like the US and

---

[32]   Such reasons include sales deficiencies, distributor deficiencies, market issues, changed in channel distribution, sales of the supplier, etc.

other jurisdictions, the goal of the MRFTA is to promote free and fair competition. [33] Currently, the MRFTA is used as a tool to curb the monopolistic behavior of Korean multinationals (chaebols) and to help accelerate good corporate governance. Currently, Korea is using the MRFTA to help establish a "level playing field" for businesses. The main features of the MRFTA are as follows:

- To make the market share more efficient by preventing the formation of monopolistic behavior
- Enforcement of the MRFTA through regulations of the Korea Fair Trade Commission (KFTC)
- Prevention of certain abusive acts by prohibiting acts that (i) unreasonably controls the sale of commodities and services; (ii) interferes with the business activities of others; (iii) unreasonably alters prices and (iv) acts or actions that substantially lessens or restricts competition.

30.2.1 Restricting Competition

South Korea's MRFTA prohibits certain collusive acts such as price-fixing, which restricts competition. This includes the pre-determination of price, control of production, acts that substantially suppresses competition, and acts that interfering with prices of resellers-i.e. resale price maintenance.[34] In vertical agreements (i.e. between supplier/manufacturer and distributor) the agreements are subject to the rule of reason approach and would be deemed "illegal" if the restrictions on competition and unfairness would outweigh the benefits of the agreement- and would hence be considered "unreasonable".

---

[33] Article 1 of the MRFTA states in part that "The purpose of this Act is to promote free and fair competition, top encourage thereby creative enterprising activities, to protect consumers…"

[34] See Article 29 of the MRFTA

30.2.2 *Unfair Trade Practices*

The MRFTA, has been greatly influenced in part by the antitrust regimes of the US and EU. As part of the influence, the MRFTA has focused on eliminating "unfair trade practices". Korea's concept of unfair trade practices is the belief that some business practices that may not appear anticompetitive are in fact anticompetitive when viewed in light of all of the facts. Thus, some practices may be "unfair" and anti-competitive event though they are not aimed at market dominance. Such unfair trade practices may include:

- Refusal to deal unreasonably
- Discriminatory treatment
- Foreclosure of competitors
- Unfair inducement of customers
- Coercive dealing
- Trading on restrictive terms
- Interference in other enterprises
- Unfair support

Types of unfair trading practices will be analyzed using two factors: (i) anti-competiveness of the action and (ii) unfairness. The KFTC's Guidelines have been established to provide guidance on which conditions would render vertical agreements illegal. Among the circumstances the Guidelines would take into consideration are:

- The number of trade counterparties
- The market share of the parties
- The purpose and intent of the restrictions
- The duration of the restrictions

Safety Zone- a safety zone exists for companies doing business in Korea. A company whose market share is ten (10%) percent or less will be considered to have a minimal anti-competitive effect.

It should be noted that at the time of printing of this book, Korea is in the midst of overhauling its antitrust laws. Korea created a task force to review the MRTA and recommend changes to the antitrust laws. As it turns out, the task force recommended a number of sweeping changes, focusing on administrative enforcement changes, civil enforcement changes and criminal enforcement changes.[35]

30.2.3 *Hot Antitrust / Competition Topics for In-House Counsel and Managers in South Korea*

- Pharmaceutical Issues- the KFTC has conducted numerous investigations into 17 pharmaceutical companies over anti-kickback violations. In 2007 the KFTC issued 40 Billion won in administrative fines for violations. In 2009, the KFTC issued over 10 Billion won in fines. In 2010 the KFTC implemented a whistleblower system to help encourage self- reporting.

  In 2010 Korea amended its Medical Device Act to introduce a dual punishment system. Under the amendment, both the manufacturer and the healthcare provider are subject to criminal prosecution if kickbacks are approved.

  Also, in 2014, the Korean Supreme Court ruled that pay for delay settlements between original drug manufacturers and generics may violate the MRFTA. Under the amended Pharmaceutical Act, the following arrangements must be reported to the KFTC:

  (i) Agreements between the market approval holder and the generic applicant with regards to a manufacture or sale of the drug;

---

[35] The task force recommendations have been considered by the Competition Law Amendment Special Committee (Committee) which was created to implement the recommendations. The Committee has made 17 specific recommendations on reforming the MRFTA.

(ii) Agreements between the market approval holder and generic applicant regarding acquisition of rights related to the first generic exclusivity; and

(iii) Agreement between the notified generic applicants related to the acquisition of rights related to generic exclusivity

Areas of concern for the KFTC

- Collaboration among competitors
- Unilateral conduct
- Abusive exercise of superior bargaining power
- Use of unfair methods of competition
- Concentration of economic power

• SEPs

In a major decision involving Standard Essential Patents (SEPs), the Korea Fair Trade Commission (KFTC) issues its decision regarding Qualcomm's market power and anti-competitive conduct on January 20, 2017. The decision set forth the KFTC's finding regarding the use of SEPs and discusses in detail potential harms stemming from Qualcomm's abuses of the SEPS. Holding that Qualcomm refused to honor its commitment to license SEPs under Fair, Reasonable and Non-Discriminatory (FRAND) terms, the KFTC ordered Qualcomm to negotiate in good faith, with its rival chip makers, renegotiate chip supply agreements with handset makers and to pay a fine of approx. 1.03 Trillion Korean Won (approx. $912.34 Million USD) as well.[36]

30.3 Risk Management Processes and Procedures

In order for companies to comply not only with antitrust laws of various jurisdictions, they will need to establish appropriate processes

---

[36] See In re Alleged Abuse of Market Dominance of Qualcomm Incorporated, KFTC Decision No. 2017-0-25, January 20, 2017

and procedures to enforce antitrust regulations and to show antitrust regulators they are in compliance. Such processes include:

- Compliance programs emphasizing antitrust laws
- Corporate policies addressing antitrust issues
- Training programs emphasizing antitrust training
- Regular interaction with the law department if there are antitrust questions
- Use of outside counsel of complex antitrust issues
- Contract management processes that require review of contracts by legal to ensure that no antitrust laws are violated

30.4 Planning

In-house counsel and/or compliance officers should consider adopting corporate policies which addresses antitrust issues. It is suggested that the company implement a compliance program which is comprised of the following processes and procedures:

1. Antitrust training
2. A detailed corporate policy outlining what conduct and behavior is permissible and not permitted based on antitrust laws and policies
3. An antitrust audit every year reviewing the results of training, employee and manager issues as well as a review of the policies
4. A contact review and management process addressing illegal and anti-competitive behavior is very important
5. A review of distribution agreements and conduct related to distributors and dealers

30.5 Risk Management Tips to Avoid Antitrust Issues

In-house counsel and risk managers must diligently train management as well as employees on not only the pitfalls of violating antitrust laws but also on avoiding such violations. It is recommended a compliance program be put in place that trains employees to limit all of their conversations and activities with competitors. Most employees who are criminally prosecuted over verbal discussions with competitors not written agreements.

❖ Remember that sales managers are always coming into contact with competitors whether at seminars, trade association meetings or in public.

To prevent violation of antitrust laws it is recommended that employees follow a set of simple rules:

- Don't discuss prices with competitors
- Don't exchange price lists with competitors
- Don't talk to competitors about bids
- Don't "talk shop" with competitors at trade association meetings or seminars
- Don't talk to competitors about customers or territories
- Don't charge different customers for the same product unless cost justified…i.e. to "meet the competition", etc.

It should be noted that the above also apples to many legal regimes in various jurisdictions, with of course, certain variances.

Summary

The implementation of an LRM program requires a risk assessment or a risk audit. Only through a risk assessment can a company identify the major areas of legal risk as well as evaluate the strengths and weaknesses in its current risk processes. Such risk assessment should only be conducted after the company has established goals and objectives in which to evaluate the results of the audit.

Normally an LRM audit would be conducted in phases. In the basic approach, which can be used as a model for the LRM audit, phases include: phase 1, in which the company decides to do a risk review; phase 2, in which the risk identification takes place; phase 3, in which tools are used to identify the severity of the risk; phase 4, in which a critical risk analysis is conducted to determine probability of impact; and phase 5, in which the action plan is implemented.

Numerous processes can be implemented to mitigate legal risk. For manufacturing companies, product liability remains a series of legal exposures. Besides basic product liability defenses, companies also have to concern themselves with design risk management processes as well. Besides design risk management processes and product liability mitigation processes, companies should also consider outsourcing of certain functions as another form of LRM, or risk management.

Many risks are inherent in a company's use of data. Risks exist everywhere, from unauthorized access of data via hacking, a stolen laptop, third-party vendors, inadequate security systems, increased regulatory oversight, and unenforced privacy policies. In today's technology-oriented society, data leakage and data privacy risks pose enormous threats to a company's financial and reputational well-being and must be taken seriously.

Part Three

Legal Risk Management Strategies: Pre-litigation

The goal of legal risk management, or LRM, is to minimize, transfer, or reduce exposure to legal risk. Obviously, to have a successful LRM program, a company must think proactively—prior to the filing of litigation or prior to the commencement of government investigations or levying of fines and penalties. What LRM strategies can be used prior to litigation that can reduce the risk of litigation? What programs and processes, if properly executed, will minimize or mitigate the threat of litigation or government investigations and audits? Many processes can reduce or minimize legal and financial exposure, but the most important are set forth in this section.

31 Employee Benefit Plans

31.1 Employee Benefit Plans Audit

One of the most important audits a risk manager/in-house counsel should conduct as part of a LRM program is an audit of employee benefit plans. Many countries offer employee benefit plans, pensions, or related schemes in accordance with local laws.

In the U.S., employee benefit plans or retirement benefit plans are subject to the requirements of the employee Retirement Income Security Act of 1974, as amended (ERISA)[37]. It is very important, for reasons set forth in this chapter that a LRM program covers an ERISA audit as well as a compliance review. Failure to do so, could subject a company in the U.S. as well as the company's board of directors to $$$ in fines and penalties, not only from the Department of Labor's standpoint but from the I.R.S. standpoint as well.

31.2 Employee Benefit Plans Review

Regulations adopted pursuant to ERISA set fort requirements respecting employee retirement and welfare benefit plans (the "Plan"), include:

---

[37] ERISA is codified at 29 U.S.C. Sec 15. However, parts of ERISA laws covering tax issues are also found in the U.S. IRS code.

- Reporting and disclosure requirements
- Fiduciary responsibility
- Administration and enforcement
- Participation and vesting

ERISA requires that health and welfare plans be set forth in a written document which describes the benefit and the operation of the Plan. The document must identify who is responsible for the control, management and operation of the Plan. The Plan must also have recordkeeping systems to track the flow of funds and written materials to be provided to Plan participants.

The general review of a compliance audit should focus on three areas:

- Fiduciary responsibility
- Plan documents
- Process, procedure, reporting and disclosure requirements

31.3 Fiduciary Considerations

ERISA sets standards of conduct for employee benefit plan sponsors and others who exercise discretion in managing a plan or plan assets. Therefore, use of discretion in administering and managing an employee benefit plan or controlling the plan's assets makes that person a fiduciary to the extent of such control or discretion. Fiduciary status is determined based upon the functions performed.

Each Plan must have a named fiduciary; however, a person does not need to be named to be a fiduciary; who jointly or severally control and manage the operation and administration of the Plan. The Plan instrument may actually designate the named fiduciary or may specify a procedure for naming the fiduciary by the employer.

ERISA sets forth the standards and rules of conduct for plan fiduciaries. Plan fiduciaries are required under ERISA to fulfill a number of duties including:

- A fiduciary must act solely in the interest of plan participants and their beneficiaries and with the exclusive purpose of providing benefits to them.
- A fiduciary must carry out their duties prudently
- A fiduciary must follow plan documents
- A fiduciary must diversify investments
- A fiduciary must pay only reasonable plan expenses

One measure of prudence is the process used to carry out the fiduciary responsibility. Acting under established written procedures which identify Plan fiduciaries and the specific scope of each fiduciary's duty provides a fundamental framework around which to develop programs designed to minimize potential fiduciary liability. Fiduciary liability therefore typically arises from the process, not the actual decision.

Normally, a company is the Plan Sponsor and named fiduciary for the employee benefit and retirement plan including a 401(k) Plan. The company will have fiduciary responsibilities for the employee welfare benefit plans. As the company acts through its' board, the board may be liable.

A fiduciary that breaches any responsibility or duty under ERISA may be personally liable to make good any losses to the Plan resulting from the breach. All fiduciaries have potential liability for the actions of their co-fiduciaries. Breaches of fiduciary responsibility can give rise to civil and criminal penalties, which can be enormous. This has been opened by the U.S Supreme Court. The U.S. Supreme Court has held that individual employee may bring an action for "appropriate equitable relief" under ERISA against an employer for breaching its fiduciary duties (Vanity Corp. V. Howe).[38]

---

[38]   Vanity Corp. V. Howe, 116 S. Ct 1065 (1996)

31.4 Settlor Considerations

Not all functions relating to the operation of employee benefit plan are fiduciary functions. The law recognizes "settlor" functions where the Plan Sponsor is acting in its employer capacity. "Settlor" functions include business decisions respecting employee benefit plans.

- Establishment of an employee benefit plan
- Determination of the benefit package
- Features to include in the plan
- Plan termination
- Plan design changes

It is important to recognize where the company's board is acting in a fiduciary capacity or on behalf of the employer in a non-fiduciary capacity. It is critical to document process the board uses to carry out their fiduciary function and that Plan procedures are followed in carrying out Plan Sponsor functions.

31.5 Plan Documents, Process, Procedures and Reporting

Deficiencies in documents, processes and procedures can lead to legal exposure and/or liability for:

- Fiduciary matters
- Tax liabilities
- Civil penalties
- Reporting and disclosure requirements apply to both Employee Retirement Benefit Plans and Employee Welfare Benefit Plans.

A company has reporting and disclosure obligations to the:

- Government
- Participants

In the U.S., Company's 401(k) Plan is normally a "Qualified" defined contribution retirement benefit plan. "Qualified" Plans can provide significant tax advantages if Internal Revenue Code requirements are met. The Internal Revenue Code requirements relate to "form" and "operation" of the Plan. The Internal Revenue Code imposes excise taxes intended as penalties on a wide variety of prohibited transactions between a Qualified Plan and an employer, trustee, or other disqualified person, subject to a number of statutory exemptions.

31.6 Compliance Audit

A compliance review should be conducted to determine what a general pattern and practice has been implemented respecting actions taken by the company with respect to both the retirement and health & welfare benefit plans usually the Human Resources Department may be involved with ERISA obligations. How has it conducted the 401(k) or Employee Benefit and Retirement Program?

As a prudent fiduciary, the process used by the company select and monitor the specialists it retains to carry out functions respecting the plans is the focus for determining whether the Board of Directors acted in a prudent fashion in selecting and retaining the advisors. A LRM Compliance audit should cover the following:

- Secure information and documents submitted to the company connection with the retention of service providers
- Obtain copies of engagement letters and service agreements
- Review compensation agreements
- Review reports supplied by or relating to the performance of each service provider
- Ensure that the agreement with the service providers sets forth the specific responsibilities of the company and the service provider under the agreement
- Consider indemnification and insurance requirements
- Document periodic reviews of service providers performance

- Review current insurance programs respecting fiduciary coverage
- Review by Laws respecting indemnification

31.7 Recommended Actions

Board considerations should encompass many areas, including:

- Establishment of a committee of the Board to oversee employee benefit plan matters
- Review of the fiduciary responsibilities and plan administration activities respecting retirement and health & welfare benefit plans
- Consider delegation of authority and responsibility for certain activities respecting the management and operation of the plans
- Establish written procedures which identify fiduciaries to whom responsibility is delegated and the specific scope of each fiduciary's responsibility

31.8 Compliance Considerations

A general employee retirement and welfare benefit plan compliance review is highly recommended in many organizations. Not only in the U.S. but elsewhere as many countries have laws and regulations concerning benefit plans. However, in the U.S. companies face great exposure if they fail to implement proper procedures and safeguards in respect to ERISA requirements. Therefore, I cannot stress enough the importance of a legal audit of employee retirement and welfare programs or benefit plan programs considering the immense legal exposure a company and /or its BOD may face.

32 Compliance

Form: Compliance Policy
Form: Compliance Manual

32.1 What Is Compliance?

Many countries now require companies to implement compliance policies for legal reasons. Some companies have implemented compliance policies for brand image and other reasons as well. A compliance program, properly implemented, not only increases a company's brand image but reinforces ethical behavior, which in turn minimizes violation of local laws by upholding compliance of financial and legal rules.

To understand compliance, one needs to review the history of compliance in the United States.

US Compliance History

32.1.1 Background

- In November 1991, an innovative piece of legislation was enacted in the United States that had a profound effect on corporate America. This has reverberated throughout the world.
- The legislation was the US Federal Sentencing Guidelines ("Guidelines").

32.1.2 *The Guidelines*

- The Guidelines are used by judges to determine the appropriate sentence for corporations convicted of a federal crime.
- According to the Guidelines, a corporation may be sentenced or fined for federal offenses connected with antitrust, securities, bribery, fraud, money laundering, criminal business activities, extortion, embezzlement, conspiracy, etc. As you can see it is quite broad and covers many "illegal" activities.

When deciding on an appropriate sentence, judges were for the first time asked to consider whether the corporation had an "effective compliance program" before the violation took place or, in other words, whether the corporation took appropriate steps to prevent and detect violations of law. Therefore, in order for courts to reduce or mitigate criminal sanctions, companies must now have a compliance program in place. The Guidelines were amended in 2004 (Revised Guidelines).[39]

32.1.3 *The Revised Guidelines*

- The Revised Guidelines recognize that effective compliance and ethics requires more than policies and procedures, it also entails a focus on organizational culture that promotes law abidance. In other words, a major focus is on compliance and ethics.
- For the first time, a set of laws creates a legal mandate for compliance. It looks at:
    - Incentives
    - Requirements
    - Guidance
    - A focus on ethical behavior

---

[39]   Federal Sentencing Guidelines for Organizations (revised and amended as of Nov. 1, 2004).

32.1.4 The Revised Guidelines

- The Revised Guidelines recognize seven elements in a proper compliance program.
- The current Revised Guidelines list seven elements of an "effective compliance program" as being:
    - Compliance standards and procedures (a code of conduct should exist)
    - Oversight by high-level personnel (the Board must oversee the program)
    - Due care when delegating authority (due care in hiring employees)
    - Effective communication of standards and procedure (training)
    - Auditing/monitoring/reporting systems must be in place
    - Compliance must be promoted and enforced consistently throughout the organization
    - There must be an appropriate response after violation detected

32.1.5 Failure to Enact Compliance

- In February 1996, in what was the largest criminal fine in US history, a New York federal court, following the Guidelines, sentenced Daiwa Bank (Japan) to pay a $340 million fine.[40]
    - The case involved a bank employee who lost $1.1 billion in unauthorized trades.
    - Prosecution arose out of a report of an unauthorized, off-the-books trading scheme—bank officials conspired to conceal the losses from bank regulators for more than two months.
    - The two main reasons for the fine:

---

[40] See United States v The Daiwa Bank, S.D.N.Y. 95 Cr. (KMW)

- "Lack of a meaningful compliance program"
- "Consequent failure to report the employee's wrongdoing"

32.1.6 Lessons

Foreign companies doing business in the United States can learn an especially important lesson from Daiwa Bank. Primarily, foreign companies doing business in the United States must realize they have to comply with U.S. laws and regulations. Daiwa Bank could have avoided the criminal fine had it followed the requirements of the U.S. Sentencing Guidelines.

32.1.7 The United States

In implementing a compliance program in conformity with U.S. law and in compliance with specific laws, a company shows it fully appropriates U.S. laws and regulations. By developing such a compliance program, a company understands in general terms the requirements of U.S. law.

32.2 Establishment of Compliance Program

The establishment of a compliance program anywhere in the world usually consists of adopting a company code of conduct, with perhaps specific policies governing local conditions. However, because of the U.S. requirements, many organizations have adapted compliance policies that conform to U.S. standards. Because of the Revised Guidelines, specific elements to a valid compliance program are required. They are:

32.2.1 US Compliance Program

- The basics—what is needed?
  - A code of conduct

- Local codes of business ethics (and other company policies) covering each country in which a company does business
- Local training on all aspects, such as antitrust, employee issues, etc.
- A system to report suspected wrongdoing to the company
- An anonymous reporting system allowing employees to report wrongdoing anonymously

32.2.2 Code of Conduct

A company's compliance programs' code of conduct should incorporate various principles. Primarily, five basic principles should be followed or reflected in the code. The five principles a company's compliance code of conduct should incorporate are as follows:

- The company complies with local laws and ethical standards of society.
- The company maintains and promotes an ethical organizational corporate culture.
- The company respects customers, shareholders, and employees.
- The company cares for the environment as well as the health, and safety of its customers and society.
- The company is a socially responsible corporate citizen.

32.2.3 U.S. Compliance Program Code of Conduct

To establish an "effective compliance program" under the guidelines and other U.S. laws, a foreign company normally goes beyond its local code or domestic code of conduct. Its employees must be familiar with the specific laws that govern their conduct in the jurisdiction in which they work.

If a company has a branch or division in the United States, it must have a U.S. Code of Ethics, which is designed to inform employees in the United States about the specific laws and standards governing their conduct. Having a compliance program is mandated by the U.S. Sentencing Guidelines.

32.2.4 *The U.S. Compliance Program Local Codes of Business Ethics (and Other Policies)*

- A U.S. Compliance and Code of Ethics (and other policies) should cover at a minimum approximately twenty-two different areas. An employee handbook should perhaps cover another forty or more.
- U.S. Code of Conduct
- Principle 1. The company complies with laws and ethical standards:
    - Nondiscrimination, anti-harassment, and anti-retaliation
    - Drugs and alcohol
    - Wage and hour laws
    - Americans with Disabilities Act
    - Employment at will
    - Political contributions and activities
    - Personal political contributions
    - Antitrust law and competitive practices
    - Foreign Corrupt Practices Act
    - Government contracts (if it does government work)
    - Government relations-dealing with government regulators
    - Government reports
- Principle 2. The company maintains an ethical organizational culture:
    - Company property, confidential information
    - Intellectual property and property of others
    - Accurate books and records
    - Computer hardware and software, e-mail
    - Confidentiality of client information
    - Accounting policies

- Conflicts of interest
- Nondiscrimination, anti-harassment, and anti-retaliation
- Drugs and alcohol
- Principle 3. The company respects customers, shareholders, and employees.
  - Procurement
- Principle 4. The company cares for the environment, health, and safety of its employees and the public.
  - Environments, safety, and health
- Principle 5. The company is a responsible corporate citizen.
  - Compliance procedures

32.2.5 Compliance Training

To have an effective compliance program, a company must also hold compliance training after it "launches" the program. Areas of training should be covered and how the training should be given is of major interest.

It is best if the company offers local compliance training covering the relevant laws and practices where people are located. Training can be given in person, online via web-based training, or by other media. It must be given on a regular basis.

32.2.6 Local Training

- Training on the code of conduct can be given by HR or by Legal.
- Local training in antitrust, anti-harassment, antidiscrimination, and anti-retaliation, ethics, illegal business practices, financial integrity, customs, etc.
- The majority of the local training will be in person and online.
- The goal is to equip employees to handle compliance issues.
- Training should help employees to identify potential wrongdoing.
- Training should help employees understand their role in the compliance scheme.

- It should let them know what to report and how to report.

32.2.7 The U.S. Compliance Program: Reporting Wrongdoing

- In the United States, having an effective reporting system has come to mean one that encourages reporting by allowing for a variety of reporting avenues including anonymous reporting systems.
- If an employee was limited to one avenue of reporting (i.e., to his supervisor), it is likely he would not report wrongdoing if his supervisor was involved.
- In the United States, a company should allow for employee reporting normally as follows.

32.2.8 Employee Reporting

All employees are required to promptly report all known or suspected violations of applicable laws or of the compliance program, including corporate policies. Reports of such violations shall be promptly made to a manager; the compliance officer, if any; HR; or to the Law Department. If any employee wishes, he or she may report violations anonymously via an anonymous e-mail (or by phone) system. All reports should be promptly and thoroughly investigated.

To the extent possible and permitted by law, the company must take reasonable precautions to maintain the confidentiality of those individuals who report legal or compliance-related violations.

32.3 Training Programs

Training programs may vary depending on the needs of a particular company. Training programs may consist of instructor-led training, Internet-based, or e-learning programs or even a combination of both. It is up to the company to decide which training program fits the needs of its employees as well as suits its budgetary constraints. In fact, companies in the United States are scrambling around trying to decide on how to handle training programs for the BOD and executive management that is required which includes deciding on what form the training should take, its content as well as the frequency of the training.

32.4 Risk Assessment of Compliance Programs

A risk assessment or LRM audit is vital in the implementation and continued success of any compliance program. Not only do the U.S. Federal Sentencing Guidelines require a periodic risk assessment of a compliance program, but conducting a periodic risk assessment has an upside as well. By conducting a periodic or annual assessment of the compliance program, not only is the company or organization receiving valuable feedback on the program from employees and management which will help it improve the compliance program, but it is also will be in compliance with the U.S. Federal Sentencing Guidelines.

By conducting an LRM audit of the compliance program, a company should be able to:

- Review and modify existing corporate processes.
- Update current compliance training, if needed.
- Modify the Compliance Department structure if needed.
- Add additional policies and or training programs.
- Add additional manpower to comply with the compliance needs of the corporation if necessary.

32.5 Legal Risk Management Reasons for a Compliance Program

In the past twenty-five years, numerous companies have been racked by scandals resulting from the absence of compliance.

To name a few:

Companies	Impact
Enron	Bankruptcy
WorldCom	Bankruptcy

Parmalat	Bankruptcy
JP Morgan Chase, Citi	>$2 B penalty fine
Adelphia	$715 M penalty fine

Individuals—Criminal	**Sentence**
Bernie Ebbers—WorldCom CEO	25 years
Dennis Kozlowski—Tyco CEO	8–25 years
Timothy Rigas—Adelphia CEO	20 years
Andrew Fastow—Enron CEO	10 years
Fronklin Brow—Rite Aid CEO	10 years

A company that fails to implement a compliance program may suffer the following:

- Indictment of executives and other managers
- Loss of resources
- Loss of market cap
- Loss of reputation
- Negative impact on the corporate brand

But also, it can affect stakeholders such as:

Stakeholders

Shareholders

Creditors

Employees

Customers

Suppliers

Local Communities

Retirees

In order to minimize or avoid many of the legal and financial issues discussed above, a company should:

- Create a basic compliance system
  - For preventing problems
  - For detecting problems
  - For responding and remedying compliance issues
- Create a culture of compliance
  - Foundation of competitiveness
  - Priority
  - Instill values of ethics
- The key to implementation
  - Senior management must commit to compliance. Management cannot keep a blind eye to problems.
  - Proper checks and balances must be created in the business processes.
  - Compliance must be built into all business processes.

In the United States, companies must implement a sound compliance system in order for directors of the company to discharge their fiduciary responsibilities.[41]

A well-drafted and implemented compliance policy can go a long way to reduce legal risk before litigation arises. World-class companies are driving compliance throughout their organizations. They understand that besides complying with legal requirements, rigorous financial and legal compliance leads to ethical actions that not only minimize legal risk but benefit the company's reputation and ultimately the bottom line, thereby protecting the company's brand.

---

[41] Carole Basri and Irving Kagan, *Corporate Legal Departments*, 3rd ed., PLI, 2004, 11–4 citing in re Caremark Int'l Inc. Derivative Litig, 698 A.2d. 959 (Del. Ch., 1996).

32.6 Real Case in Point – WorldCom

Besides Enron, WorldCom remains one of the greatest corporate scandals of the twentieth century. A prime example of an ethical failure in upper management.

Once, one of the largest telecommunications companies in the U.S. WorldCom saw its value decline during the dotcom investment & Fiasco of the late 1990s. WorldCom's revenues decreased while expenses for running its fiber optic network increased.

The CEO, Bernie Ebbers, had taken WorldCom public in 199 with annual revenues of $39 Billion. Ebbers, an extravagant spender never cut back on his lifestyle and saw it threatened when WorldCom's fortunes began to diminish.

In 2000, Ebbers instructed his CFO to report false revenues and use other financial tricks to mask WorldCom's balance sheet. Amongst the ways WorldCom's management masked the declining financial condition of the company was by falsely claiming corporate earnings growth and profitability to push up the value of the stock. The fraudulent actions were accomplished by the accounting department "underreporting line costs" and inflating revenues with false accounting entries. WorldCom's assets had been inflated by approx. $11 Billion USD. Internal auditors found out and reported Ebbers' actions to the SEC. The SEC started investigating.

During that time Ebbers also encouraged shareholders to buy more stock knowing the value of the company was decreasing.

Once it was found that the SEC was investigating and the WorldCom BOD forced Ebbers to resign, WorldCom shares lost 90% of their value. WorldCom declared bankruptcy, investors lost billions of dollars and over 17,000 people lost their jobs.

Though internal auditors picked up Ebbers actions, it was too late.

Questions:

• Does your company have compliance systems in place to prevent a WorldCom disaster?

- Are systems in place to prevent fraudulent behavior by upper management?
- Is your BOD sufficiently informed to provide proper oversight?

32.7 Real Case in Point – Enron

The most famous business scandal in recent memory is the Enron scandal. Both the CFO and CEO were convicted of various felonies including securities fraud and conspiracy to inflate profits[42]. Apparently, both the CFO and CEO used off-the-books partnerships to disguise Enron debts and then lied to investors about Enron's' horrible finances while selling their own shares.

When Enron disintegrated, its bankruptcy erased approx. $60 Billion in investors' stock value and left more than 5,000 employees jobless. The employees' retirement and pension accounts were totally destroyed leaving them with no retirement fund.

The major crime of the CEO (Kenneth Lay) was to advise employees while Enron was collapsing to keep their stock while he was selling his own. In other words, he knowingly destroyed the lives and savings of thousands while he padded his own bank account.

The CFO, Jeffrey Skilling, however, committed a more heinous crime of creating of the book's partnerships to disguise Enron's debts.

Both the CFO and CEO showed extreme immorality, some of the damage could have been prevented if appropriate compliance systems were in place to prevent the fraudulent behavior of top management.

Also, had the Board of Directors exercised appropriate oversight responsibility, the Enron scandal may not have occurred. However, because the Board was denied access to important information nor did it appreciate the information it did receive, the CFO's off-the-books partnerships were never questioned. Though the BOD did approve procedures for management appraisal of Skilling's partnerships, nothing was followed up on. The BOD failed to properly scrutinize the bizarre

---

[42] *Buchholts and Carroll, Business and Society, 7th Ed, South-Western (2006), p 256*

nature of Skilling's partnerships and never questioned the CFO as to the results of the probe into the partnerships.

The primary cause of the Enron catastrophe was a combination of unethical and illegal behavior at the top of the management combined with poor corporate governance of the Board of Directors[43].

Questions:

- Do you have compliance processes in place to prevent an Enron type scandal?
- Is your BOD sufficiently informed to provide proper oversight?
- Are systems in place to prevent fraudulent behavior by employees of your company?

---

[43]   *See Stearns and Steiner, Business, Government, and Society 12th ed, McGraw-Hill (2009), p594*

33   Anti-Bribery Issues and Concerns

33.1 Importance of Anti-Bribery

Though anti-bribery laws are front and center these days, the major anti-bribery law, the FCPA, has been around since 1977. This law as well as pressure from the US government has resulted in a number of anti-bribery laws being implemented and enforced in numerous jurisdictions. Anti-bribery risk is now a major risk many international companies face when doing business in the US and elsewhere.

Obviously, compliance programs need to cover anti-bribery laws and resulting concerns as no two anti-bribery laws are the same. Here are a few anti-bribery laws to consider when forming a compliance program as well as overall legal risk management.

33.2 US- Foreign Corrupt Practices Act (FCPA)

Under the FCPA, it is illegal for anyone doing business in America to give anything of value, directly or indirectly to a foreign official to obtain or retain business. Payments to a government are not illegal, payment to a government official to win or retain business is. Some payments are of course permitted, such as grease payments to facilitate normal or routine governmental action.

The major risk related problems under the FCPA is that the DOJ has expanded the enforcement of the FCPA outside of the US, while other jurisdictions have not. Remember, the FCPA prohibits US companies from making improper payments of gifts to foreign government officials, politicians or political parties. It also requires companies to keep accurate records of transfer of assets whether international or domestic. All associates and agents of US companies must comply as well including subsidiaries and international companies doing business in the US.

33.3 South Korea-The Act on Prevention of Improper Solicitation and Receipt of Money (Kim Young Ran Act)

The Kim Young Ran Act (Act) not only implements an anti-bribery law that is quite drastic, but it may now be enforced against teachers, quasi-public officials including public hospital employees as well as companies that have violated the Act. The Act strengthens Korea's current corruption laws and regulations by focusing on four areas: (i) the expansion of acts that may be punished; (2) the expansion of the definition of "public official"; (3) the prohibition of improper solicitation without payment of money; and 94) liability provisions to ensure corporate accountability.

According to the Act, a public official, journalist, teacher or administrator of a private school can be subject to imprisonment up to three years or a penalty of KRW 30 Million or less for receiving a favor with a value of more than KRW 1 Million regardless of whether the favor was given as a bribe or was related to the recipient's work. Even if each favor is worth less than KRW 1 Million, if the favor was given in connection with the recipient's work administrative fines can be imposed.

33.4 Anti-bribery Claims- Internal Investigations

To mitigate exposure to the criminal penalties of domestic and foreign anti-bribery laws, it is obvious that companies whether based in Korea, the US, the UK, or elsewhere need to establish a robust corporate compliance program as well as revise the ones already established in order to meet the higher standards of conduct now required. But establishment of compliance programs will not completely protect the company if the wrongdoers are not identified. So early identification of corporate wrongdoers must also be a necessity in order to limit a company's civil and criminal liability under the anti-bribery statues. This means that besides considering compliance guidelines, or a code of conduct, companies are now under pressure to implement guidelines that cover internal investigations too.

Conducting an internal investigation can be emotion-charged, time consuming process that requires expertise and effective planning. Managers and other staff who investigate claims such as bribes, corruption and employee fraud should be prepared to conduct interviews and document the investigation in a proper and thorough manner. The ultimate goal of an investigation is to enable the company's decision –makers to resolve matters fairly and effectively. The immediate goal of an investigation is to obtain the facts. Therefore, to be effective, an investigation must be:

- Thorough and accurate
- Fair and impartial
- In compliance with the requirements of law and
- the company's ethics program
- Commenced and completed in a timely manner

33.5 Next Steps

So, companies are now forced to take drastic action as well as ask the really tough questions concerning compliance and internal corporate policy. Such questions include:

- Does the company have a compliance program in place to address the FCPA and other anti-bribery laws?
- Is there a training program in place to cover the various anti-bribery laws?
- If a training program is not in place, is the company willing to establish a program that covers anti-bribery?

- Does the company have an internal investigation policy in place?
- What steps has the company taken to address various risks posed by non-compliance with anti-bribery laws?
- Is Upper Management involved in implementing a robust compliance program to address anti-bribery concerns?

34 Record Retention

Form: Records Retention Program

34.1 Information Retention

Information retention, or "records retention," as it is normally called, is one of the largest sources of potential legal risk (and related financial risk) that companies face. What records a company saves, destroys, or erases may in fact determine the company's fate in litigation. Massive governmental fines and penalties have been levied against companies because of records that were improperly kept or that were uncovered in antitrust investigations, antidumping investigations, etc.

A business must consider the risk of keeping documents, especially electronic documents such as e-mail over an extended period of time. Obviously, a business wants to protect valuable information as long as it has value. On the other hand, an organization has to be sensitive to the legal risks posed by saving records and documents past legal requirements of a particular situation.

In essence, we have a balancing act. How does a company balance the needs of business with legal requirements? The issue is not really a legal problem per se but a business problem with legal issues. The legal risk, however, of a nonexistent information retention program can be enormous, and, therefore, should be properly addressed in an LRM program.

How does a company handle retention of documents? What legal requirements exist, and how are they implemented? Strict mandatory standards exist in some countries.

In the United States, the law requires an information retention policy (IRP) that

- retains information at least as long as required by law,
- is applied consistently and systematically,
- allows quick retrieval, and
- can be suspended effectively, if required.

What are the risks of noncompliance?

- Huge fines and penalties
  - The act of losing documents that may be considered evidence in litigation or failing to preserve evidence once legal proceedings appear reasonably likely to occur may damage a company financially and/or its reputation. Note what happened to Arthur Andersen and Enron, etc.
- Huge cost of dealing with information in legal proceedings
- Huge expense of keeping too many documents, especially e-mail
- Not properly implemented

Many companies have an IRP, which, unfortunately, is never properly implemented or followed by employees. Thus, the IRP may at least be ineffective or, at worst, not recognized by courts as a legitimate IRP. This opens the door to fines, sanctions, and worse. Make certain if your company has an IRP that it is properly implemented and followed. If your company does not have an IRP- create and implement one now!

34.2 Risk Assessment: A Suggested Action

A company must ensure it has a viable business / legal oriented IRP in place. A risk assessment must be conducted to determine if one exists. Usually, when a company conducts a risk assessment it will find:

- No suspension procedure exists.
- There has been no auditing of documents.

- The retention policy, if it exists, is antiquated and not equated for the current electronic environment.
- E-mail is not handled correctly.
- The IRP has not been properly implemented or communicated.
- Employees not only are unaware of the IRP but are not following it.

34.3 E-mail

E-mail has become a very important concern when implementing an effective information retention policy or IRP. This is primarily due to E-discovery issues resulting from litigation, which will be discussed later in Chapter 21. The main issue involving e-mail is how long e-mail should be maintained on a computer hard drive before it is deleted. E-mail issues may entail the following:

- No proper archiving of e-mail
- Not properly backed up if needed
- Not properly deleted (i.e., if not accidentally lost, it may be kept forever, resulting in huge costs to review and produce)

An example of potential E-discovery costs because of E-mail is as follows:

1. Preservation		
Preservation notices		$5,000
2. Collection		
Collection from data sources		$11,000
3. Staging		
Preprocessing		$2,000
Processing		$11,000
4. Review		
Contract attorney review		$50,000
Hosting		$10,000
5. Production		$15,000
	Total	$99,000

In line with the above referenced E-discovery cost allocation, the table set forth above is a typical example of costs directly associated with a review of ESI for discovery:

- This cost example is based upon a typical review of electronic content to provide a frame of reference.
- This example is for a review of content collected from twenty-five custodians with thirty gigabytes of data.
- The costs are mainly for the discovery review and production life cycle and exclude legal and consulting fees.

34.4 Action Plan

Once a company has conducted a risk assessment of its IRP, it should implement an action plan to address any risk posed by inadequacies of the IRP. At a minimum the following steps are recommended:

- Draft a comprehensive IRP that addresses all documents, including electronic documents.
- Clean up any old information. Records that are no longer required to be kept legally should be destroyed or deleted unless valid business reasons exist to keep them.
- Upper management should approve of the new IRP.
- Departmental retention coordinators should be appointed to drive the new IRP in each department.
- The new IRP must be rolled out to all employees. This may entail marketing the IRP to each department.
- There should be periodic reminders via e-mail, brochures, or posters reminding all employees of the IRP.
- There should be quarterly status meetings with all department coordinators.
- Annual audit: there should be an annual compliance audit to check on the IRP, especially e-mail.

35 Management of E-mail

One of the major business and legal risks a company faces is e-mail. E-mail is now the primary source of all office communication. Over 80 percent of all corporate communications is via e-mail. Over 95 percent of all corporate data created is comprised of e-mail. In fact, over 75 percent of an organization's IP resides in e-mails and attachments. E-mail has become so pervasive in a company that more than 40 percent of all data is not connected to a paper format or tangible medium—it just remains ESI.

The risk inherent in e-mail is due to its instantaneous publication. In other words, e-mail is instantaneous, efficient, and quite user-friendly. The problem is not only does it take up a great deal of space on a company's server, but it is wrongly assumed to be private by most employees. This poses great risk to a company. Let's look at the risks of e-mail.

- E-mail can be forwarded to unintended recipients who get on the e-mail chain.
- Many companies have implemented policies that define e-mail residing on company computers as company property and specifically allow access to knowledge or content of the writer or recipient.
- E-mail is "discoverable" in litigation.
- E-mail memorializes tentative/preliminary opinions that cannot always be explained away.

- E-mail, especially in the U.S. provides a ready source for potential "smoking gun" evidence that can be used against the writer and company.
- E-mail establishes a fact/activity trail based on e-mail date/time stamps—plaintiff lawyers can use e-mail to build detailed histories.
- E-mail is hard to delete once sent.
    - Computers maintain a FAT ("file allocation table"); deleting e-mail may only remove the file name from the FAT.
    - Data in whole or part can reside in various locations on the hard disk until "overwritten."
    - Data is overwritten on a random basis.
    - Reconstruction of deleted files is possible through forensic bit stream analysis.

Therefore, a company must view e-mail as a necessary evil—one that is a good, efficient business tool that brings with it inherent legal risks.

35.1 Management

A company needs to manage the legal risks of e-mail in several ways.

- E-mail must be part of the document or records retention program. A well-drafted records retention program will cover e-mail destruction, e-mail preservation during litigation, and under other circumstances.
- E-mail training

    A company must train its employees as to the risks of e-mail. Employees must be trained to assume:

    - E-mail will be requested in subpoenas or through discovery or otherwise inadvertently or purpose fully disclosed to third parties.

- E-mail will be obtained by people seeking to use them against the company.
- If e-mail can be misconstrued, it will be misconstrued.
- E-mail policy

  A company must create and implement an e-mail policy and associated processes informing employees that it will monitor e-mail and take action against those who send harassing, malicious, or offensive e-mail to others.

35.2 Training

E-mail training should be made part of the compliance training program. Private attorneys as well as governmental entities can use e-mail against companies in lawsuits or investigations, such as:

- Product liability lawsuits
- Sexual harassment lawsuits
- DOJ antitrust investigations
- FCC or CPSC product safety investigations
- Other governmental investigations

The press, external critics, and watchdog groups may also use e-mail against a company as well.

- Training should mandate employees treat e-mail with care.
- Users treat e-mail too casually and should be cautious.
- E-mail should be treated in the same manner as a memo or letter.
- Employees should be encouraged to reread e-mails and think carefully about their contents before they send the e-mail.
- E-mail should only be circulated to those who need to know.
- Company e-mail should only be used for business reasons.
- E-mail should not be used to transmit trade secrets or other form of IP to third parties without executive approval.

- E-mail should not be used to restrict a company's rights or enlarge its obligations.

35.3 E-mail Issues

A company needs to take e-mail management seriously. Though a convenient form of communication, e-mail is hard to delete and can be used by third parties against a company in litigation or by the government in an investigation. It is too easy to use. A LRM program must address e-mail management issues. Such issue can range from litigation issues to data and records management issues as well.

36 E-discovery

Form: E-discovery Policy

36.1 What Is E-discovery ?

One of the most important LRM processes a company needs to implement is the E-discovery management process. But why?

E-discovery is basically the right of any party in litigation (especially in the United States) to demand electronically stored information (ESI). Of course, a party's right to ESI during litigation is subject to the local laws and legal norms of where the lawsuit is brought. In some jurisdictions it is rare; in others it is used often. When it comes to US litigation, however, the lack of adequate e-discovery processes can be fatal. Foreign companies or individuals doing business in the United States (and some U.S. companies too) fail to realize the importance of ESI and E-discovery until it is too late.

36.1.1 E-discovery in the United States

US law recognizes a party's right to seek ESI in discovery. It mandates disclosure of a copy and/or location of ESI and also allows the requesting party to specify form(s) of production of the ESI documents. If the forms are not specified, the default forms are as stored or reasonable format. The burden of providing ESI can be staggering for a variety of reasons such as:

- Cost of locating all ESI
- Time and energy to locate all relevant ESI
- Time and energy to collect and review ESI
- Cost of production of ESI

The problem facing companies when dealing with ESI is that ESI-related technologies have become numerous and complex. The ability to locate, retrieve, collect, review, and produce relevant ESI (including e-mail) may determine a company's future, once it is involved in litigation. The reasons for this include:

- Some reports estimate that approximately 80 percent of costs of litigation are related to discovery, including E-discovery.
- Litigation involving E-discovery in the United States can be costly.
- Failure to have an adequate E-discovery process can be fatal.
- US Federal Rules or Civil Procedure and US case law (*Zubulake v. UBS*, etc.) have created significant issues and costs.[44]

36.2 E-discovery Obligations: US Laws and Case Law

The Federal Rules of Civil Procedure (FRCP) defines a party's ESI obligations in federal litigation.

- E-discovery

- Preservation of evidence
    - Federal Rules of Civil Procedure (FRCP) early focus on parties' obligation to preserve evidence as early as possible
- Rule changes address e-discovery
    - Early consideration of discovery plan
    - Early consideration of privilege issues

---

[44] Zubulake v. UBS Warburg LLC, 217 F.R.D. 309 (S.D.N.Y, 2003). Note there are five Zubulake cases in total.

- Accessibility of electronically stored information (ESI)
- Formats for production of ESI
- Federal Rules of Civil Procedure
  - Rule 26
    - Committee note: "a responding party should produce electronically stored information that is relevant, not privileged, and reasonably accessible, subject to the (b) (2) C limitations that apply to all discovery.
    - "The responding party must also identify, by category or type, the sources containing potentially responsive information that it is neither searching nor producing. The identification should, to the extent possible, provide enough detail to enable the requesting party to evaluate the burdens and costs of providing the discovery and the likelihood of finding responsive information on the identified sources ..."
- Preservation of evidence
  - Litigation hold
  - Zubulake V [*Zubulake v. UBS*, 229, F.R.D. 422 (S.D.N.Y. 2004)]
    - Requires outside counsel to make certain that all potentially relevant information is identified and placed "on hold."
    - "To do this counsel must become fully familiar with her client's document retention architecture. This will invariably involve speaking with information technology personnel who can explain system wide back up procedures and the actual (as opposed to theoretical)

implementation of the firm's recycling policy. It will also involve communicating with the 'key players' in the litigation, in order to understand how they stored information ..."

- Preservation of evidence
  - "The obligation to preserve evidence arises when the party has notice that the evidence is relevant to litigation or when a party should have known that the evidence may be relevant to future litigation ..." (*Fujitsu Ltd. v. Federal Express Corp.*, 247 F3d 423, 436 (2d Cir. 2001)

Not only does the "hold" requirement apply to a company's ESI but to backup tapes as well. The court in Zubulake addressed this issue:

- Litigation hold
  - Zubulake V [*Zubulake v. UBS*, 229, F.R.D. 422 (S.D.N.Y. 2004)]
    - "As a general rule, that litigation hold does not apply to inaccessible backup tapes (e.g., those that are maintained solely for the purpose of disaster recovery) ... which may continue to be recycled on the schedule set forth in the company's policy. On the other hand, if backup tapes are accessible (i.e., actively used for information retrieval), then such tapes would likely be subject to the litigation hold ..."

36.3 Information Technology (IT)

In order to comply with the E-discovery rules and regulation as well as case law in the United States, a company (including its in-house counsel) must closely look at the IT network in order to locate where all relevant ESI is located. Only after a company thoroughly searches and collects data can it then review and collate it.

36.4 Management of E-discovery Process

There are five basic steps to the E-discovery process that must be or should be managed by in-house counsel (or outside counsel if no in-house counsel exists) together with appropriate IT personnel and related management.

The five steps are:

- Preservation: Complying with the duty to preserve evidence. This includes litigation hold orders, hold reminders, retaining data, and preserving related ESI.
- Collection: Gathering ESI documents necessary to respond to the subpoena. Concerns are the data map, size of the data collection, indexing the data, and collecting the data.
- Processing: Calling and preparing documents for review. Concerns de-duplication of ESI, as well as narrowing down the relevant ESI through key words, file type, data type, etc.
- Review: Categorizing and redacting documents. Documents may be categorized as relevant, privileged, or confidential. This needs attorney review.
- Production: Delivering documents to the other side. The document format (TIFF, PDF, and native platform oriented, etc.) must be decided.
- Each of the five steps entails processes and a procedure that should have been implemented prior to an LRM assessment or review. If not implemented prior to an LRM review, they need to be implemented ASAP.

36.4.1 In Order to Find All ESI, the IT Department Must Consider Its Networks, Which May Include:

- IT network
  - Network topology and content maps
  - Server/router list
  - Host servers
  - IP address

- Purpose of servers
- Work stations
- Physical locations where backup media stored
- Data storage and destruction systems and practices
- ASPs
- PDAs
- System of key players and key employees
- Accessibility/inaccessibility of records

36.4.2 An ESI Action Plan

Companies need to take the risk of ESI-based litigation seriously. Failure to do so will lead to catastrophic results. Therefore, it is suggested a company implement an action plan regarding ESI prior to litigation. If an action plan is not in place prior to litigation, it may be too late. Such plan should consider the following steps:

36.4.3 Proposed Plan

- Form a task force team to assess the current status of ESI processes within the company.
- Task force should have representatives from:
    - IT
    - Legal
    - Contract management
    - Risk management
    - Outside E-discovery counsel
- Arrange a task force meeting.
    - Review ESI rules.
    - Review status of company's past, present, and future litigation.
    - Select in-house e-discovery coordinators.
    - Review company's:
        - IT systems
        - Network topology and content maps

- General characteristics of data
- Applicable policy intention protocols
- Focus on data storage and destruction systems and practices
- Perform inventory of company's ESI and paper records.
- Identify all types of ESI.
- Identify all obsolete unneeded records that are for reasons unknown still being preserved.
- Identify all custodians of the ESI.
- Identify all locations of all data repositories.
- Consider current IT architecture and systems to facilitate ESI retrieval and litigation holds.
- Prepare employee training program on ESI and ESI policies.
- Select two technical IT E-discovery coordinators.
- Identify and retain outside experts and E-discovery vendors:
  - Determine what outside services, if any, may be required immediately or in the foreseeable future.
  - Review experts previously used by the company.
  - Integrate experts and vendors into various tasks of the team.
- Prepare and implement a customized E-discovery litigation response plan and procedures to identify, preserve, collect, process, review, analyze, and produce ESI.
- Coordinate with outside counsel on handling all technical e-discovery issues.

A well-thought-out ESI action plan is critical to the survival of many corporations, especially those doing business in the United States. As Ralph Losey, in his book *Introduction to e-Discovery*, points out,

"Today millions of British Pounds and US Dollars are being spent on e-discovery cures. This expense is a harsh reality of litigation."[45]

36.5 Real Case in Point - Zubulake v. UBS Warburg LLC

The most import E-discovery case in the U.S. is Zubulake v. UBS Warburg LLC, 217 F.R.D. 309 (S.D.N.Y. 2003). This case has set the tone for all other E-discovery cases.

Laura Zubulake, the plaintiff, sued her Swiss employer for gender discrimination and illegal retaliation. She alleged she was treated differently from her male counterparts, belittled and had her professional responsibilities taken away[46].

During litigation, it was discovered that Warburg tried to deleted emails and deny everything happened. The jury awarded her $18 million in compensatory damage and $19 million in punitive damages.

Zubulake litigation resulted in 5 cases all important to E-discovery and showing how important E-discovery rules are. Primarily, the cases taken together stand for several rules that parties in litigation in the U.S. must now follow. They are:

- The court may order sanctions against a party if it relocates its duty to preserve evidence, including e-mails
- Parties have a duty to preserve all relevant evidence including evidence found on back-up tapes
- Outside counsel must make certain that all potentially relevant electronic information is identified and placed on "hold" or in other words – protected. All relevant information must be retained.
- Costs of restoring back-up tapes or legacy systems are to be allocated between the parties using certain criteria.

---

[45]   Ralph Losey, *Introduction to e-Discovery*, Chicago (ABA Publishing, 2009), 16.

[46]   Id, 441

- Outside counsel must become "fully familiar" with his or her client's architecture. Also, outside counsel must take steps to monitor compliance to confirm all sources of discovery, including E-discovery are identified, and reviewed.

Not only does the court Zubulake place a duty on parties to preserve all relevant information including ESI, it also places the burden on outside counsel to ensure compliance with the preservation obligation. This is broken down into 4 distinct responsibilities:

  - Counsel must instruct all employees to produce electronic copies of their relevant files
  - Counsel must ensure all backup media containing relevant information is identified and stored in a safe place
  - In cases where there are a small number of back-up tapes, counsel should take physical possession of them
  - Where there are a large number of back-up tapes, those tapes should be segregated and placed in secure storage
- A party has an obligation and duty to suspend routine document destruction and ensure a litigation "hold" is put in place when it reasonably anticipates litigation

Questions:

  - What duty does a company have when it anticipates litigation in the U.S.?
  - What duty does a company have to preserve back-up tapes or other forms of storage media when it anticipates it will face litigation in the U.S.?
  - What duty does outside counsel have to ensure his or her client preserves ESI when it is likely the client will be sued in the U.S.?

37 Document Management

In the previous chapters we have discussed data privacy issues facing companies as well as E-discovery risks a company faces. However, all of the issues and legal risks they pose can be considered subsets of the overall data management issue a company faces. In other words, how does a company identify, define, protect and manage its data? A document management program will, of course, also encompass E-discovery and data privacy concerns.

37.1 The Corporate Landscape

When a company considers a data and document management program, it must look at the program from the business risk and legal risk standpoints.

- Business rationale and risk: Protecting a company's most valuable asset: information—data and documents and inherent risks.
- Legal rationale and risks: Strict laws and regulation-based requirements, especially for data and document retention and inherent risks.

The two above issues are of course linked. The business issue concerns access to and the efficient use of data as well as preservation of data. Therefore, what are legal issues and accompanying risks associated with a company's business rationale for the use of data and documentation?

The legal issues and risks concern primarily data as electronic evidence.

37.2 Electronic Evidence

A company sued in the United States and perhaps elsewhere, even if handling a dispute through arbitration, will have a number of legal concerns and risks to consider, such as:

- Obligation to produce
  - Court orders to produce
  - Discovery obligations
  - Rules governing production of data and documentation
- Penalties for nonproduction
  - Fines/penalties
  - Preclusion
  - Presumption of guilt by the jury of finder of fact
- Spoliation claims

In considering the above legal concerns over electronic documentation and data, often called ESI, or "electronically stored information," a company's efficient use of data is made problematic by virtue of the numerous platforms/locations for storage and transmission of ESI. Such platforms include:

- Desktop and laptop computers
- File and mail servers
- Databases
- Backup tapes and archival media
- PDAs
- Voice mail
- Instant messaging
- Voice-over IP

37.2.1 Magnitude of ESI

To give an idea of the problem facing a company when storing data, consider the following quote.

> "A floppy disc ... is the equivalent of 720 typewritten pages of plain text. A CD-ROM can hold up to 325,000 typewritten pages. Large corporate computer networks create backup data measured in terabytes ... each terabyte represents the equivalent of 500 billion typewritten pages of plain text."[47]

Risks facing a company when dealing with ESI include:

- Automated deletion of ESI over time because of volume
- Limited access to backups and legacy systems
  - Sparse
  - Cost
  - Retained knowledge
- Failure to follow rules regarding E-discovery, such as the failure to initiate a litigation "hold"

37.2.2 Legal Risk Management Objectives When Dealing with ESI

A company's primary objectives when dealing with ESI prior to litigation are:

- Handling ESI discovery obligations in a cost efficient/time efficient manner
- Initiating required litigation "hold" requirements
- Prevention of spoliation (destruction or loss of ESI) problems or spoliation claims

---

[47] *Manual for Complex Litigation*, 4th Ed, Sec 11.446, available on the Internet at http://www-fjc.gov/public/home.nsf/pages/470.

37.3 ESI Requirements

To avoid fines, penalties, and even loss of litigation in the United States, a company's documentation retention program (DRP) must show the following requirements:

- A retention policy must be in place and must be followed.
- Corporate IT personnel must be involved.
- The program must allow for suspension of auto-delete programs when needed.
- Must be able to identify "key players"—interview them and preserve their ESI.
- Litigation holds must be properly issued and reissued from time to time.
- The program must create a defensible record of compliance with retention policy and litigation hold processes.

37.3.1 Litigation Hold

There are several risks and issues surrounding a litigation hold. Risks surrounding proper issuance of a litigation hold include:

- When is it triggered? The trigger of the duty to issue a litigation hold is when litigation is "reasonably likely" (i.e., it is ambiguous).
- A company must take into consideration the company's auto-delete processes. What are they?
- Communication with IT is essential.
- A company must quickly and clearly communicate to all relevant employees and vendors who provide data management the scope of the hold and importance of compliance.

37.3.2 Duty to Locate Relevant Information:

If a company is involved with litigation in the United States, it has a duty to locate all relevant information, data, and documents—including ESI. This can be quite onerous, as it requires:

- Familiarity with document retention policies
- Involvement with IT personnel
- Communication to "key players" of litigation hold
- Location and retrieval of all relevant information

The legal risks facing a company that fails to handle the above requirements in an economical/efficient manner can be tremendous. Companies have been sanctioned millions of dollars for failing to abide by ESI requirements or, even worse, have lost the respective lawsuits, covering even more. It is inexcusable to lose any kind of major litigation because of a lack of properly developed document management system. What can a company do to mitigate the legal risks surrounding document management to comply with US requirements?

37.4 Plan of Action

A company must take the following steps to develop an adequate data and document management plan:

- Assess the company's current use of technology documents.
- Locate all in the company's possession.
- Use technology to leverage legal requirements.
- Retain experts or outside consultants to above or to help implement systems/processes.
- Implement policies and procedures addressing all legal risks posed by ESI.

37.4.1 Risk Assessment of ESI

To implement an appropriate plan of action, a company must conduct a risk assessment of its processes and capabilities by:

- Seeking proposals of vendors (outside experts)
- A top-to-bottom analysis
  - ESI and paper documents
  - Hardware and software

- Management of data
- Retention of data
- Litigation holds
- Disaster preparedness

37.5 ESI Implementation

The legal risks facing companies in today's legal and regulatory climate, especially in the United States, are enormous. Failure to implement a data and document management program that not only addresses a company's business concerns, but legal obligations as well can be disastrous. The development and implementation of an LRM program addressing these concerns is not a luxury but a necessity. It is highly recommended that a company implement a data and documentation management program that addresses ESI and all of its issues.

38 Implementation of a Crisis Management Strategy

Any discussion of LRM would not be complete without a brief discussion of crisis management. Crisis risk management (CRM) itself would be a topic for a book. There are numerous books on the topic. Nonetheless, for purposes of this book and a LRM discussion it is a fitting topic to discuss. Without effective management of a corporate crisis, a company's future would be in doubt. Any LRM program should consider the development of a crisis management strategy for foreseeable events and the implementation of crisis risk management within the organization.

38.1 Crisis Defined

What is a crisis? A crisis can be considered to be a major unpredictable or catastrophic event that has potentially negative results. A crisis, in other words, is a major unpredictable event that may significantly damage or impact a company or organization by harming its brand, reputation, or public image. The problem with a "crisis" is that not only can't it always be forecast or predicted, a crisis can and will affect stakeholders, which can determine the fate of the company.

The past decade can be considered the decade of the "mega crisis." Many people have been affected (some have died) because of the crises or mega-crises that have happened. Examples include:

- Coke and Pepsi were implicated in tainted products in India.
- Enron, WorldCom, and Tyco were accused of financial scandals.
- The World Trade Center towers in New York were destroyed.
- The financial and housing collapse and major recession of 2008.
- Toyota implicated in recalls because of brake issues.
- The tsunami affecting Thailand and Indonesia, resulting in deaths of approximately 250,000 people.
- The Fukushima Daiichi nuclear disaster which is still ongoing
- Major banks having their credit card customers' names stolen by computer hackers

There are numerous kinds of crises that a company should be prepared to handle, especially in an international context. Among them are financial crises, natural disasters, product failures, workplace violence, cyber-attack, or hacking, and, of course, terrorism.

It is undisputable that a major crisis can pose serious threats to a company, and, therefore, the crisis must be managed. Crises can result in (a) government fines, (b) loss of retailer confidence, (c) loss of investor confidence, (d) loss of employee confidence, and (e) massive civil litigation, including class actions.[48] In other words, the end of the company!

The problem facing any risk manager or in-house counsel is that the media in today's society has become very anti-business. As this anti-business culture of attack has gotten worse over the last twenty years, a crisis can no longer be handled by a simple PR or marketing statement. A full-fledged crisis management operation must be put in place. Damage control is now a very serious matter for any potential crisis, no matter how small. Today, more and more companies have to consider issues that negatively affect the company's brand and how best to counteract them.

---

[48] Robert W. Littleton and Thomas R. Cherry, *"International Crisis Management," International Corporate Practice*, Carle Basri, editor, New York: PLI 2011, 8–3.

It has been said that a company has twenty-four hours to put a strategy into place to handle a crisis. Some now say that because of the Internet, a company only has a few hours to address the situation. The impact of a company's strategy or lack thereof will probably be felt in ten to twenty days—or even less. Companies without an adequate strategy have failed to recover from the crisis.

In-house counsel must realize they are not just a lawyer but in fact are a crisis/legal risk manager. Therefore they need to act quickly with the crisis management team (if there is one) to address civil liability issues, identify the mistakes that may have caused the potential liability and fix them, identify the government regulations, if any, that should be complied, as well as determine what insurance policies are affected and whether the insurers need to be informed of the crisis. Remember, counsel should move quickly to address and manage any of the potential complaints that may result from the crisis event. This should all be part of a grand crisis management strategy. So, what should a crisis management strategy consist of?

38.2 Crisis Management Strategy

Companies that successfully manage crises have used four or five basic steps to prepare for a crisis to the extent possible. They include the following steps:

- Identify the major areas of vulnerability the company faces.
- Develop a plan for dealing with potential threats.
- Form a crisis management team to deal with or handle threats.
- Simulate crisis scenarios of potential threats to prepare the company.
- Learn from the experience of managing the crisis.

Other companies have used a variety of steps to handle crises, including:

- Avoiding the crisis through proactive steps
- Preparing for the crisis through preparation and planning
- Properly reacting as soon as the crisis exists, and
- Resolving the crisis

To help put everything into context, a company should realize that crises, including international crises, occur in stages. The crisis management strategy should be prepared to deal with the stages as they unfold. Each stage requires certain responses from the company, and each stage has a certain impact upon a company.[49] Typically, however, a company does not have a crisis management strategy in place, especially one that can handle the various stages of a crisis. Many times, a company is caught sleeping without a strategy and fails to adequately manage or resolve the crisis, which may severely impact the company. Usually, a poorly managed crisis follows a similar pattern:

- Early indications of a crisis starting—perhaps reports from the Service Department indicating product failure or serious defects.
- Warnings of the upcoming crisis are ignored by company management. Maybe the Service Department's warnings go unheeded by management.
- The crisis explodes, overwhelming management as deaths or serious injuries are reported due to product failure or product defects.
- Management tries to resolve the crisis quickly but without success as it failed to consider the ramifications of the crisis and how to handle it.
- The company fails to take adequate measures to handle the crisis as the crisis continues to unfold as reported by the media.
- The company suffers the consequences of an outraged media, public, and even some or all stakeholders.

---

[49]   Id,8:4.

- The company's existence and brand is severely threatened or put into jeopardy as its stock plummets and lawsuits are filed causing its reputation to be severely tarnished.

38.3 International Crisis

In today's world, many companies do business internationally. Because of international considerations, an international crisis is harder to manage than a domestic crisis. As it is more complex, companies caught up in an international crisis have to pay more attention to international, cultural, and communication issues than they would in a purely domestic scenario. Cross-border crisis management has become very important. Therefore, an international crisis requires a number of steps, including:

- Planning for an international crisis
- Appointing a crisis manager to handle international issues
- Establishment of a crisis management team equipped to handle international crisis
- Knowledge of foreign situations as they impact the company
- Communications
- Cross-border management of the crisis
- Having appropriate international legal counsel on the team

The principle focus of any crisis management strategy, especially in an international contest, is communications. All crisis management plans call for effective crisis communications, which many times are not always executed properly. Inadequate or failed communications lead to bad publicity, unhappy stakeholders including employees, and potential disaster. An effective crisis communication strategy is necessary for any international crisis. Call in an outside crisis PR consultant if needed.

A number of processes are needed to implement an effective crisis communication strategy to manage an international crisis, including:

- Creation of the crisis communication team.

- Identification of key spokespersons who will speak for the organization. Who are they? What are their roles?
- Training in relevant cultural issues, if the crisis involves other cultures.
- Establishment of communication procedures and protocols. Who communicates to whom and why?
- Identification of key messages to be communicated to key stakeholders and groups.
- Decision as to what communication methods should be used. Do they involve the Internet, TV, radio, etc.? May be decided by the geographic location of the crisis.
- Effective use of social media
- Retain the use of a well-respected outside Crisis PR professional
- Be ready to handle the crisis as it unfolds. Generally, if all steps have been properly implemented the company should be prepared.

38.4 Communication Components of a Crisis Management Plan

As stated above, communications is important. Therefore, a communications plan must take into consideration proper communication to numerous entities, including:

- The media
- Employees
- Crisis Management Team
- Government
- Websites
- The public
- The stakeholders (internal and external)

38.5 Considerations

When establishing a crisis management strategy, a number of questions must be asked.

- How many disputes or potential disputes are involved?
- Can the disputes be resolved quickly? If so, how?
- How many participants are involved?
- How many stakeholders are involved?
- How is the best way to communicate effectively to the media and stakeholders?
- Who should the spokesperson be?
- Should Upper Management be the face of the company?
- Should there be more than one spokesperson?
- What are the facts surrounding the crisis?
- How many cultures or jurisdictions are involved?
- What regulatory obligations, if any, need to be fulfilled?
- What insurance notification requirements need to be fulfilled?

A company that has an effective crisis management strategy in place will be able to handle a crisis when it happens. Those companies who are not ready to handle crises or who fail to handle them properly not only will fail to prosper but may also fail.

38.6 Real Case in Point – Toyota

Toyota was involved in a series of recalls from 2009-2010 as a result of numerous cars experiencing unintended acceleration. By 2010, Toyota recalled 9 million vehicles worldwide. The major problem Toyota faced was that it failed to grasp the enormity of the situations surrounding the recalls and therefore committed numerous media blunders. In effect, Toyota had spent millions of dollars to build up the Lexus brand name and lost all credibility by failing to adequately handle the crisis. See *Crisis Communications: The Definitive Guide to Managing the Message* by Steve Fink.

As Toyota responded to the major recall and resulting media crisis in a very inadequate way, it was faced with numerous lawsuits, loss of brand value and a tarnished reputation. Toyota dealerships in the U.S. lost an estimated $2,470 million in revenue. Toyota lost as much as

$2,000 million from lost output and worldwide sales. In fact, Toyota stock decreased by 15% between January 25 and January 29, 2010.

Toyota's inept response to the crisis caused by alleged unintended acceleration and brake issues can be seen as a prime example of not how to address and manage the impact of a crisis. A summary of the case is as follows:

August 28, 2009, 4 people were killed in a 2-car collision involving a Lexus near San Diego, CA. The NHTSA's investigation revealed that the vehicle was wrongfully fitted with a rubber floor mat (meant for a SUV) that was not secured by retaining clips. The mat may have trapped the accelerator pedal causing the spring not to release. Prior to the accident, another customer had complained to the dealership about the floor mat trapping the accelerator & pedal while driving. The NHTSA's report also indicated the accelerator pedal may have been stuck due to other reasons.

On October 18, 2009, the Los Angeles Times published an article covering claims of unintended acceleration in Toyota vehicles. The Los Angeles story not only points out that at least 5 accidents have been caused by unintended acceleration in Toyota vehicles since 2007, but that hundreds of complaints had been filled with the federal government.

On November 2, 2009, Toyota voluntarily recalled 3.8 million vehicles by sending letters to customers asking them to remove the driver floor mat. Toyota claimed the mat was the sole cause of the unintended acceleration. However, the NHTSA issued an unusual statement claiming the investigation was not closed until Toyota "effectively addressed the defect" and that removal of the mat was an interim measure." Toyota publicly apologizes for its claim.

On November 4, 2009 Toyota issued a press release denying claims by the media that a problem exists with its "drive-by-wire electronic throttle system[50]."

---

[50]   *Motortrend, January, 2010*

On November 8, 2009, the Los Angeles Times once again reported on the Toyota matter claiming 1,200 complaints of unintended acceleration had been made to Toyota which it had ignored.

On November 29, 2009, the LA Times reported that unintended acceleration complaints on the Lexus ES 300S dramatically increased after 2002 and that 19 deaths had been attributed to unintended acceleration in Toyota vehicles since 2002. Toyota had no explanation but claimed the electronic throttle system was not at fault.

On December 5, 2009, Toyota still claimed floor mats were the main cause of unintended acceleration claims but that is contradicted when on December 26, 2009 a Toyota Avalon crashes into a lake after accelerating out of control. All occupants were killed. Floor mats were ruled out as the cause as they had been taken out and placed in the truck.

The LA Times continued its report that Toyota had been hiding defects from customers and had not taken actions to solve the unintended acceleration problem.

Though Toyota finally began recalling millions of vehicles in late 2009 and January of 2010, the reputational damage had been done. The public was outraged over Toyota's perceived failure in not taking effective action to solve the unintended acceleration problem. Toyota's sales plummeted, the brand and reputation was tarnished.

Question:

- What should have Toyota done to prevent the crisis?
- Does your company have and effective crisis management process in place?
- Are you ready if a Toyota type crisis hits your company?

39 Crisis Management: Hypothetical Case in Point

Cell phone disaster

PanStar is the newest cell phone company in country X and the fastest growing cell phone company in the world. Its hit cell phone, the "Cinnamon Stick," has sold five million units in India, its largest market. It has sold two million units in country X and has sold three million units in the United States, its second-largest market. Its annual sales for 2012 exceeded $75 million US. Not bad for a start-up.

As a new start-up company, PanStar depended on venture capital. It found financing with a US venture capital company—the Equity Venture Capital Group (EVCG) in New York. EVCG has invested $25 million in the start-up and was in the process of providing another loan of $25 million to finance expansion. Soon PanStar would list itself on its country's stock exchange. It could then expand to other countries. The CEO of EVCG, Mr. Overby, was very happy about EVGC's investment and thought the loan would be available by September 1.

On May 1, 2011, President Park was informed by Mr. Kho, his head engineer, that several faulty battery chargers were found, which could cause the cell phone battery to overheat.

The problem was isolated and identified to the faulty manufacture of the battery chargers by PanStar's main subcontractor, I-Risk, located in Mongolia. It appeared only a few faulty battery chargers were sold, and I-Risk thought it had corrected the problem. No problem was expected, as only a few faulty battery chargers were produced, and overheating was usually not that serious.

On July 1, 2011, President Park received a frantic phone call from his major distributor in India, Mr. Raj Samsoran. He had received word that one of the cell phones had just exploded, killing the cell phone owner, a boy of twelve years of age in New Delhi. He promised to look into it ASAP!

On July 2, President Park was informed that the Indian Product Safety Commission was outraged over the cell phone explosion and was blaming PanStar. It wanted to immediately ban the sale of all PanStar cell phones in India. It called for an official investigation of the alleged incident. It also wanted to impose fines.

On July 3, Mr. Overby of EVGC called President Park about the Indian cell phone situation. Obviously, if the cell phone batteries were defective, it may be hard to get financing. EVGC was starting to question PanStar's products. Was investing in PanStar a good idea? Should it provide the loan or not?

On July 4, a reporter from a local TV station contacted PanStar's PR Department wanting to interview President Park about the "exploding" cell phones. A TV station from the United States wanted to interview him as well. So, did an Indian TV station.

July 5, President Park knew he had to act fast if he wanted to handle the crisis. Otherwise, the company faced ruin. He called in his management team—his head of communications; his head of Sales, his VP of operations, his head Service safety engineer, and his CFO. He asked for advice. What steps should be taken with the following in mind:

- What steps should be taken by the crisis management team to resolve the crisis?
- What steps should the Communications Department take, if any, regarding the crisis?
- Are there any international issues that should be addressed? If so, what are they?
- What stakeholders are affected by the crisis and how should their concerns be addressed?

Summary

As LRM should be used proactively to reduce the threat of legal risk, a company needs to think of strategies that can be used prior to litigation to reduce risk. Such strategies that can be used include the implementation of a compliance program, creation of a records retention program, use of an e-mail management program, implementation of an e-discovery policy or process, a data management program, and the creation of a crisis management process.

The use of a compliance program can be an effective risk management tool. A compliance program, if properly implemented, will not only increase a company's brand image but will reinforce ethical behavior among the employees, which has positive benefits. This, in turn, helps minimize legal risk and exposure.

One of the principle reasons a corporation faces legal exposure is its failure to manage information, whether in hard-copy form or in electronic form. Electronically stored information (ESI) poses numerous problems, as it is hard to manage. Not only should a company implement an information retention policy, but it should also address issues caused by ESI, including e-mail issues.

E-discovery issues, if left unchecked, may result in enormous costs and expenses if a company fails to implement an E-discovery policy, especially if it faces litigation in the United States. It is very important for a company as part of its LRM program to implement an E-discovery plan that can mitigate exposure to costs, fees, and expenses.

Notwithstanding the implementation of a compliance program, a crisis management strategy needs to be in place. A CRM program is becoming more important as an LRM tool because of the numerous media attacks and/or culture of attack in which most businesses operate in today's environment.

Part Four

Legal Risk Management and Litigation

Though a company may have implemented legal risk mitigation, avoidance, or even LRM shifting strategies and processes, there will come a point where litigation, especially in the United States, is inevitable. Though pre-litigation risk management strategies are vital to minimize the exposure of litigation risks, managing litigation properly is essential for a satisfactory outcome. Companies that fail to properly manage outside litigation face potential out-of-control lawyers and out-of-control legal fees and costs. Also, if not properly handled, any failure to hire law firm based on a comprehensive plan will result in lack of coordination, little continuity, lack of consistency, and even separate law firms taking contradictory positions when dealing with different divisions. Sometimes corporations rush to hire lawyers based on areas of expertise without looking past a short-term objective. A company that fails to optimize its use of legal support services ends up hiring numerous law firms for numerous areas such as tax, customs, litigation, employment, etc. This results in increased costs, and chances for successful resolution of litigation or commercial disputes may disappear. Therefore, this section of the book stresses basic litigation management concepts, as that is also of utmost importance.

It should be noted that processes developed to defend against litigation must take into consideration a number of issues, especially if more than one division or subsidiary is subject to potential litigation in the United States or elsewhere. Such processes should include the following litigation considerations, especially these companies or division operating in the U.S. marketplace.

- Multiple group companies can be named as defendants. These companies will need coordination of defense and discovery matters.
- Maintaining corporate compliance.
- Litigation respecting same products in multiple jurisdictions.
- Insurance coverage: Is it adequate? Risk Management or Legal needs to review insurance coverage.
- Communication: Are communication protocols set up to facilitate effective and efficient communication between relevant departments, especially in case of a crisis?
- Internal Investigations: Is there a complaint and investigation procedure protocol?
- Centralized management of litigation must be implemented for:
    - Effective coordination of legal defense efforts in order for the companies and attorneys to avoid duplication of cost and effort from case to case.
    - Coordinated use of witnesses, answers and interrogatory responses, documents, deposition materials, and research and briefs on legal issues.
    - Assurance of consistency of actions taken at every phase of the litigation, including pleadings, discovery and responses, discovery motions, and settlement strategies.

- Proper minimization of disruptions to the company's business by internally coordinating fact-finding.
- Development, implementation, and coordination of a defense plan.
- Coordinated activity respecting financial considerations, such as:
  - Reserves
  - Disclosure to auditors

For cases where multiple group companies are named as defendants or where actions respecting the same product are filed in multiple jurisdictions, an effective litigation management process can provide a central site for:

- Preservation of evidence, documents, files, and records
- Use of document depositories and computerized storage
- Coordinated or cross-referenced numbering system for documents
- Coordination of protective orders and procedures for handling claims of confidentiality and privilege

An LRM program must also:

- Establish complaints and claims handling procedures and controls.
- Establish claims processing procedures.
- Establish record-keeping guidelines.
- Establish e-discovery process controls.

From the above, it is apparent that the role legal risk management should play in litigation is important. Only a well-thought-out LRM program that considers all the above-mentioned issues and concerns will be successful.

40 Corporate Structure Issues

Companies, especially multinational companies or conglomerates with several subsidiaries, can effectively mitigate risk through the use of a holding company. The creation of a corporate structure that uses a holding company can limit and isolate liability and legal risk arising from the operations of individual subsidiaries. This is especially true of companies doing business in the United States through subsidiaries or multiple operations.

40.1 Holding Company: Liability Containment

US corporations generally have liability limited to their assets, and stockholders are not personally liable for the debts of the corporation. A US corporation is generally subject to suit in the United States only in the state of its incorporation and in states where it does business. These principal features of the US corporation generally result in containment of the liability for that corporation's debts or acts to the corporation itself without attribution of liability up the corporate chain of ownership.

The prospect of enormous punitive damage awards against corporations by American juries and the possible imposition of large civil fines alone demonstrate the need for maintaining corporate formalities and utilizing a holding company structure that cuts off liability at the subsidiary level. The holding company structure isolates and confines liability to the subsidiary. The presence of one or more US holding companies between the subsidiary and the ultimate foreign parent serves as a further buffer to protect the parent from liability exposure in the United States. A related, but equally important, limited liability strategy centers on the foreign parent. Specifically, to protect its own assets, it should avoid direct US contacts, so it is not subject to the jurisdiction of courts in the United States. Rather, business should be conducted through its subsidiaries.

40.2 Centralized Management of Regulatory Matters Applicable to Subsidiaries and the Group or Parent as a Whole

Many regulatory and compliance matters are measured or regulated on a controlled group basis. Since the activities of any entity down the ownership chain can affect the whole group or ultimate parent organization, usually certain elements of control reside at the holding company. This precludes "stray" arrangements from being adopted on an ad hoc basis. As required, the holding company can access information generally not available to various group members.

The holding company can put together more effective arrangements (e.g., master contacts) for use by group members to obtain the best terms. Immigration can also be effectively managed by a single source as opposed to numerous conflicting sources.

Centralized management of regulatory matters applicable to subsidiaries also has other benefits, such as the followings.

40.2.1 Tax Planning and Minimization

The holding company structure offers the benefit of centralized planning and control over US tax liabilities. Considerations include the following:

- Consolidating country and group management and reporting
- Federal tax
- State and local taxes

- Excise, property, and other taxes

40.2.2 Holding Company Structure Promotes Efficiency and Minimizes Redundancy in Certain Areas, thereby Generating Cost Savings, to the Extent Centralized Services Are Provided to the Entire Group

- Legal
- Risk management and insurance
- Other administrative efficiencies provision (i.e., specialized legal services to group companies)

40.2.3 Holding Company Structure Facilitates Synergies and Efficiencies between Subsidiaries and Operating Groups through Knowledge Sharing

- Transfer of technology
- People mobility
- Teaming on projects
- Shared services
- Employee benefits
- Insurance

40.2.4 Risk Mitigation through a Holding Company

As part of an LRM plan, companies need to consider the holding company structure, especially in the United States. A holding company structure can promote the centralized management of risk mitigation and promote the ease of transfer or sale of assets, if necessary.

With the recent explosion of adverse liability judgments against foreign companies in the United States, especially in product liability areas, it is in the best interests of corporate conglomerates to effectively limit their liability through a holding company structure. Obviously, limiting a potentially onerous judgment to a subsidiary would be a desirable goal of the corporate parent.

40.3 Potential Issues Involving Holding Companies

The use of a holding company structure in the United States is not without its drawbacks. Among the drawbacks are:

- Taxes on a state level
- Costs of running a holding company structure
- Proper corporate formalities must be followed

40.3.1 Legal Significance of the Corporate Structure

One of the major features of a corporate organization in the United States is that it insulates shareholders from personal liability for the debts of the corporation. Therefore, under normal conditions, a corporate parent will not be held liable for the obligations of its subsidiary. The court will not impose liability upon a parent for the obligations of its subsidiary in the absence of compelling legal reasons. However, under certain circumstances courts will hold the parent or stockholders liable. It will, in other words, "pierce the corporate veil" and go past the subsidiary and hold the parent liable. The major legal doctrine allowing the courts to do this are set forth below.

- Fraud

If a subsidiary is being used by the parent as a vehicle to perpetuate a fraud or crime.

- Alter ego

If there is such a close relationship between the parent and the subsidiary that the former may be said to be the "alter ego" of the latter.

Though fraud is usually not a major concern of conglomerates, the alter ego doctrine can be. Courts will sometimes treat a wholly owned subsidiary as an instrumentality of the parent, hence alter ego if the parent fails to respect corporate formalities necessary for the proper formation and function of a subsidiary.

Therefore, if the parent exerts too much control over a subsidiary, and the subsidiary does not follow corporate formalities, an alter ego situation can exist.

To determine if an alter ego situation exists, courts will look at a number of factors indicating control, such as:

- Stock ownership
- Officers and directors
- Financing
- Responsibility of day-to-day operations
- Arrangements for payment of salaries
- Whether the parent corporation uses the property of the subsidiary as its own
- Minimum compliance of general corporate law

A court may be inclined to invoke the alter ego doctrine if it finds a subsidiary disregards minimum corporate formalities.

Specifically, corporations in the United States are required to hold annual stockholder meetings, elect officers, annually file a franchise tax return, maintain separate corporate minute books, and maintain separate accounting records. Failure to follow these processes can result in a court holding that the subsidiary is merely the alter ego of the parent.

To avoid this, the holding company needs to do the following:

- Maintain separate corporate records for each subsidiary.
- Segregate the funds of each subsidiary.
- Maintain separate books of account for each subsidiary.
- Assure each subsidiary is properly charged for the centralized service provided by the holding company.
- Keep all minute books up to date.

41 Use of Outside Counsel

When using outside counsel, most companies, especially those that have affiliates or subsidiaries, need a comprehensive approach. Unfortunately, many companies hire law firms on a case-by-case or ad hoc basis. Sometimes divisions of the same company hire different law firms without thinking about potential issues of legal talent and failure to obtain high-quality legal services on a consistent and reasonably priced basis.

If a company has an in-house Law Department, it is incumbent on the in-house Law Department to develop processes to select and use outside counsel on a consistent basis with a focus on quality, reasonable fees, and, of course, success. Such success is normally the result of a long-term relationship in which outside counsel becomes a member of the company's "team," learns the business, and can, therefore, provide timely legal and business advice.

If a company does not have an in-house counsel, it must look toward retaining a law firm, which in essence acts as an in-house counsel. In other words, the law firm becomes an "outside general counsel." By hiring an outside general counsel, a company obtains a firm that can consistently and responsibly evaluates legal issues, decide how to handle them, and implement a comprehensive legal strategy.

The concept is analogous to a building contractor. Just like a building contractor knows the overall status of a building, the outside general counsel knows the complete legal requirements of his client. When a building contractor does not have the expertise to build part of the building, he calls in a subcontractor. Likewise, when legal services outside the area of expertise of the outside general counsel are required, he recommends that another law firm be retained to handle special or specific matters.

41.1 Centralization

A company either has in-house counsel or it does not. To successfully handle legal issues facing most companies these days (especially those involving litigation and the legal process), the use of outside counsel must be centralized. If a company has many divisions or subsidiaries, a department should be empowered to oversee all legal matters. There are numerous advantages to centralization of outside counsel or the legal function:

41.1.1 Advantages of Centralization

- One organization has an overview of all legal issues confronting the company and can properly advise management on legal issues.
- Efficiency: Whether in-house or outside, efficient and fast response to legal issues is necessary.
- Use of a single law firm as outside general counsel can result in monetary savings.
- Centralization of legal services lends itself to the centralization of the company's legal records, documentation, and information, creating a more efficient process.
- Centralization of legal services allows for a more efficient review of data, resulting in the proper use of information and development of an appropriate strategy.
- Investment: Whether a company is large or small, it needs to look at use of outside counsel as an investment. Picking the right outside counsel and developing a long-term relationship with such counsel will pay dividends in the long run.

Efficient and timely use of outside legal services, whether such use of outside legal services is picked by an in-house lawyer or by a company manager or officer, relies on whether outside counsel is the right fit for the company. There are many law firms around, but not all are the right fit. Picking the right law firm or outside counsel depends on a number of factors. Many times, a company picks a law firm because of a personal relationship between a company officer and a lawyer in the firm. Or maybe the firm has done a good job in advertising. The trouble is, without going through a process to determine the acceptability of a law firm, picking outside counsel can be hit or miss.

42 Picking the Law Firm: The Value Added Proposition

Whether the company is large or small and whether it has an in-house Law Department or not, picking the right outside law firm is essential. This is especially true if the company does not have in-house lawyers and opts to pick an outside general counsel. There are many law firms to pick from. But only a few really can add value and really benefit the company. The company or organization needs to ask various questions when looking for law firms that can add value.

- Does the law firm understand my business or is it willing to try and understand my business?
- Is the law firm willing to operate like a "building contractor" and let me know if other specialized law firms (subcontractors) are needed?
- Is the law firm willing to make a commitment to my company by becoming a "partner"?
- If I am picking an outside general counsel, does the firm have general, broad capabilities to handle my issues, and if so, is the firm willing to "audit" the legal processes of my operations?
- Can the company or its in-house lawyers work comfortably with the outside law firms? Will they help me for the long term?
- Is the law firm willing to work with the company managers on a regular basis?

- Will the law firm, operating as an outside general counsel, be willing to interview and select other outside law firms on select matters, if needed?
- Will the law firm be willing to become a go-to law firm by offering reasonably priced solutions to my legal problems, such as using a blended rate or success fee, or do the partners think they can all charge $1,000 per hour?

In other words, is the law firm willing to become your partner? Will it invest significant resources in becoming your go-to law firm? Will it add value?

42.1 Finding Law Firms

Before a company or a company's in-house lawyers can pick the right outside law firm, a search for the right firm must be conducted. This entails a process more sophisticated than just looking at legal advertisements in the newspaper or on TV. Several tools are useful in helping find appropriate law firms and lawyers. These tools or procedures can assist most companies in finding the right firm if implemented.

First, however, a company has to assess it needs and decide what kind of firm it wants. Does it want a large firm that can handle most issues or a boutique small firm that specializes in one area of law? It could want a medium-sized regional firm that can handle many issues but does not have offices in every major city yet has a large regional presence. Regional firms can be very cost effective when dealing with certain issues.

On the other hand, Kevin Quinley, in his book on litigation management points out that large law firms have many advantages in that sheer size of the firm will guarantee there are enough lawyers that can handle most cases.[51] Therefore, if a company has many or very serious lawsuits requiring a large team or staff of lawyers and legal

---

[51]   Kevin M Quinley, *Litigation Management*, Dallas: International Risk Management Institute (1995)

assistants, a large firm is best. So, if General Motors is sued in a class action over faulty brakes, etc., a large firm is best equipped to handle that kind of litigation.

Be that as it may, larger firms are not always the best answer. Smaller firms, including regional ones, will many times be more flexible when it comes to billing and perhaps be more responsive, especially when the matter is not major litigation. Small or regional firms may provide more personalized service tailored to a specific client. I would use regional firms if possible, as such firms are usually cheaper and provide a similar quality of service—sometimes even better quality—as do the large firms. However, sometimes it is best to use a national or large firm, or even a multinational law firm if there are international issues and concerns involved.

Large firms tend to have more resources to handle large and complex matters but have, like any large organization, certain processes and procedures that may not allow them to operate as cheaply and efficiently as smaller firms. Large firms often have a bureaucracy that renders them less flexible and nimble than a small or regional firm. However, as large firms tend to have more offices and more lawyers, it may be advantageous to use these firms when the scope of litigation or the seriousness of the matter requires such resources. So, as stated above, before picking a law firm, a company must assess its legal requirements. Is it "bet the farm" litigation or a less serious matter? Does it require a national or international presence, or is the matter isolated to a smaller geographic area?

42.2 Thoughts on Selecting the Appropriate Law Firm

There are a number of things a company can do to pick the best firm for its legal matters if it does not have a GC. Some of them are discussed below.

- Ask around the industry. What law firms, if any, represent or have represented similar companies in the industry?

- Industry or trade journals—even newspapers—may mention firms that are familiar with the industry.
- Law firms maintain websites that contain information about the firm and its abilities. A search on the Internet may list firms with lawyers that have a specialty you are looking for.
- What does the local business community say about the particular law firm? What do your peers or colleagues say?
- If you have used a law firm in the past for a different matter, maybe it can recommend a firm, if needed.
- What firm or firms do your colleagues recommend, if any?
- If you have an outside general counsel, that firm should handle the matter.

Once you have located three or four firms, set up a meeting. Not only do you want a firm that can handle your matter, but you need a firm or a partner at a firm that you trust and are comfortable with. To find the best firm and/or partner, you should ask a number of questions regarding the firm and, more specifically, the partner. In essence, conduct a reference check on the law firm. I would suggest the following questions:

- What kind of billing arrangements does the firm expect? Does the partner bill by the hour or on a project basis? Or both?
- Staffing: How will the partner staff the case?
- How busy is the partner? Can he take the case?
- Will the firm pay enough attention to your case?
- What experience does the firm and/or partner have in dealing with cases such as yours?
- How committed is the firm to you? Does it want to enter into a long-term relationship?

At the end, prior to picking the firm, you have to ask yourself:

Am I impressed with the firm and, more importantly, am I comfortable or impressed with the partner or lead attorney with which I met? Can I work with them? Do I trust them with my legal problem or lawsuit?

When a company retains a law firm to handle a specific matter, it can lead to a long and perhaps expensive relationship. This is especially true in the USA, where USA stands for "You Sue Anyone"! It is imperative, then, to find a firm that can not only efficiently handle the legal matter at hand, but one that has the best interests of the company at heart. Can the firm add value to your case? What is the firm's value add?

What I recommend at the end of the selection process, when you have narrowed down your search to one or two firms you like, is to conduct a reference check. Do not be afraid to ask the law firms for a list of former clients. Contact the clients, if possible, and ask them how satisfied they were with the firm. The law firm may think it did a great job for the client, but, in fact, the client may have a different opinion of the firm's abilities or a different opinion of the partner in question. A reference check often helps uncover issues regarding the firm's services, but it is not guaranteed. Still, it is a method that may at least help you satisfy any open questions you may have and help you make a decision as to which firm to use. Remember to pick the firm you are most comfortable with.

42.2.1 Picking the right law firm in Korea

Picking a law firm in Korea has been the topic of a number of articles and books. Tom Coyner's book, "Doing Business in Korea" for example describes the trials and tribulations of picking the right law firm in Chapter 30 of the book. He opines that some (if not many) domestic and international lawyers are commercially incompetent, as many Korean attorneys fail to appreciate the commercial context in which they offer counsel.

Failure of appreciating or understanding the commercial environment in which one operates is not unique to Korean lawyers. I've witnessed firsthand lawyers in other jurisdictions including the US act as if they were giving legal advice in a vacuum. However, some of the fault in how Korean lawyers operate has to be placed at the feet of Korean law schools who until recently failed to emphasize the commercial /international nature of the legal practice in Korea by only emphasizing domestic law. As Korea's economy is primarily export driven, this has led to a less competitive legal market than other jurisdictions in Asia such as Hong Kong and Singapore.

Picking the right law firm in Korea is like picking a law firm in other jurisdictions. It is up to the manager or in-house counsel to meet with Korean lawyers and determine if the firm is a good fit. In Korea, be particularly careful as only a handful of firms dominate the legal market. Sean Hayes in his Korean Law Blog has also written about selecting Korean counsel as why it is important to pick a commercially competent one.[52]

---

[52] See Sean Hayes at: https://www.thekoreanlawblog.com/2018/10/best-korean-law-firms-fees.html

43 US litigation

The main issue facing companies involved in U.S. litigation is that U.S. litigation compared to litigation in many other countries is quite unique and expensive. U.S. litigation is not only complex but can be quite costly, onerous, and burdensome. The key element of U.S. litigation is that it is notice-based pleading in a common law setting, which means the facts of cases are to be developed through a complex discovery process in which lawyers for the parties play an adversarial role. Unlike in many countries, courts in the U.S. usually act as more of an umpire and will let the attorneys for both sides actively and aggressively handle the case.

43.1 Discovery

Discovery, by its very nature, takes up time, adds a great deal of expense to the cost of litigation (for both parties) and can lead to the disruption of business.

The kinds of discovery vary but are primarily limited to the following formats:

- Depositions
  - Oral examination
  - May involve written questions

- May involve key employees and/or officers of the company
- Interrogatories
  - Answers to written questions posed by the other side
- Production of documents and things and entry upon land for inspection and other purposes
- Production of ESI
- Physical examination of the evidence

It has been noted that discovery in the United States is like no other discovery process elsewhere. The United States, in fact, provides litigants a much greater ability to review all broadly relevant documents than any other jurisdiction in the world. The expense, delay, and business disruption associated with US discovery are unparalleled.[53]

43.2 Jury Trials

The USA, unlike most civil law jurisdictions, uses a jury system for civil proceedings. That means a jury composed of six to twelve people selected from the local area will decide the facts that are in dispute, effectively deciding the outcome of the case. The judge acts basically as an umpire by deciding legal questions. The problem this presents is that a group of ordinary laypeople from the area will decide the outcome of the case, no matter how technical or difficult it is.

The fact that a jury will decide the outcome of the case adds an element of unpredictability. Regardless of how strong the evidence is, a jury verdict is never guaranteed. Litigants, whether the plaintiff or defendant, often decide to settle, regardless of the strength of the merits of the claim or defense to the claim due to unpredictability, the cost and expense of trial, the potential disruption to business, and the negative publicity.

---

[53]   Donald Donovan, *Introducing Foreign Clients to US Civil Litigation* (International Litigation Strategies and Practice, ABA Publishing, 2005), 34.

43.3 Absence of Fee-Shifting Statutes

Unlike many countries, the United States does not usually have fee-shifting statutes allowing the prevailing party to shift its legal fees and expenses to the losing party. Each party to a litigation bears his or her own legal expenses unless a statute or contractual agreement provides that the prevailing party should be awarded attorneys' fees. Courts usually refuse to award attorney fees to the prevailing party in absence of such contractual stipulation or statutes.

The absence of fee shifting, in most cases, is extremely important. The prevailing party in litigation may very well lose financially if the amount awarded at trial does not exceed the cost of litigation. This combined with the other costly factors of litigation, such as discovery, creates a litigation system that is costlier, time consuming, and burdensome than most litigation systems in other countries. Just because a party wins at trial in the U.S. doesn't mean the party wins financially. Be careful about litigation in the U.S.

43.4 Strategy

In the case where parties are unable to resolve the dispute prior to litigation, a litigant must develop a winning trial strategy. In the U.S. such strategy will be based on complex rules of evidence allowing or disallowing the admission of certain evidence, including testimony or documents, etc. The parties will obviously try to position themselves to be in the strongest position possible up to and during the trial, regardless of whether an out-of-court settlement is finally reached. What does this strategy mean to most litigants? It means:

- Loss of time.
- Expense.
- Potential interruption of business.
- The cost and expense of business interruption.
- Potential bad or negative publicity.

- Negative impact on the company's brand image
- Potential loss of reputation.
- In the United States, trials are public. Does the public exposure of a trial matter to you?
- As trials are public, the media often plays a part in reporting and influencing the case. Do you want this?

43.5 Class Actions

Another unique aspect of US litigation is that of class actions. In the United States, groups of claimants are able to sue as a class. Such litigation is called a "class action," and it exposes corporate defendants to potential life-threatening litigation where enough class members are involved. A class action could consist of thousands of claimants represented by one claimant. If a company is sued in a class action, it is potentially exposed to a jury award in the millions of dollars. Another issue is that there could be more than one class action or multiple class actions in a number of states. The potential legal exposure and high transactions costs of numerous trials are great. Class actions have in fact led to the destruction of companies and have forced certain manufacturing industries to leave the U.S. marketplace.

43.6 LRM: US Litigation

To properly manage civil litigation in the United States, companies need to implement LRM strategies and processes by either creation of an in-house Law Department or a Risk Management Department that is capable of overseeing or managing outside litigation. Depending on the legal exposure of a company, it can be a full-time job. This management function will be key in properly coordinating litigation to avoid excessive costs, duplication of effort, and minimization of disruptions to a company's business, as well as setting an effective trial strategy.

What many foreign companies doing business in the United States fail to appreciate is that an outside litigation lawyer does not necessarily have the company's best interests in mind during litigation. A litigator wants to win, regardless of the cost. Many companies have paid millions of dollars to law firms during litigation when a resolution to the dispute was available had the parties tried to actively settle the case. Remember, a trial lawyer's business is trial work and not settlement.

An in-house legal manager or risk manager, representing the company's best interests, can help facilitate settlement once a legal risk assessment as to the validity, cost, and expense of litigation is made. In fact, during trial, a settlement is still possible and can be facilitated by in-house counsel or risk management. Therefore, the Law Department or the appropriate risk manager (if no Law Department exists) or controller should maintain control and oversight of any litigation. A LRM program can be very helpful in managing the legal risk process as well as providing litigation oversight.

43.6.1 *Reasons for an Internal Legal Risk Management Process*

Companies facing U.S. litigation are often exposed to excessive fees and costs, massive business disruption, lengthy litigation, and the unpredictability of the jury system. Though, obviously, outside litigation counsel is necessary in most cases, an in-house Law Department can save the company great sums of money by managing the litigation process. Such management involves the assessment, management, and potential transfer of risk through various LRM strategies, including:

- Effective coordination of legal defense efforts in order for the company to avoid duplication of costs and effort from case to case
- Coordination of witnesses, answers and interrogatory responses, documents, and depositions
- Acting as the central site for all facts, positions, decisions on legal issues, and motions
- Development, implementation, and coordination of a defense plan

44   Legal Fees and Costs

A company, wherever situated, will eventually be subject to litigation, government investigations, fines, employee actions, etc. To properly defend itself will require the use of law firms, especially in the United States. However, as explained in the preceding chapter, legal fees and costs can be excessive. The financial well-being of a company may depend upon how well it is able to manage outside legal fees and costs.

As part of an overall LRM program, a company's Law Department must implement processes to control, reduce, and manage outside legal fees and costs. By utilizing legal risk management tools, a Law Department or Risk Management Department can proactively reduce legal fees and costs.

44.1   Tools for Reducing Legal Fees

- Processes that can measure the performance of outside counsel
- Processes that track legal costs and expenses
- Use of KPIs that measure the Law Departments metrics
- Creation of a contract management system, which standardizes contracts and forms
- Negotiation of legal fee agreements with outside counsel
- Use of outside billing guidelines, which prevent excessive billing by law firms

44.1.1 KPIs

Key performance indexes (KPIs) are an effective way to measure a Law Department's metrics as well as use and effectiveness of outside counsel. I recommend a corporate Law Department to establish at least ten to twenty KPI metrics to get a good picture of the effectiveness of not only the Law Department but outside counsel. This can be reflected in the dashboard on your computer monitor. Typical examples would be:

- Law Department's total expense
- Law Department's total expense as a percentage of revenue
- Number of active litigation matters
- Number of new litigation matters
- Number of closed litigation matters
- Law Department's fees for outside counsel
- Total external spending on litigation matter
- Cycle time to resolve claims
- Estimated dollar savings through use of legal risk management tools
- Percentage of legal matters that receive a management—specific post-mortem review

There are other KPIs to use, but the above metrics can be used to help quantify the number of litigation matters, average time to resolve matters, total legal costs, and savings through LRM processes. The more processes put in place to measure performance from a risk management point of view the better. KPIs not only measure the effectiveness and efficiency of a law department but can be used as a tool to improve the effectiveness of the Law Department.

45 Litigation: Hypothetical Case in Point

The Gold Connection

Five-Star Electronics began selling the GoldBug stove in its home territory of the country of Albanon in 2011. In March 2012, the CEO of Five-Star Electronics decided to sell the product in country XXX. The GoldBug stove heats gold ions, killing bacteria. Some said it was a good disinfectant and would also kill bacteria in stoves—maybe even severe acute respiratory syndrome, or SARS.

Prior to this, Five-Star, in conjunction with outside experts, consulted with the XXX Environmental Protection Agency (XXX EPA) and state regulatory bodies to get a determination on whether the stove needed to be registered in XXX as a pesticide or simply classified as a pesticide device. If it was only a pesticide device, no XXX federal registration would be required. If the Gold was classified as a pesticide and not a pesticide device, GoldBug would come under EPA regulations in XXX. Once under EPA regulations, others might also take notice about the "gold" issue, which could impact sales in those countries as well.

The XXX EPA made a determination that the stove was a device and didn't require registration. Five-Star thought it was in the clear. Mr. Kim, CEO and president of Five-Star XXX, told his VP of sales (Mr. Smith) to ready the launch of the product in the XXX market. If successful in XXX, they would sell it in Mexico and in Canada. It was expected to be a big success and propel Five-Star to the top of the home appliance market in XXX.

Mr. Smith ordered his marketing team, under the supervision of its director, Mr. Walsh, to start a marketing campaign. Without consulting with Five-Star's Law Department, the marketing campaign was begun. After all, the EPA approved it, right? What could go wrong?

On May 12, Five-Star received news that several state EPA agencies opposed the classification of the stove as a pesticide device and thought it was a pesticide. Several environmental watchdog groups, such as Those Against Gold (TAG), began pressuring the state agencies to review the state classification. The state agencies began pressuring the EPA to change its position. Mr. Smith heard about the state EPA agencies but opted to do nothing, thinking the matter would go away.

On June 1, Five-Star was informed that the EPA changed its position on the GoldBug stove and would now require registration of the machine as a pesticide. The registration process could take more than a year, during which time Five-Star would not be able to sell any units. President Kim was told by his boss, the CEO of the parent company, Mr. Park, to "solve it." Too much money was at stake. In fact, the GoldBug factory could shut down. And besides, the competition was coming out with its new and improved stove soon. Something had to be done.

On June 15, Mr. Smith met with his marketing team behind closed doors. Perhaps he screwed up when he failed to talk to the Law Department. The Law Department would be very upset if it found out what had happened. Luckily, Mr. Smith was told by Mr. Walsh that his nephew knew a district officer of the EPA. Maybe they could resolve the matter prior to getting legally involved and spending money to handle the matter. They decided to contact Mr. Walsh's nephew. Maybe they could work out a deal. Perhaps if they didn't do anything, the EPA would let them sell the washing machine, or at worst maybe pay a simple fine.

On June 30, Mr. Walsh's nephew put a call in to his friend at the EPA, Mr. Black. What could be done? Could they negotiate a deal? Mr. Black was not very sympathetic. He had been told by his boss to take a tough stand against gold infringers. Because Five-Star had not done anything to resolve the issue until now, the EPA was contemplating bringing an "agency action" against TriStar. The fine could be $5 million.

Unable to resolve the issue, Mr. Smith went to his in-house lawyer and explained the dilemma. Mr. Smith was told by his lawyer they were looking at fines of over 5 million US dollars. The main problem was that Five-Star, in an effort to grab market share, already had signed a 100 million US dollar supply agreement with its most favorite customer, Acme Electronics. Acme Electronics had already advertised the product and had placed advertisements in the local circulars and local newspapers. The store had made room on its floor for the new GoldBug stove.

To make matters worse, Acme Electronics decided not to buy similar products from the competition. It was too late for Acme Electronics to cover its losses if it could not take shipment of the GoldBug.

It was obvious they had to come up with a strategy to resolve the current dispute(s). What dispute resolution strategies should they consider and why?

- Who are the parties to the dispute?
- What dispute resolution mechanisms were used?
- If litigation is used, how expensive would it be?
- If litigation was used, where would the litigation be brought?
- If litigation was used, how would XXX pick a law firm and how would it control outside legal costs?

46 Management of Outside Counsel

46.1 Cost Containment Strategies

Form: Outside Billing Guidelines—see Appendix B

Law firms charge different rates for different legal issues. Fees charged for an acquisition will be different than fees charged for litigation. The issue facing an internal law department, risk manager, or corporate manager in general, when charged with the task of managing outside firms, is, of course, management of fees and costs in relation to the legal matter being handled by the law firm. Law firms, as service providers, can get out of control if not properly managed. There are many horror stories involving excessive billing by law firms.

I remember a case involving a well-known multinational law firm that issued its unsuspecting poor client an invoice for $250,000 without any explanation of the services provided. The invoice simply said, "For Services Rendered—$250,000." The client was obviously shocked. How do you go to your CFO or CEO with invoice in hand and ask that the company pay it? What will accounting say? There are numerous ways to contain and control costs. One of the major strategies in which a company can control costs is through the use of outside billing guidelines.

46.2 Outside Billing Guidelines

More and more in-house Law Departments are requiring this use when providing legal services. Most guidelines set forth basic principles that a law firm must follow, such as:

- A description of services
- What a proper invoice should look like
- When the law firm should invoice the company
- What services can be invoiced
- What a firm cannot invoice for, such as legal research, copying fees, postal fees, or work done by junior associates

Firms normally like to bill excessive fees for their young associates just out of law school. Most young associates bring little or no value to a project except the ability to do basic research. In essence, firms try to train their young associates while billing clients. This has been the standard practice for many years. But why should you have to pay for that? It is recommended that you refuse to pay for any work done by a junior associate if that associate has recently graduated from law school and has not been sufficiently trained to handle basic issues. Control your costs!

Another way law firms bill excessively is overusing the "team" concept. Many legal matters require a team of several lawyers, such as a partner who oversees a matter; a senior associate, who does most of the research and writing; and perhaps an expert in certain areas. However, on complex matters such as litigation, many law firms love to create large teams consisting of many lawyers who bill on issues regardless of adding any value. Be on guard for firms to try and overuse the "team" concept. Billing guidelines should stress that a company or its in-house Law Department must approve the lawyers a law firm wishes to put on the team.

A number of issues the outside billing guidelines should address to avoid excessive fees and costs are:

- Requirement of a case plan and budget
- A proposed strategy for handling the case
- Identification of significant activity the outside law firm expects
- A discovery end date and anticipated trial date
- Requirement that the firm gets approval from the company before filing motions
- Requirement that the law firm justify staffing
- Refusal to pay for summer associates or interns

46.3 Monthly Reporting

Not only should companies require law firms to invoice in accordance with billing guidelines set by the company, but they should also require the firm to report exactly what it did on a monthly basis. By demanding monthly reports from a firm, it is possible to get a monthly narrative on the exact services provided. This helps not only put the services a law firm has provided in perspective but can help a company question unreasonable invoices. Was the hundred-page memorandum of law on anti-trust issues necessary when a five-page executive summary would have been more practical?

Remember, unless managed properly, a law firm can easily exceed its proposed budget. It must be held accountable to a reasonable budget and not be allowed to charge excessive fees and costs. It is up to the company to manage fees and costs. It is up to you!!

47 Use of Negotiations

47.1 What Are Negotiations?

Negotiations are an often underutilized LRM tool. Used as a dispute resolution mechanism, negotiations can be used to resolve disputes, internal and external to a corporation, prior to such disputes turning into legal disputes such as litigation. It is another tool to avoid the risk of litigation or arbitration and can minimize legal costs and expenses that might otherwise occur.

Negotiations can be simple or complex, depending on the subject matter. International negotiations are the most complex as they involve different cultures, languages, legal systems, and viewpoints. Nonetheless, all negotiations, whether domestic or international, will involve strategies, knowledge of the facts and issues, an understanding of the other side's viewpoints, and, above all else, an understanding of the problem and risk at hand.

47.2 Stages of Negotiations

Negotiation can be defined primarily as a decision-making process whereby two or more parties resolve their disputes or differences by advancing their interests vis-à-vis each other. Negotiations may be broken down into several distinct stages:

- The beginning or the pre-negotiation stage
- The middle or the negotiation stage
- The final or the post- negotiation stage

All three stages are crucial to successful resolution of a dispute or potential dispute that could lead to the risk of litigation. Let's discuss each stage with a few examples.

47.2.1 The Pre-nnegotiation Stage

Prior to negotiating with the other party or counterparty, a party must understand the facts, identify the issues involved, and map out a strategy to deal with negotiations. Though it may seem easy, this stage actually involves numerous steps. Each step may involve several processes or sub-processes as well. The basic steps are as follows:

- Determining the problem at hand
- Determining the interests of all parties involved
- Identifying possible solutions
- Deciding upon negotiation strategies
- Understanding your best alternative to a negotiated agreement— sometimes called the BATNA, first coined by Roger Fisher in his book on negotiation[54]

Knowing your BATNA sets the bottom floor of any deal, as it will set the range of a possible settlement. Usually, no party will agree to a negotiation that offers less than the party's BATNA. By way of example:

BATNA—ABC Company

---

[54] See Roy Lewicki, Bruce Barry and David M Saunders, Negotiations, NY: McGraw-Hill, 2010, p 10 which discusses BATNA as set forth in the book by Roger Fisher, William Ury, and Bruce Patton, Getting to Yes: Negotiating Agreement without Giving In, 2nd Ed, (Penguin, 1991).

Tristar wants to enter into a supply contract with ABC Company to sell TVs at 15 percent above margin. ABC wants to purchase TVs at 5 percent above margin. Tristar knows it can sell all of its TVs to Best Bros. Company at 12 percent above margin. Tristar's BATNA is 12 percent above margin.

Once a party understands the facts, has defined the dispute to be resolved, and knows his or her BATNA, the party needs to develop a negotiation strategy. There are two basic strategies negotiators use in negotiating dispute:

- Position based- competitive in nature
- Interest based- cooperative in nature

47.2.2 Competitive-Style (Position-Based) Negotiation

Negotiations maybe conducted in a competitive manner whereby parties state their positions and negotiate from those positions. It is considered a win/lose strategy or position-based strategy. It is the most common form of negotiation strategy that everyone is familiar with, though not the most effective, as it focuses only on the negotiating a party's wants and needs and does not address the needs and wants or desires of the other party. Many people not familiar with negotiating will tend to follow the competitive style approach, which in many situations will not succeed.

47.2.3 Cooperative-Style (Interest-Based) Negotiation

Negotiations may also be conducted as a cooperative process or interest-based process whereby the parties focus on solving each other's problems and addressing both parties needs and desires. It is, in other words, a win/win strategy or interest-based negotiation strategy.

Parties may use one or the other negotiation strategy of win/lose, or both, or hybrids of both if needed. It is common to use both strategies in one negotiation. Using the strategies depends on how parties perceive negotiations and often whether they want a short-term relationship or long-term relationship with the other party.

In many situations, it is imperative to know the BATNA of the other side. This may facilitate negotiations, as the parties may try to solve each other's problems. Failure to solve your counterpart's main concerns and issues may lead to failed negotiations. Of course, your counterpart has his or her own BATNA. Here is an example of what companies may face when negotiating.

- XYZ Company in Korea wants to distribute product XXX in Thailand. Thailand's laws prevent direct sales. XYZ wants to find a distributor that can distribute its product XXX.
- Bainai is willing to become a distributor. It costs $1 million in investment and setup costs to distribute product XXX. To recoup its investment, Bainai wants a five-year exclusive contract.
- XYZ knows it can find other distributors later, but it needs a distributor now. It does not want to sign an exclusive arrangement with Bainai. What if Bainai is a poor distributor?

Question:

- What win/win solutions can XYZ and Bainai propose to each other so each can meet its BATNA, or solve each other's interests?

47.2.4 Negotiation Stage

The negotiation stage or middle stage of the negotiation process involves numerous decisions too. Once parties have finalized the pre-negotiation stage, decisions still have to be made involving such issues as when, where, and how negotiations will take place.

For instance, parties may start negotiations via e-mail to negotiate minor items before concluding negotiations over the phone. Or they may start negotiations over the phone and wrap up with face-to-face negotiations. Or they may start with using email to negotiate minor items, phone conferences to settle some other items and then meet face to face to conclude the most important items and issues. Therefore, decisions have to be made on how to negotiate to one's own advantage.

During the negotiation stage, internal and/or external parties and stakeholders may play a part in the outcome. Decisions must be made whether to include them or not. If third parties are involved in negotiations, one or both of the main parties may try to develop coalitions. Third parties may, in fact, add more problems and issues to negotiations or at least bring an added dimension to the discussions.

Parties must also decide upon a venue for negotiations. Many parties prefer a neutral site. However, those negotiators in a strong position may prefer negotiations to be held in their own office. It is all about tactics and to a certain degree perception of the other party's position.

47.2.5 Post-negotiation

An equally important stage is the last stage of negotiations or the post-negotiation stage. This stage results in an agreement or resolution. Hopefully, an enforceable one at that.

Parties must also decide whether to reduce an agreement to writing or leave it verbal—or a little bit of both. There are several sub- processes in this stage, such as concluding an agreement, drafting it in writing, and having the parties review it and approve it. Of course, each party may need its home office or upper management to approve the agreement as well.

Parties may want their respective Law Departments or outside lawyers to review the negotiated agreements. Agreements need to be reviewed to determine if they indeed resolve the dispute, and if the agreements are enforceable. A non-enforceable agreement usually does not solve the matter in dispute.

47.3 Miscellaneous Issues

There are a number of miscellaneous issues that parties need to consider when using negotiations as an LRM tool. As negotiations are in fact voluntary, they require the informed consent or assent of the parties. This leads to a number of questions that must be asked.

- Do you resolve the dispute now or wait until a later date? Is now the right time to resolve the dispute?
- Do you use this as an on-going process or see it as a onetime event?
- How many people will participate in the negotiations? Will there be several teams?
- What do you really hope or want to achieve?
- Does the other side want to come to the table?
- What does the other side really want or hope to achieve?
- What is the other side's BATNA? Can you find it out? Can you guess it?

So, both parties must decide if they want to negotiate, and if so, when, where, and how. Maybe delays will benefit one or the other party or maybe not.

It is obvious that negotiation is an important LRM tool. However, to be adequately used as a method to decrease risk of litigation, the parties on both sides (of the negotiation) must be adequately trained in negotiation techniques and must have a proper negotiation mind-set. If the parties come to the table properly prepared, ready to negotiate and seek an amicable outcome, negotiation can be a powerful resolution process and risk mitigation tool. If not, it may lead to a lost opportunity and an unfavorable result.

47.4 International Negotiations

In international negotiations, culture and national or regional characteristics play an important part when thinking about negotiation strategies and tactics. It is helpful to understand different cultures and respect them when negotiating. So, when you are preparing for negotiations in an international context, think about the attitudes and characteristics of your counter party sitting across the table from you, whether they are Asian, North American, Latin American or European. For instance:

- What attitudes do they have towards negotiating?
- What are their attitudes towards protocol?
- How prepared are they?
- How focused are they on the negotiations?

Certain characteristics of nationalities in a negotiation setting has been observed and commented on by numerous authors in the past. I obviously want to steer away from stereotypes, but generalities are helpful when getting ready for international negotiations to a certain point. Here are a few general characteristics I've observed in international negotiations. Of course, they are no exhaustive and not always correct or on point.

47.4.1 *Regional Characteristics in International Negotiations*

1. North America

- Attitudes towards negotiations: Many Americans take the "time is money" or "bottom line" approach.
- Protocol: Many American negotiators do not take protocol seriously, as they like to use an informal approach. This is reflected in:
    - The downplaying of status
    - The downplaying of dress
    - The downplaying of formalities
    - Using first names when talking, dropping titles

- Approach: US negotiators tend to be more focused on short term gains rather than long term success. Notice the number of failed JVs between US and Asian companies over the years.
- Relationships: The US negotiator seems to care less about long term relationships than about immediate results.
- Note: Remember, when dealing with Americans, the American negotiator will usually be pragmatic, will care about practical solutions that will get results, will not expect the final deal to change at the last minute and will expect the contract or agreement once signed to be final and binding. Americans do not expect the deal to change simply because circumstances may have changed.

2. Latin America

- Attitudes towards negotiations: The Latin American negotiator will look upon negotiations in a more serious light than his US counterparty and will expect negotiations to be slower paced.
- Protocol: I've noticed Latin Americans to be more formal than US negotiators, but not as formal as Asians. Protocol to a certain degree is based on socializing first.
- Approach: Latin Americans believe in establishing a relationship with their counterparts first. Work, in essence, comes after socializing.
- Relationships: The Latin American negotiator will expect to establish a relationship with his or her counterpart.
- Note: When dealing with Latin American companies, remember things happen more slowly in Latin America. Expect some potential issues when dealing with government entities.

3. Japan

- Attitude towards negotiations: The Japanese negotiator considers business relationships to be very important. In fact, the early stages of negotiations might be used just to establish a business relationship more than anything else as the Japanese will normally use initial meetings to understand their counterparts.[55] It is worthwhile to note that Japanese negotiation styles have been the topic of a number of articles, one of the most famous being "The Japanese Negotiation Style: Characteristics of a Distinct Approach" by John L. Graham, Negotiation Journal, April 1993. One of the interesting findings in Graham's works and substantiated by my own experience is that Japanese tend to be more polite in negotiations than negotiators from other Asian countries. Normally, they will not resort to threats or warnings when negotiating whereas negotiators from other Asian countries, such as Korea, may do so. In fact, you may never hear the Japanese say "no" in negotiations.

- Protocol" Japanese negotiators tend to be very formal in how they approach negotiations, so protocol is very important to them. Be careful as a relaxed style might offend them. This will be seen in:
    - How they dress (usually very formal)
    - The use of titles
    - The structure of meetings/negotiations to include written agendas, etc.
    - Politeness- they can be less direct or forthcoming that you expect.
- Note: Your Japanese counterpart will expect to renegotiate the contract if circumstances change. Also, you should avoid making your Japanese counterpart lose face, etc.

4. China

- Attitude towards negotiations: Personal relationships are of great importance in Chinese society. So, in negotiations, small

---

55   See Kiss, Bow or Shake Hands: Asia by Terri Morrison and Wayne Conway, Adams Media (2007) for an excellent discussion of Japanese cultural manners.

courtesies and follow up presents may be expected (though times are changing) in many situations. They will negotiate in good faith only if they trust you. To them, negotiations require a great deal of time and planning.

- Protocol: Formality is important. Also, remember, they do not like negotiating with low ranking and/or non-decision makers.
- Note: To your Chinese counterpart, patience, harmony and a long-term relationship involving trust is very important. He or she will not like major changes in proposals or abrupt changes in negotiation strategies. They will not accept unreasonable demands and will expect to renegotiate deals if circumstances change.

5. Korea

US and Western based negotiators have to a certain degree underestimated Korean negotiators over the years. This is due to a misguided perception of Korea (especially in the US) as a backward, poor, underdeveloped country recently coming out of a civil war. Of course, this is far from the truth. In the last 30 years, Korea has undergone rapid development and transformation from a poor country to a developed one. Korea is now the 11th largest economy in the world, larger than many European economies.

Korea is a country with a culture of more than a 3000-year (older by some accounts) history. Bronze Age clans definitely appeared around 900 BC, though of course pre-Bronze age peoples go back much farther.[56] Until recently, its society was based on Shamanism, Confucianism, and Buddhism. Today, it is approx. 40-50% Christian, and 30% Buddhist. It is still a rather conservative society, having been greatly influenced by Confucianism over the years. Therefore, when dealing with Korean counterparts, the above reflections should be taken into consideration.

---

[56] See: The Koreans, Michael Breen, St. Martin's Press, NY (1998)

- Attitudes towards negotiations: Koreans approach negotiations in a collective manner. Korea, as a high text culture, believes in the collective. Being too independent is not good. Individualism is not so important. It's not therefore about the negotiator as much as the group. Your Korean counterpart may be more direct or less polite than you expect. Korean negotiators are known for being more direct than the Japanese. However, your Korean counterpart (regardless of Western appearance) will be bound by Confucian values or attitudes and the hierarchical nature it brings. Generational respect and authority are important. Working for the welfare of the group or company is more important than individual glory or profit.
- Protocol: Protocol is important. Following rules of etiquette will help your Korean counterpart determine if you are trustworthy. Age is also important (though less so than in the past) i.e. the older you are the more authority one has.
- Relationships: Relationships are very important. In Korea, societal relationships are still dominant such as:
    - Respect for the elderly
    - Welfare of the group is the main concern
    - Relationships are not based on equality but are determined by age and title
- Note: If circumstances change, your Korean counterpart will expect to renegotiate. Relationships are more important than the bottom line. Culture also play a part in Korean negotiations. For more on Korean culture, see my blog: Negotiating with Koreans at www. Seoullegalriskmgmt.com.

Perhaps the most comprehensive book on doing business in Korea, which includes an excellent chapter on negotiations, is Thomas Coyner's book "Doing Business in Korea: An Expanded Guide", Seoul Selection (2010). In his chapter on negotiating business in Korea, Coyner points out that the Korean business climate is quite unusual due to its Confucian background as well as its recent Japanese colonial rule.

This, Coyner asserts, has resulted in a unique set of rules that should be understood if one is to be successful in negotiating deals with Koreans.

47.4.2 Success in International Negotiations

For successful negotiations in an international context remember the following principles:

- Confirm the agenda, time, place and language of negotiations
- Don't always expect negotiations will be in English
- Know when to come to an agreement on issues
- Spell out terms, penalties, milestones, etc. so your counterpart is really on the same page
- Have the right team (inside and outside experts or SMEs) including people respected by both sides. Key: Does your counterpart respect you and your team?
- Be sensitive to the interests and needs of your overseas counterpart. Remember BATNA!

Note: Mistakes not to make in international negotiations include the following:

- Not allocating enough time for negotiations
- Having little knowledge of your host country
- Having insufficient understanding of personal relationships in your host country
- Having a poor understanding of the decision-making process of your counterpart's organization (and maybe yours too)
- Failure to get buy in from your home office. Will they commit or not?

48 Negotiation: A Hypothetical Case in Point

The Glass Works

Fine Glass, a US LCD manufacturer, was approached by Dong A Glass Company out of Korea to create a joint venture in country X. The JV was to be 51 percent owned by Fine Glass with 49 percent owned by Dong A. The purpose behind the JV was the creation of an LCD panel manufacturing facility. Dong A (though in the TV business) did not have access to leading edge LCD panels. Fine Glass was known for its LCD panel-making technology. This facility would be state of the art. It would compete with its major competitors anywhere in the world. The parties discussed the JV to be 75 percent funded by Dong A, with Fine Glass providing all technology and 25 percent of the remaining start-up capital.

Fine Glass was interested because a JV facility would give it access to Asian markets. Besides it would have 51 percent ownership of the JV. What could go wrong?

Fine appointed its VP of international investment, Mr. Brown, to be the point person. He soon realized there would be issues because part of Fine's LCD IP was owned via a joint development agreement by the Japan Glass Company out of Tokyo, Japan. Brown decided to approach Japan Glass about the JV. Japan Glass was interested. After several weeks of phone calls and faxes, Brown met with Mr. Kosigi of Japan Glass in Tokyo to discuss its involvement with the JV. Japan Glass did not want to invest in the JV but wanted a technical assistance agreement where it could charge the JV a 10 percent royalty. It wouldn't have to worry about repatriation of investment capital.

It was decided the JV was to be headquartered in country X. But for tax purposes and lower manufacturing costs, the parties, including Dong A, soon realized it made more sense to put the physical plant in country Y. X had just completed a tax investment treaty with Y that made investment very attractive. Also, labor costs would be cheaper. Dong A had thought about building an LCD TV factory in Y. Perhaps the JV could be built in the same corporate park where the TV factory would be built.

One problem was that the place where the JV could be built in country Y would be decided by the Y Land Development Corporation, (YLC) a semi-governmental-owned agency assigned the task of approving foreign investment in country Y.

Mr. Brown was dispatched to Seoul to start negotiations with Dong A and Japan Glass. Upon his arrival, he went directly to his hotel. While checking in he suffered a minor heart attack. The meeting was postponed, and Mr. Brown returned to the United States for treatment. Mr. Brown's replacement, Mr. Smith, was tasked with completing the deal. He had no international experience but was next in line for Brown's position.

Smith was under pressure. The delay in meetings because of Brown's heart attack could delay the JV because of the foreign investment process. Also, Smith found out that the country Y land development company was recommending Y own 51 percent of the manufacturing facility in Y, regardless of who owned the JV.

Japan Glass was getting nervous. Its joint development agreement with Fine was legally binding. But if it provided technical assistance to the JV in Y (it would receive a 10 percent royalty), would its IP (patents and trade secrets) be honored by the factory in country Y?

The meeting was set for April 1. Dong A rented out meeting rooms at a major hotel in X, as it did not have adequate office space for meetings. Mr. Park would lead the Dong A team. He spoke English and Korean as well as Japanese. All parties gathered to discuss the creation of the JV, the negotiation of the technical assistance agreement, and the foreign investment application process, etc.

- If you are Mr. Smith, how do you prepare for the negotiations?
- If you are Mr. Park, what cultural differences do you expect to see in the negotiations?
- If you are Mr. Kosigi from Japan Glass, how do you expect to negotiate your issues?
- If you are Mr. Smith, what would you do differently than in a regular domestic transaction?
- In which language would you conduct the negotiations?
- Should an interpreter be used?

49 Use of Arbitration and Dispute Resolution

49.1 What Is Arbitration?

Arbitration is a contractual mechanism that parties use to avoid litigation. As it is a contractual mechanism, the parties are free to determine the procedural requirements, number of arbitrators, governing law, and other key provisions, etc.

In other words, arbitration is a procedure that the parties select instead of availing themselves of a judicial system of a particular country, state, or province.

The primary characteristics of arbitration are:

- The parties select the arbitrator(s).
- It is a consensual process.
- It is a private process.
- It is a neutral process.
- It issues a final decision, with normally no appeal rights.
- It is very cost effective.

49.2 Justification for Arbitration

The main reasons that make arbitration a very attractive process over litigation, especially in the United States, are primarily: (1) it is a neutral process, (2) arbitral decisions are easily enforceable, (3) it offers flexibility (the ability to control and minimize electronic discovery and cost), and (4) the arbitrations are sophisticated. Flexibility, sophistication of the arbitral process, and enforceability are set forth in more detail below.

- Flexibility: One of the most fascinating qualities of arbitration, both domestic and international, is its inherent flexibility. That quality principally arises from two sources: the fact that the contract of the parties creates the jurisdiction of the arbitrator, and the necessity to adapt to the procedural requirements of the claimants and respondents. Examples of flexibility include provisions for the type of arbitrator required, and rules regarding the admission of evidence and discovery of facts. That is particularly important for any company that engages in business in the United States due to the explosion of discovery requirements regarding electronic documents. US courts impose stringent requirements for the maintenance of electronic documents (such as e-mails) and enforce severe penalties for violating these rules. These rules are particularly onerous on companies that have documents stored in various countries and locations. The arbitration clause negotiated can protect a party from such requirements while still maintaining due process and the ability to prove one's case.

- Sophistication of arbitrators/process: Although arbitrators usually have legal training, they come from many different backgrounds—law professors, practicing lawyers, judges, government officials, etc. This fact creates an opportunity for the development of a sophistication that flows from the combing of many different experiences and points of view. Moreover, because all arbitral tribunals are ad hoc in the sense that they are created for a specific case and cease to exist when that matter is determined, an experienced arbitrator encounters numerous significant collegial experiences on a level and variety that is not available to the judge. This leads to a willingness to devise solutions to procedural and substantive matters that are sophisticated in the sense that they are worldly wise and are prepared to accept complexity. For example, if a dispute is of a technical nature, the parties can require that the arbitrator be experienced in specific fields (e.g., engineering, employment law, or commercial actions of a particular type). This leads to sophisticated techniques of questioning expert witnesses, as well as other obvious benefits.

- Enforceability: It is a truism that an award issued by an arbitral tribunal and a judgment rendered by a court are worth very little unless it can be enforced. Happily, arbitral awards are easily enforced. Sometimes, in certain circumstances, they are more easily enforced than court-rendered judgments. In the United States, the enforcement of arbitral awards is guaranteed by the Federal Arbitration Act and numerous state laws. Indeed, if an international dispute exists between parties of different countries, the New York Convention (signed by the United States and most other nations) makes enforcement of arbitral awards easier than court-rendered judgments by virtue of limiting the defenses that may be interposed to enforcement of the arbitral award.

- Arbitration has long been viewed favorably as a dispute resolution mechanism for international disputes. This especially holds true for disputes in Asia.[57] In the past decade, arbitration in Asia has greatly increased which is an outcome or result of the rapid increase in trade.[58]

49.3 Arbitration Process: General Characteristics

General Characteristics: The arbitral process begins with the arbitration clause. When drafting an arbitration provision, several options are available. For example, an arbitration clause can include

---

[57] Bryan Hopkins, "A Comparison of Recent Changes in the Arbitral Laws and Regulations of Hong Kong, Singapore and Korea," *KLRI Journal of Law and Legislation* 3, no. 1 (2013).

[58] Id

a provision first requiring mediation prior to proceeding with an arbitration. Thus, under this scenario a party can go to mediation, and if there is an agreement, the process ends there. If not, then the parties proceed to arbitration and a final award. The arbitration clause must also deal with the place of arbitration, the language of arbitration, and the type of arbitrators to be selected. The place of arbitration can be important, particularly in international disputes, because the law of the venue of the arbitration will be applicable on procedural matters where there is a dispute among the parties.

Arbitration clause: The first step in the arbitral procedure is the drafting of the arbitration clause. The following are the essentials of any arbitration clause:

- Include a mediation requirement if desired (strict time limits should be imposed, and an administrative body selected to manage the mediation).
- A broad description of what is covered (e.g., "and dispute that arises from or is related to" a particular contract). This is important to make sure that the obligation to arbitrate is not avoided by a party arguing that a particular dispute is not covered by the arbitration provision.
- An institution to administer the arbitration (e.g., the International Chamber of Commerce (ICC), the American Arbitration Association (AAA), the London Court of International Arbitration (LCIA), etc. This is important to ensure that the process is not unduly delayed.
- Place of arbitration (make sure that the laws of the venue are arbitration friendly and provide for finality of the award).
- Arbitration award must be final.
- Number, process of selection, and qualifications of arbitrators.
- Law applicable to the dispute.
- Discovery concerns (how many depositions, limitations on e-discovery, etc.).
- Ability to obtain provisional remedies (e.g., injunctive relief) from courts without waiving rights to arbitration.

- Confidentiality.

49.3.1 Arbitral Procedure

Upon a dispute arising that is covered by an arbitration clause, the procedure regarding filing a demand or request for arbitration is simple. First and foremost, the rules of the administrative body selected to run the mediation must be consulted. However, the (very) general procedural steps are as follows:

- In the event mediation is called for in the arbitration clause, initiate mediation with a recognized mediation body. Several administrative bodies, such as the ICC (International Chamber of Commerce) and AAA (American Arbitration Association), provide for mediation rules as well. Typically, a demand for mediation with a statement of the dispute and a filing fee are filed. The opposing party will then be entitled to file its own statement. The parties attempt to agree on a mediator; if not, the administrative body will select the mediator. The mediation is to be governed by strict time limits, at the conclusion of which the arbitration process can begin.
- A demand/request for arbitration is filed with the appropriate arbitral body, accompanied by a filing fee. What is included in the demand/request for arbitration is determined by the applicable rules and judgment of counsel at the time of filing. Typically, the respondent will have to file its answer and will be responsible for half the costs of the arbitration. (Consumer arbitration differs significantly in this regard.)
- Arbitrators are selected, and the arbitration process begins. The production of documents and other evidence begins as circumscribed by the arbitral clause. In many circumstances, direct testimony will be provided in written form, and only cross-examination and limited redirect is allowed at the final hearings. Prehearing memorials are typically filed. A final

hearing is held, after which the arbitral tribunal will issue a
final award.
- Upon the issuance of a final award, if the losing party does not
  voluntarily comply with the award, then the award is presented
  to a court of competent jurisdiction, where it is confirmed and
  will be enforced as any other court judgment.

49.4 Arbitral Institutions

A number of arbitral institutions have become popular, especially
in the international context. Many countries have their own arbitration
laws as well as arbitral bodies that administer arbitration. The most
popular are:

- The International Chamber of Commerce (ICC)
- The American Arbitration Association (AAA)
- The International Center of Dispute Resolution (ICDR)

Many companies that do business in Asia use the arbitration rules
of Singapore (SIAC); Hong Kong (HKIAC) or Seoul (KCAB). To
date, more arbitrations are beginning to take place in mainland China,
as well. The increase of arbitrations in the Asia –Pacific countries are
directly related to the increase in trade and rapid economic growth of
the Asia region. This is expected to continue.

49.5 Arbitration Clause

The arbitration clause is the most important part of any contract
when the parties are negotiating the use of arbitration.
A well-thought-out arbitration clause should contain:

- If possible, a mediation requirement—to possibly avoid
  arbitration
- A broad description of what is covered
- An institution to administer arbitration (ICC, AAA, ICDR, etc.)

- Place of arbitration (the laws of the venue should be arbitration friendly)
- An understanding that arbitration awards are final
- Number, process of selection, and qualification of arbitrators
- Applicable law
- Discovery concerns (limitations to E-discovery and use of ESI)

In light of the current climate, no one wants to incur costs associated with arbitration of litigation if avoidable. To help avoid arbitration or potential excessive costs, I recommend the following:

- The arbitration clause should also require a period of time (thirty days, etc.) where the dispute is first escalated to executive management to discuss. You will be surprised how easy it is to settle a dispute when the senior-level management, who understand the "big picture," gets involved.
- As stated before, try to make use of mediation as well. Having a neutral party look at a claim and provide an objective opinion on the claim could lead to a speedy resolution.
- Make certain the arbitration rules and administrative body fit the scope of the deal. How expensive is the deal?
- Limit the scope and length of arbitration as well as the discovery permitted. Limitations on discovery can help not only speed up arbitration but limit and control costs.
- Think about negotiating a prevailing party cost/recovery expense provision in the clause. This would certainly cause the parties to think more about settlement of a dispute instead of arbitration.
- In-house counsel must manage and control arbitration costs. Outside counsel needs to understand the need to control costs and should agree to an arbitration budget. A well-thought-out arbitration budget is very important. The costs of arbitration will depend on how well in-house and arbitration counsel manage the process.

49.5.1 *Korea's Arbitration Changes*

Korea has recently revised its arbitration laws by updating the Korean Arbitration Act (the "revised Korean Arbitration Act"), as of November 30, 2016.[59] Also it should be noted that the revised Korean Arbitration Act was implemented during the same time that the new international arbitration rules were adopted by the Korean Commercial Arbitration Board (KCAB). Along with the new KCAB international arbitration rules, the revised Korea Arbitration Act further updates the legal framework for arbitration in Korea and helped create an even more arbitration-friendly environment.[60] Korea's revision and modernization of its arbitration laws and regulations came at a time when other arbitration jurisdictions in Asia were modernizing or updating their arbitral laws as well. The revised Korea Arbitration Act closely tracks the 2006 UNCITRAL Model Law on International Commercial Arbitration.

The revisions have been discussed in detail in a number of articles and books on Korean arbitration.[61] Some of the most significant and important changes in the revised Korea Arbitration Act are set forth below.

49.5.2 *Changes to the Writing Requirement for Arbitration Agreements*

The revised Korea Arbitration Act follows Option I of Article 7 of the 2006 UNCITRAL Model Law. Therefore, the revised Korea Arbitration Act recognizes an arbitration agreement regardless of the existence of a formal agreement as long as both parties intended to refer the case to arbitration. Such intent can be inferred from emails, etc. This

---

[59] See Jae Hyun Kim and Bryan E. Hopkins, *Recent Changes to the Korean Arbitration Act and its Comparison with Singapore: Korea's Potential to Become an Arbitration Hub,* Journal of Arbitration Studies, Vol 26 No.3 (2016)

[60] Id

[61] Andrew White, Yulchon LLC, *Revision of Korean Arbitration Act,* Lexocology, June 29,2016

revision is a reflection of the recent international trend to remove the requirement of having to prove the existence of an arbitration agreement through a writing. The language of the revised Korean Arbitration Act is very similar to the 2006 Model Law and therefore should be more familiar to non-Korean parties and their international counsel.[62]

49.5.3 Interim Measures by a Tribunal

Interim measures are temporary measures taken by the arbitral tribunal to maintain the status quo. Such interim measures could be injunctions, etc. The revised Korean Arbitration Act adopted the 2006 UNCITRAL Model Law regime on interim measures, including the section on enforceability. In fact, Korea is now one of the few countries that closely adheres to the Model Law's enforcement regime for interim measures so that it can be actively used in arbitration practice.

There are several differences between the revised Korean Arbitration Act and the Model Law's interim measures regime however. The two major differences are: (i) only interim measures issued in arbitrations seated in Korea may be enforced by Korean courts; and (ii) the provision for preliminary orders (which do not exist within the Korean legal system) is not part of the revised Arbitration Act.[63] Many countries such as Hong Kong, Austria, Germany, France, Switzerland and United Kingdom etc. have also adopted the interim measures in arbitration proceedings.

49.5.4 The Taking of Evidence

Before the revised Korean Arbitration Act was enacted, an arbitral tribunal could either take evidence on its own, or alternatively, the tribunal could entrust the court with the taking of evidence.[64] The revised Arbitration Act, however, has expanded the choices of the

---

[62] Id
[63] Id
[64] Id

arbitral tribunal. That is, under the revised Korean Arbitration Act, the court may become more involved with the tribunal in taking evidence by ordering witnesses to appear before the tribunal or ordering parties to submit the requested documents to the tribunal. This important amendment in the revised Korean Arbitration Act allows a means of interim relief to the parties and the tribunal that was previously unavailable under the previous Arbitration Act.

49.5.5 Simplification of Recognition and Enforcement of Arbitral Awards

Considering how inconvenient it was for the parties to arbitration to have another hearing in order to enforce the final and binding arbitral award, the revised Korean Arbitration Act provides that the process of recognition and enforcement of arbitral awards will now be carried out through the issuance of an order. This will provide greater assurance to parties and their counsel that enforcement proceedings will be concluded in an expeditious manner. The new process should will be simpler and more efficient than in the past.

49.5.6 Implications of the Revised Korean Arbitration Act

In consideration of arbitration friendly factors such as the geographical location of Korea and the fact it is active in international trade through numerous Free Trade Agreements etc., Korea will most likely become a major arbitration hub in Asia. It is expected that the revisions made to the Korean Arbitration Act will help establish Korea as a major arbitration center in Asia.

50   Arbitration: Hypothetical Case in Point

Mining Coal

XXX Construction had just finished a profitable year. It had completed the luxury skyscraper in Mumbai and had also finished building a new SBR plant in Saudi Arabia. However, due to a shortage of steel from its supplier of steel, The Steel Company, it was limited in future projects. So, Mr. Shin, president of XXX Construction, decided to go into the steel business.

XXX obtained bank financing from its bank, Acme Bank, for $100 million to buy an old steel mill owned by YYY Steel. Terms of financing included a guaranteed repayment of $10 million to Acme upon the completion of the first construction project using steel from the YYY facility.

One problem that XXX had was, of course, lack of natural resources. To make steel, XXX needed iron ore and coal for the furnaces. XXX was able to source one hundred thousand tons of iron ore per year from Kazakhstan. However, XXX could not source coal as well.

Luckily, President Shin's GM, Mr. Lee, called. He had a source in China that should be able to provide coal. Mr. Lee contacted the Homin Mining Company and was able to negotiate a supply contract for two hundred thousand tons of coal per year. According to the contract between XXX Construction and Homin, the coal would be delivered to XXX's carrier (a ship) at the port of Hunan every Friday starting sixty days from execution of the contract. The supply contract was signed on

March 1, 2010. President Shin was very happy, as a worldwide shortage in coal was expected in 2011, and he had firmed up a source of supply.

Knowing that he had iron ore and coal, Shin set about executing construction agreements, which would use the steel made by the newly acquired YYY Steel plant. One of the contracts was with the Premium Office Tower Company for the construction of a modern luxury office /hotel building in downtown New York City. The steel was to be delivered to the construction site in NYC on July 1, 2012. Because of the construction permits, unions, and tax benefits provided by NYC, construction had to be commenced no later than June 1 and finished on June 1, 2013. Failure to complete construction on time would result in holdback penalties of $100,000 per week to be levied against XXX. Shin was confident the schedule could be met. What could go wrong?

On May 1, 2012, Mr. Shin received a frantic call from Mr. Lee. The coal from China was not delivered. In fact, it may not be delivered for at least another eight months due to logistical problems. Homin Mining did not realize the train from its mine could not deliver the coal to the port of Hunan because train tracks had not been laid all the way to the port. The tracks stopped twenty miles from the port. The port of Hunan was responsible for the track. No construction of new tracks was scheduled until 2013. To make matters worse, there were no roads on which to have the train offload onto trucks.

Among the problems:

- Due to a worldwide shortage of coal, YYY Steel could not produce any steel for at least four months. It found a new source of coal in Brazil, but it would take three months to have it delivered. The coal was selling for $150 per metric ton instead of $100 per metric ton from China.
- The ship sent to pick up the coal in China was being charged demurrage charges of $10,000 per day for every day it stayed at the port of Hunan.
- The construction schedule of the new office building in NYC was threatened.

- If XXX could not perform on schedule, it would have to pay a penalty and still had to think about repaying part of the loan to Citibank.

XXX faced massive losses. Its steel mill, YYY Steel, was in trouble. Also, it faced penalties and fines if it could not complete the construction of the office building in NYC on time. It was four months behind schedule. Its carrier also faced demurrage charges as well.

Mr. Shin called up his lawyer, Mr. Smith. Mr. Smith had reviewed the supply contract with Tsingtao and the construction agreement with Premium. Mr. Shin wanted to know what kind of dispute he was looking at and what his options were. Both agreements contained an arbitration clause. The supply contract's arbitration clause stated in part:

> All disputes arising out of or in connection with the present contract shall be submitted to the International Court of Arbitration of the International Chamber of Commerce and shall be finally settled under the rules of arbitration of the International Chamber of Commerce by arbitrators appointed in accordance with said rules.

Upon reflection, Mr. Smith realized the supply agreement was silent as to where the arbitration was to take place, number of arbitrators, and governing law.

- If XXX is forced to arbitrate its claim against Homin for damages, what concerns does it have?
- Should XXX expect three arbitrators or one arbitrator?
- What language will the arbitration be in?
- Where will the arbitration take place?
- What issues does Homin face?
- What advantages are there to arbitration over litigation?

51 Management of Litigation

Form: Litigation Plan and Budget

Management of litigation, like management of most business processes, begins with a business plan and a budget. In this case, prior to trial, when a company seeks an appropriate law firm to represent it, it needs an acceptable litigation plan and budget. Law firms many times will try to push back on the request of a budget, claiming legal costs are hard to predict. This, of course, is not the case. Experienced lawyers, whether in the United States, Europe, or Asia, are very familiar with the legal costs in their own geographic region as well as costs and expenses associated with the particular issue, such as patent litigation or class actions. Certain costs may be hard to quantify, such as defense litigation costs (which may depend on how aggressive a plaintiff is in trial), but for the most part, law firms can provide a litigation plan and budget using approximate or ballpark figures.

Effective management of litigation will depend on a well-prepared litigation plan and budget. This, in turn, depends on the proper identification of potential litigation issues and a plan for potentially adversarial proceedings. Questions that should be asked when discussing the plan and budget with outside counsel include:

- Is this matter an actual or potentially adversarial proceeding?
- Will this matter result in potential commercial litigation?
- Will this matter result in potential regulatory litigation?

- Will this matter lead to governmental litigation?

51.1 Kinds of Actions

An accurate litigation plan and budget will depend on the nature of the proceeding or legal matter at hand. Such matters can be classified as follows:

- Commercial litigation
    - Antitrust and trade disputes
    - Bankruptcy and creditor actions
    - Class actions (product liability, etc.)
    - Labor and employment
- Regulatory proceedings
    - Governmental inquiry/informal visit
    - Investigations
    - Subpoenas
    - Government enforcement proceedings
    - Administrative tribunals
    - Internal corporate investigations

Certain costs will be associated with the nature of the dispute. For instance, commercial litigation costs will be dictated by the cost of discovery, including: depositions, interrogatories, production of documents and things, and physical examinations, etc. Costs involved with regulatory proceedings will involve governmental investigations and internal corporate investigations and perhaps parallel proceedings, criminal as well as civil litigation.

51.2 Litigation Management Tools

Litigation management depends upon the in-house legal team or risk manager actively assessing and managing litigation by using an effective litigation management process. The litigation management process should utilize management processes as well as LRM tools.

For a corporation to effectively manage litigation, management needs to understand its role as litigation manager. If it hands over the entire litigation management process to the outside firm representing it, the costs will, of course, substantially increase! The law firm must be managed! The risk manager, corporate manager, or in-house lawyer (General Counsel, etc.) must understand his or her role as a litigation manager. That includes use of management functions and LRM tools.

- Management functions
    - Effective coordination of legal defense efforts to avoid duplication of costs
    - Coordination of use of witness and discovery
    - Serve as the central site for all facts, positions, and decisions in legal issues
    - Development and implementation of a defense plan
    - Internal assessment of facts
    - Point of contact for regulators
- LRM tools
    - Litigation budget
    - Coordination of documents
    - Use of employee interviews
    - Insurance
    - Use of defense plan
    - Early case assessment
    - Alternative fees
    - Outside billing guidelines

52   Litigation Management during Trial

Effective litigation management during trial depends on the company's attitude toward litigation as well as its controls over the law firm. Trials, especially in the United States are quite expensive and could involve the future existence of the companies involved.

Trials by their very nature are very costly. Normally, lawsuits settle prior to trial, as both sides know that juries can be fickle. Some companies will, therefore, never want to go to trial (or try to settle during trial), and some will decide to fight and go to trial. Many times, it is more advantageous for parties to litigation to settle prior to trial, as trials become extremely expensive.

Disadvantages of trials include:

- High transaction costs
- Length of proceedings
- Negative publicity
- Business interruption
- Unpredictability of juries
- Lack of finality—always the loser will appeal

If a company decides to go to trial, it must control the outside law firm, manage the process, and understand the potential dangers (including cost and expenses) it faces. Prior to trial, the company needs to ask trial counsel a number of questions, including:

- What is the true evaluation of the case?
- What is the approximate cost of trial?
- What are the chances of settlement before trial?
- What are the main strategies of litigating the case?
- What witnesses and experts will be needed?
- How long will the trial last?
- What are the chances of winning?

If a company knows it only has a 30 to 40 percent chance of winning at trial, is the dispute worth going to trial for, or is settlement a better option? A company is in a better position to decide whether it should go to trial upon proper evaluation of the case. LRM tools can help this.

52.1 Evaluation of the Case

At the beginning of litigation and selection of the law firm, the risk manager or in-house lawyer must assess the case—the strengths, weaknesses, costs, etc., involved. Case evaluation is very important. Evaluation can be made through an early evaluation by outside counsel, knowledge of potential costs, use of employee interviews, and formulation of a plan/budget. When a company has a good idea on the chances of winning, potential costs, and weaknesses of the case, it is in a better position to determine whether to proceed to trial. Therefore, at the beginning of litigation, the company or organization should obtain a thorough evaluation of the case and use internal tools to assess the cost of a trial. Is the cost of litigation worth it?

Risk analysis of litigation can be a useful tool in evaluating a case. One such tool that is often utilized is the decision tree. A decision tree analysis can be used to evaluate the probability of outcome of certain events during trial. Each event can then be analyzed in the context of the probability of the entire outcome. As Carol Basri and Irving Kagan point out, a decision tree risk analysis allows "a rigorous and systematic method of analyzing and preparing cases from inception."[65]

52.2 Fees during Litigation

Obviously, the litigation budget should address the fees and costs of going to trial; a law firm's fees at trial skyrocket for a number of reasons, including:

- The number of lawyers involved.
- Time: Most trial lawyers will work long hours during a trial, so fees will add up. This is especially true if the trial is a complex one involving patent disputes or antitrust claims.
- The cost of expert witnesses.
- The cost of motions during trial. Motion practice can be very expensive.
- The cost of producing documents during trial.
- Note: If you are spending $100,000 per month before trial, you may spend $500,000 during trial, especially if it lasts longer than you or your outside counsel originally thought.

52.3 Evaluation of Discovery Costs during Trial

Discovery costs in litigation are usually the largest part of the total cost of litigation. Discovery costs (in the United States) can add up to 50 percent or more of the total cost of litigation. Depending on the trial, discovery costs can increase, especially if there are spoliation issues or document destruction issues. Corporations must constantly monitor discovery issues during litigation to prevent surprises. A spoliation motion at trial could be very costly, consuming time and expense not originally anticipated. Don't just rely on outside counsel to handle all discovery issues.

---

[65] Carole Basri and Irving Kagan, *Corporate Legal Departments*, Third Edition (New York: Practicing Law Institute, 2004), 14–24.

52.4 To Settle or Not Settle?

There will come a time during litigation, especially at trial, where it may be advantageous to settle the case instead of continuing with the trial or going to the verdict phase of the trial. Some companies will want to settle early in the process and some later. It depends on the strategy of the company and how it views its chances of winning. It also depends on advice of the trial counsel the company has hired, as well as other factors, such as pressure from the judge, lack of confidence in the jury (do they appear to dislike you or your lawyer?), and overtures from the other side. More importantly, it depends on what is in the best interests of the company. Outside counsel will not necessarily think about the best interests of the company. The law firm, or your trial counsel, will want to win! That's expected. That what they want to do! In fact, you probably retained the outside law firm to win. But winning may not be in the company's best interests. Settling a case prior to trial may not only save the company money, time and expense but may also prevent negative publicity thereby saving the company's brand. Do not get so caught up in the emotion of litigation that you forget to settle when it is to your advantage.

52.5 Evaluation of the Trial

Effective management of litigation during the trial process requires an up-to-date evaluation of the trial. This requires close contact with the outside counsel handling the trial, observing the trial (how does your trial counsel look at the trial?), constant feedback from your litigation lawyer or team, and involvement of management. The litigation manager of a company needs not only to stay involved throughout the trial but must update management on a daily basis.

A risk manager, litigation manager, or in-house counsel must manage the litigation process, especially during trial. It is important that the risk manager or in-house counsel stay connected with the trial counsel and consider doing the following action items during trial:

- Get a summary of the trial from trial counsel or the trial counsel's team every night if possible. Are there are any surprises in how the case is proceeding? If so what are they?
- Monitor the jury. If a jury is deciding the case, how does the jury look? Do you think the jury is interested in the case and your side of the argument?
- Determine if the defense strategies used in trial are working. If not, is it time to settle?
- Determine if settlement is the best option. Use the decision tree analysis to help make Alternative Dispute Resolution (ADR) decisions.
- Trials can be very expensive. Success depends on a number of factors including the following:
  - Facts of the case.
  - Trial strategy. Is it working?
  - Correct evaluation of the case prior to trial.
  - Correct evaluation of the case during trial.
  - Attitude of the judge towards your case
  - The makeup of the jury.

Successful management of litigation during the trial depends on use of LRM tools such as case evaluation, coordination of witnesses, and trial strategy. If a company fails to properly manage litigation during the trial phase, it can lead to increased costs, expenses, business interruption, and, of course, defeat. Therefore, use of litigation management tools such as a decision tree analysis, document coordination system, or early case assessment process is very important.

Summary

LRM processes are numerous and diverse. Such processes can touch upon all departments of a company. The problem in-house counsel or risk management face is that it is not without cost. In order to properly implement an LRM program, executive management has to understand it and approve its implementation.

In other words, in-house counsel or risk management must sell it to the BOD. This can be done with empirical data showing historical legal costs, insurance costs and probable legal fees based on potential legal exposure.

Part Five

Legal Risk Management: Evaluation of the Process

53   Legal Risk Management: Evaluation of the Process

53.1 Selling Legal Risk Management to the Organization

A discussion of legal risk management (LRM) in the proceeding chapters has illuminated the numerous processes and procedures that should be applied. LRM processes are not only numerous and diverse, but can, if accepted and implemented by the organization, provide an effective way of mitigating and/or eliminating legal exposure and prevent claims, litigation, and fines. The problem for any corporate risk manager or in-house counsel is to sell the LRM process to management. It is not without cost and expense.

Most organizations have yet to fully embrace, implement, and internalize risk management concepts, let alone LRM processes. Studies have shown corporations have yet to fully embrace risk management concepts and have failed to implement an enterprise wide risk monitoring and reporting system. How do you sell LRM to the organization? First you need to quantify the legal risk and exposure to enable the CFO and other executives and perhaps board members to understand the significance of the exposure the organization faces.

53.2 Quantify the Legal Exposure

Quantifying potential legal exposure is fairly easy. One can look at historical legal costs, expenses, and related jury verdicts, fines, etc., to determine a base line for future legal costs and expenses. If an historical record of legal costs does not exist, numerous reports and surveys exist on how to average legal costs and expenses via a particular industry. Your insurance broker may have summaries of legal costs for your industry. At least it should have a historical summary of insurance related claims. Once one has enough empirical data to show potential exposure, it is easy to show potential legal costs. In fact, a number of companies in the legal industry have issues benchmarking reports breaking down the average legal costs and expenses in particular industries. This can be a great tool to use when showing management what costs and expenses are normally incurred by companies.

The CFO of any organization is numbers driven. If you can provide, in effect, "the bottom line" to the CFO, he will be inclined to approve a budget for LRM processes. Be prepared and have facts and figures to support your request.

53.3 A "Teaching Moment"

Do not be afraid to use crises, disasters, lawsuits, government investigations and fines, etc., to your advantage. Companies, especially large companies, tend to throw resources at perceived problems and exposure once a crisis happens. A crisis may be an event that will justify legal spending.

Use such an unfortunate event or crisis to not only explain why the LRM program is needed but use it as a "teaching moment" of what not to do. Take advantage of it! Remember, sometimes organizations move slowly until they perceive a threat of financial loss or exposure. Then, once the company perceives a threat, they throw money and resources as it.

If the CEO, CFO, etc., turns on the TV and sees your company's product shown in a negative light, which is a good time to request a budget for risk management or an LRM program. Teaching moments are often good tools to use as well.

54 Internalization of Legal Risk Management

Most companies have yet to internalize legal risk management. Though many companies have some LRM processes in place, those normally are few and far between. Also, though organizations may have a few processes in place, they are usually not coordinated with each other internally. Sometimes departments do not communicate with each other as effectively as they should.

To be completely effective, a company has to internalize LRM processes. What does this call for? Basically, a company internalizes the LRM process when:

- LRM is embedded in the corporate decision-making process.
- The identification of early warning indicators are based on key LRM processes.
- Effective use of LRM tools on a regular and /or daily basis.

A company internalizes the LRM process when it not only fully implements the LRM process and uses tools to identify all major areas of legal risk but also uses it in the decision-making process.

Only when a company is willing to fully embrace legal risk management can it reap the benefits of preventing, mitigating, controlling, and transferring legal risk.

55 Review of Legal Risk Management: Justification

At the beginning of the book, we discussed the concept of legal risk management or LRM, and why it is important that organizations such as corporation should adopt it. As you can see from the many areas covered in this book, from risk insurance to compliance and law firm management, LRM is not only a broad area, but it consists of many diverse processes and tools. A company cannot emphasize only one aspect of LRM and forget the rest. After all, the goal of LRM is to prevent, manage, mitigate, and transfer legal risk, allowing a company to control its own future. Taking a proactive stand with regard to risk allows a company to control its destiny instead of reacting to events!

These days, companies are exposed to unprecedented attacks from many sources. Governments want to increase taxation and regulation; the media wants to attack companies, and, of course, people are accustomed to looking at companies as the "root of all evil." To defend itself against attack from many sources, a company has to implement as well as internalize a culture of "legal risk management." A well designed, implemented, and internalized LRM program can control legal risk, allowing a company or organization to prosper.

It is hoped that this book has, in some small way, contributed to the understanding of risk management from the legal perspective. Hopefully, it arms a risk manager or in-house counsel with enough ammunition to not only justify an LRM program to upper management of an organization but to obtain adequate resources to implement it. Good luck!

Summary

Though a company should be proactive and implement LRM processes before litigation happens, it can still mitigate costs and expenses by implementing processes during or in anticipation of litigation. This involves litigation management's use of corporate structures to transfer risk and manage outside counsel.

Companies can transfer legal risk or mitigate legal exposure through the appropriate use of the corporate structure. For multinationals or those organizations with subsidiaries, the use of a holding company can help insulate a company by isolating liability to individual subsidiaries. Obviously, however, drawbacks have to be considered, including costs and having to use proper corporate formalities.

Once a company realizes it will face litigation, the most important LRM processes it will have to use are those involving litigation management. In other words, what processes are in place to pick a law firm, manage the law firm, and control legal costs and expenses? Only with a robust LRM process that requires a company to properly manage outside counsel can the company avoid lengthy litigation and the resulting excessive fees and costs.

A number of tools can be used to manage litigation. Standard LRM tools include the use of a litigation budget, use of a defense plan, outside counsel billing guidelines, and early case assessment.

Conclusion

Legal risk management (LRM) is very similar to the concept of ERM, or enterprise risk management. ERM is the management of risk across a corporation; LRM is the management of legal and corporate risk across a corporation. As such, it impacts all divisions and departments and requires constant implementation and the support of executive management. Only with the support of management can LRM become truly imbedded in the decision-making process of the organization.

In-house counsel and risk managers alike, whether in the Compliance Division or Insurance Department, need to take ownership of this important and vital concept. A company without a LRM process operates at risk and faces great exposure.

It is hoped that this book, in some small way, contributes to the understanding of risk management from the legal perspective. Hopefully it arms a risk manager or in-house counsel with enough ammunition to not only justify an LRM program to upper management of an organization but to obtain adequate resources to implement it.

For more information on this topic please see my blog at www. Seoullegalriskmgmt.com

About the Author

Bryan E. Hopkins
Lee & Ko

Bryan Hopkins is Special Counsel to Lee & Ko in Seoul, Korea. He also taught as a professor of law at Sejong University in Seoul, Korea. From 1999 to 2010 he was VP and General Counsel of Samsung Electronics America. Prior to working at Samsung Electronics America, he was Assistant General Counsel at Kumho Petrochemical in Seoul, Korea. He has published several books on legal risk management and articles in the *Asia-Mensa Counsel* magazine, as well as the *KLRI Journal of Law and Legislation* in Korea. He has extensive experience in antitrust, compliance, e-discovery, litigation management, and risk management. He received his Juris Doctor from Florida State University in 1980.

Appendix A

Loss Control
Policy and Procedure Manual

- Policy Statement

It is, and shall continue to be, a primary objective of each of its divisions and subsidiaries to provide customers with safe and reliable products and services. Our employees must be committed to fulfilling these needs. Each operating division is responsible for maintaining effective control of the conditions necessary to meet the safety needs of our customers and control product claim losses.

- Program Objective

To increase the awareness and effectiveness of product loss control and claims defense programming through the development and application of effective procedures and controls.

- Organization: Responsibility

Company vice presidents and officers are responsible for the development, application, and maintenance of Products Loss Control – Claim Defense Programs, consistent with the guidelines of this policy, at each of their respective operating locations.

In turn, the administration application and maintenance of such programs on a current and continuous basis rests with the individual company/division chief operating officers.

Depending upon circumstances, a company/division chief operating officer may appoint a representative to coordinate activities on his or her behalf.

All policy statements, Products Loss Control Programs, and related formal announcements and directives concerning individual programs should be approved and signed by the respective company/division chief operating officer. (See sample Policy Statement – exhibit A attached.)

Will issue general policies and procedures, monitor activity, and provide coordinating assistance with the broker and insurance company.

- Products Loss Control – Claim Defense Committee

Each division/subsidiary should, either independently or in conjunction with related group members, establish a Products Loss Control – Claim Defense Committee. The company/division officer, or where applicable their appointed representative, should chair the Committee.

Committee membership will vary depending on the type of operation (manufacturing, service, etc.) and the size of the operation. Each Committee should include the company/division representative (chairperson), the loss control representative, and sufficient membership to provide representation from all strategic departments (i.e., R&D, engineering, design, QA, QC, manufacturing, marketing, service, purchasing, shipping and receiving).

It is anticipated that most committees will have a membership of from three to seven. The minimum is two active members.

Joint committees formed within a related group shall consist of a minimum of one-member representative from each involved operating location. Under these conditions, each of the company/division representatives must serve to coordinate the program directly with all affected departments and personnel within their operation.

Joint committees should also include representatives of all strategic departments.

The purpose of the Products Loss Control – Claim Defense Committee is to:

- Develop a formal written program
- Implement the program through education and training.
- Provide administrative surveillance and technical product safety assistance and guidance throughout the operation.
- Monitor claims activity.
- Identify real or potential problem areas and institute corrective activity.

[Note: ADD MORE ITEMS HERE IF NEEDED]

Committee meetings should be scheduled and conducted on a regular basis. It is anticipated that, depending upon need, meetings will be scheduled either monthly, semi-monthly, quarterly, or semi-annually. Each operation should, at a minimum, conduct semiannual meetings to review their program. All operations should prepare complete minutes of all meetings and forward copies to the Director of Litigation and Risk Management.

- Research—Design—Development

Research, design, and development of products and services should include both safety and reliability considerations.

Personnel assigned to these activities should possess necessary academic and experience qualifications and meet applicable registration or certification requirements.

Formal hazard/failure evaluations should be conducted on all new products and services. Every possible hazard/failure that could result from use, misuse, or modification should be identified and eliminated whenever possible. Identified danger that cannot be designed out should be identified and given individual attention in the form of special warnings and instructions.

Design efforts should be directed toward meeting or exceeding all applicable safety standards and regulations. These may include federal, state, and local codes and regulation, industry and trade standards, technical society standards, and others that may be applicable to a given product or service.

Laboratory and field tests should be conducted to verify product and service safety and reliability. Where required (or desirable), independent laboratory testing and/or certification should be utilized. Product and service certification by industry or trade associations should also be considered.

All tests, evaluations, findings, and decisions relating to the above should be documented and retained.

Modification of design of existing products and revision of service procedures should include the same considerations.

Procedures should be developed for regular review of established product and service lines to ensure that they continue to meet subsequent safety and reliability standards and regulations.

- Quality Control—Standards and Procedures

Written quality control standards, including specifications, should be developed for all components, materials, and processes critical to product and service safety and reliability. Material specifications should comply with national and/or company standards and meet the requirements of all applicable safety standards.

All purchases should include specifications, regulatory standards, and all other company acceptance criteria that must be adhered to by the supplier. Incoming materials and components should be checked to ensure that they meet minimum standards. Purchase orders should contain provisions for warranties as to the fitness of the products and/or services, compliance with applicable standards, and indemnity agreements to either eliminate or transfer the risk.

Formal procedures for process controls and quality checks should be established. The standards and procedures should be made available for control use in the form of a quality control manual. Educational and training programs should be established as necessary to ensure effective performance.

Quality checks and final tests should be conducted as often as necessary to ensure that applicable standards and specifications are met. Employees conducting checks and tests must possess the necessary skills to certify acceptance. All equipment and tools used for quality control should meet current requirements for product safety and reliability and be maintained in proper operating condition.

Quality checks and final test date relating to the safety and reliability characteristics of products and services should be recorded and maintained so that, within the bounds of good practice, the condition of the products or service can be verified.

As necessary and feasible, parts, materials, units, packages, tools, and equipment crucial to safety should be permanently identified.

- Certificate of Insurance—Vendors Endorsement—Hold Harmless (Indemnification) Agreements

Selection of subcontractors and suppliers should include consideration of their financial responsibility for liability losses.

A certificate of insurance should be obtained from every subcontractor. Certificates should include specific coverages (i.e., products, completed operations, automobile, contractual coverages, etc.) and certify amounts of liability of not less than limits currently carried by.

An individual analysis of the extent of potential liability should be conducted whenever a subcontractor's coverage is less than that of the Company. When the loss liability potential is greater than the amount of coverage, the subcontractor should be requested to increase coverage, or other subcontractors with satisfactory insurance coverage should be solicited.

A determination of a vendor's insurance coverage should be made prior to the purchase of products for eventual resale. If it is determined that sufficient coverage exists to provide acceptable insurance protection for the risk involved, a vendor endorsement should be requested and obtained before actual resale of any items. If sufficient insurance is not available, the vendor should be requested to supply adequate coverage, or other vendors with satisfactory insurance coverage should be solicited.

In many instances the Company and its subsidiaries are required to enter into contracts containing some form of hold harmless (indemnification) agreement. Although there are many types of hold harmless agreements, they generally fall into three broad categories.

- Limited forms hold the other contracting party harmless for claims arising out of your negligence.
- Intermediate forms hold the other party to the contract harmless against claims where both of you may be jointly negligent.
- Broad forms indemnify the other party to the contract even where he is solely responsible (negligent) for the loss.

[NOTE: ADD MORE INSURANCE PROCESSES HERE IF NEEDED]

- Manuals, Instructions, and Labels

Operator's instruction manuals should be developed for all equipment. They should provide instruction for safe use, storage, operation, and maintenance.

The manual should identify the standards of performance in respect to safety that the product should achieve after proper preparation.

Operating instructions should be complete and easily understandable. They should contain special instruction in the use of safety devices and protective equipment. All associated hazards should be clearly identified. The operating instructions should detail the procedures that will protect against these hazards, in direct and understandable language and, as necessary, in illustrations.

Operating instructions should include maintenance instructions, and parts lists servicing instructions should clearly specify the steps necessary to assemble, install, use, and maintain the product in a safe and reliable condition. Special attention should be given to the care of safety devices. All service work performed by the company should be fully documented and retained.

Warnings and caution statements should be included in the manual and on the products and/or the product container in the form of labels or tags. They should, for example, contain statements that:

- Highlight correct methods for assembly, installation, use, and maintenance, and indicate the level of skill or training needed.
- Stress the dangers of not following the printed procedures and instructions.
- Describe the product's limitations.
- Warn against modification of the product and parts substitution.
- Warn of misuse and hazard to the user.
- Specify maintenance procedures and frequency.
- Project the useful life of the product.
- Instruct the user in the care and use of safety devices and protective equipment and warn of potential consequences.
- Recommend antidotes or emergency procedures when applicable.

Labels and warnings must comply with federal, state, local, and industry regulations and standards. The copy should be clear, conspicuous, and complete. Special attention should be given to the physical durability of the materials used for labeling and warning.

Manuals and labels should be reviewed regularly to ensure compliance with regulations and standards. They should be maintained current to warn users of new dangers discovered. Previous purchasers should be warned by the best means available when future developments make a change necessary for safety purposes.

All manuals and labels should be reviewed and approved by the Product Loss Control Committee and legal counsel before actual use.

- Marketing—Sales and Advertising

Sales and advertising materials should accurately describe products and services. Literature and exhibits used in sales promotion, advertising, or public relations should judiciously reflect necessary accident prevention features, such as safe operating practices, proper projective devices, and approved guarding.

Sales, distributor, dealer, installation, and service personnel should accurately picture products and services. They should be included in educational activities concerned with product safety responsibilities. Sales and other technical representatives should not be misrepresented as being more expert than they, in fact, are.

All proposed advertising literature should be reviewed for technical accuracy and exaggerated statements. Terms such as "maintenance free," "absolutely safe," "foolproof," and "nontoxic" should be avoided. All sales and advertising materials should be reviewed on a regular basis.

Disclaimers and limitations of warranties should be incorporated into sales literature and sales agreements whenever possible.

All advertising should be reviewed and approved by the Product Loss Control Committee and legal counsel before distribution.

- Packaging and Shipping

Written standards should be developed for the packaging and shipping of products. Applicable federal and state standards and regulations governing the identification, packaging, and shipment of regulated products must be included. Company safe packaging and shipping standards should be developed for all products.

Formal procedures should be developed to ensure completeness of shipments, including compliance with shipping and safety standards. Special attention should be directed toward ensuring that all information and instruction manuals, labels, warnings, and safety devices are included in the shipment. It is recommended that final inspection checklists be developed and utilized.

Education and training programs should be established as necessary to ensure effective performance of shipping personnel.

- Communications

Product safety should periodically be an agenda item for operations and staff meetings at all organization levels.

A program for timely investigation and dissemination of information regarding product incidents, safety suggestions, complaints, accidents, and claims should be developed and communicated throughout all departments and field activities.

- Complaints and Claim Handling

The definition of a complaint or claim, for the purposes of this program, is any verbal or written report of personal injury, property damage, or other claimed loss allegedly resulting from a direct or related failure of any company-provided material, product, work, or service. Also include for control purposes all apparent or alleged malfunctions or failures regardless of the presence of an actual claim for loss.

Conversely, complaints of claims that do not relate to the functional use or safety of a product should be excluded.

A written procedure for handling product or service complaints and claims should be developed. Included should be effective controls to ensure that:

- All complaints and claims are immediately referred to an individual expressly designated to receive claims.
- Each incident is properly described and accurately recorded.
- All complaints and claims are immediately recorded on an incident log.
- Each complaint or claim is promptly and thoroughly investigated and processed.
- Whenever possible, the product is obtained for examination.

- Each incident is reviewed by the Product Loss Control Committee
- A determination of action necessary is made and corrective action taken
- All employees, sales representatives, dealers, and installation and service personnel are informed of the procedure for handling complaints and claims
- All information relating to complaints and claims and subsequent investigations, discussions, decisions, and corrective or follow-up activity is properly recorded and preserved

[NOTE: ADD MORE CONTROLS HERE]

- Claim Processing

All claims are to be processed in accordance with the Company's rules and regulations. Immediate notification by telephone is required on all bodily injury and serious property damage liability claims.

Internal reporting procedures should be developed to ensure that all claims are properly processed.

The names of individuals assigned reporting responsibilities should be properly communicated.

- Record Keeping

Formal guidelines should be established for record retention. Specific instructions should be communicated to employees for their guidance in dealing with the preparation, storage, and retention of records, samples, and test results that are related to product/service loss control.

The basic "rule of thumb" for record retention is at least the life of the product.

Product/service loss control records should not be destroyed without the express permission of the Products Loss Control – Claim Defense Committee. If in doubt the Committee should seek counsel's advice.

- LEGAL

Legal counsel should be utilized to alert the Products Loss Control – Claim Defense Committee and local management of existing laws and changes affecting Product Loss Control.

Counsel should review all contract and sales agreements for elements of potential liability.

All printed material such as labeling, advertising, and operating or maintenance manuals should be approved by counsel. All warranties should also be reviewed.

Council's approval should be secured before printed material or product information is actually disseminated.

Review assistance is also available from the Company's insurance broker.

Policy Statement

_____, an operating division of _____, recognizes its responsibility to provide customers and consumers with safe and reliable products and services.

To this end, we have established a formal Products/Services Loss Control Committee. The prime objective of this group is the establishment and maintenance of an effective control program designed to eliminate or effectively control injury or loss potential. As Chief Operating Officer, I will chair this Committee.

Every employee plays a critical part in Loss Control. All employees must be committed to fulfilling customer needs with safe and reliable products and services. Please give your total support to this effort.

The importance of providing safe and reliable products and services cannot be overemphasized. If we do not maintain quality, we let our customers down. We depend on our customers for business. Show them they can depend on us, every day, in every way.

Date: (Signature)
                          (Chief Operating Officer)

Date: (Signature)
                          (Vice President)

Appendix B

Requirements for legal counsel retained by or on behalf of XYZ Company Ltd.

Note: THIS IS A SAMPLE OUTSIDE BILLING GUIDELINE FORM. YOU ARE FREE TO ADD MORE RESTRICTIONS AND QUALIFICATIONS OR DELETE AS MANY AS YOU WANT

- **Introduction**

The following guidelines and rules are designed to guide outside counsel (hereinafter, "Counsel") retained to represent XYZ Company Ltd. ("XYZ") and/or its subsidiaries and affiliates (collectively, "XYZ") in assisting XYZ to manage its legal affairs. These guidelines intend to help Counsel produce effective and efficient results for XYZ, in a fair and cost-effective manner.

XYZ may find it necessary to amend these guidelines or add others during the course of an engagement as appropriate to manage legal matters properly. Prior notice will be given, and the matter discussed with Counsel if such action is deemed necessary by XYZ. Questions regarding these rules and guidelines should be directed to XYZ.

- **General Guidelines**

Media communication policy: Counsel will not communicate with any media outlet or respond to any inquiries for information from any media outlets regarding XYZ and/or its customers, claims, or other legal matters, without prior approval from XYZ. Media inquiries should be directed to Attn: GC, XYZ Law Department.

Outside Coordinating Counsel-Product Liability Matters: XYZ has selected outside coordinating litigation counsel for certain product liability matters. XYZ expects that other Counsel assigned to matters managed by coordinating counsel will:

- Provide copies of reports and other communications to coordinating counsel.
- Respond to requests for information and document from coordinating counsel.
- Work with coordinating counsel to develop XYZ's claims and defense, including, but not limited to, the following: discovery responses prepared on behalf of XYZ, depositions of XYZ personnel, discovery and investigation of claims, selection of defense experts, and challenges to adverse experts. XYZ believes that cooperation in this regard is critical to ensuring that strategies undertaken on XYZ's behalf are consistently undertaken in the various cases in which XYZ is involved.

- **Initial Requirements for New Engagements**

Engagement Letters: Unless instructed otherwise, within seven (7) days of Counsel's receipt of an assignment from XYZ, Counsel must provide SAE with an engagement letter. XYZ expects that Counsel will not charge XYZ for the time and expenses associated with preparing engagement letters. Engagement letters must set forth the following information:

- Confirmation of the assignment and scope of work.

- Counsel's agreement to follow and abide by the within Guidelines, as well as other applicable corporate policies and procedures.
- Counsel's personnel who are proposed for the assignment and their billing rates, consistent with the within Guidelines pertaining to "Staffing of Matters."
- Counsel's verification that it has not identified any actual or potential conflicts of interest arising from the engagement or that such conflicts have been resolved in accordance with the within rules and guidelines and applicable rules of professional conduct.

Case Plan and Budget: Within fourteen (14) days of Counsel's receipt of an assignment from XYZ, Counsel must submit to XYZ a Case Plan and Budget that sets forth the following data, which XYZ will review with Counsel on a timely basis after the engagement is made:

- Counsel's assessment of XYZ's potential liability, including a discussion of the relative liabilities of XYZ and/or its subsidiaries.
- Counsel's knowledge about adverse counsel and the local jurisdiction.
- A proposed strategy for defending or prosecuting the case.
- Identification of significant activity anticipated by Counsel, including removal to federal court, factual investigation, motions and discovery, and an estimated completion date for each significant activity.
- Identification and assessment of prospects for early resolution of the case, including settlement and dispositive motion practice.
- For litigation matters, a discovery end date and an anticipated trial date.
- A budget for the anticipated work during the engagement, with apportionment of the budget to anticipated tasks.

- **Reporting to XYZ**

In addition to the initial case reporting described above, XYZ expects that Counsel will communicate with XYZ on a regular basis, at least quarterly, to apprise XYZ of significant developments that occur during a case. Counsel shall also be responsible for updating the case plan and budget quarterly. During the case, XYZ may request monthly updates on significant events or milestones identified by XYZ.

Significant events about which Counsel should report to XYZ include depositions (summaries should be provided), and summaries of expert reports, opinions, testimony, and other important events. In particular, before filing any dispositive motions, Counsel must advise XYZ of Counsel's intent to file any such motions and provide draft motion papers for XYZ's review at least two (2) weeks prior to the anticipated filing date.

Pre-trial reports: For litigation matters, unless otherwise specified by XYZ, at least ninety (90) days prior to a scheduled trial date, Counsel must submit to XYZ a detailed pre-trial report, which includes a description of the important issues for trial, and the relative strengths and weaknesses of the positions of parties regarding those issues. Thereafter, Counsel will provide monthly written status reports up to the trial date.

Copies of documents:

- Copies of the following documents, when generated, should be sent to XYZ: pleadings; orders; research memoranda (where authorized); legal briefs and motion papers; expert reports; and medical reports.
- In addition, Counsel should send transcripts of depositions of XYZ personnel to XYZ.
- Deposition transcripts should be sent to XYZ in ".txt" or ASCII format, with copies of any exhibits in Adobe PDF or ".tif" format, via electronic mail.

- Counsel should send such documents other than deposition transcripts to XYZ electronically (in Adobe PDF or ".tif" formats, via electronic mail or otherwise) wherever possible, to minimize the costs of transmission and to accommodate Samsung's electronic record keeping systems.

Budgetary matters: Counsel must contact XYZ to advise that Counsel's fees or expenses are expected to exceed the case budget or an approved updated case budget, at least fourteen (14) days prior to the rendering of an invoice containing the fees or expenses that exceed the case budget. Counsel's communication to XYZ in this regard must include the amount of the expected overage, and a detailed explanation of the reason(s) why the case budget or an approved updated case budget would be exceeded, if the overage is approved by XYZ. XYZ will review such communications from Counsel and will determine whether or not to permit the reported overage.

Counsel will respond to all other requests from XYZ for information and documents in a timely manner.

- **Staffing of Matters**

XYZ reserves the right to review and modify Counsel's proposed staffing of matters handled on behalf of XYZ. For the sake of efficiency, Counsel should make every effort to limit the number of professionals performing work on matters for XYZ to the lowest levels consistent with Counsel's professional responsibilities.

Changes to and Continuity of Personnel: Counsel must first seek and receive Samsung's permission to modify (additions and substitutions) the case staffing outlined in the initial case report. If Samsung approves such staffing changes, then XYZ will not reimburse Counsel for time associated with educating new staff members to the facts and background of the matters, unless the staffing changes are occasioned solely by substantive developments in the matters that call for the addition of personnel.

Experience levels of attorneys assigned to XYZ matters: Counsel may not assign lawyers who have less than three (3) years of experience in the field of practice relevant to a matter, without prior approval from XYZ.

Summer Associates/Interns/Clerks: The tasks performed by such personnel will not be paid for by XYZ, absent special circumstances and prior approval by XYZ.

Paralegals: Counsel will not assign paraprofessionals, paralegals, or legal assistants to matters assigned by XYZ without prior approval from XYZ.

Administrative/clerical tasks: XYZ firmly believes that administrative/clerical tasks are part of Counsel's overhead and costs of doing business and will not be paid for by XYZ. "Administrative/clerical tasks" include, but are not limited to, filing, date-stamping, indexing, copying or scanning documents, and/or making travel arrangements.

Intra-office conferences: XYZ will compensate Counsel only for the cost of the most senior person's participation in the conference. Please note that Counsel who spend more than ten percent (10 percent) of their billable time annually on intra-office conferences will be closely reviewed by XYZ.

Multiple counsel at particular billable events: Counsel should consult with SAE regarding anticipated needs for attendance of multiple billers at particular events. Without prior approval, XYZ will compensate Counsel only for the cost of the most senior person's participation in the event.

Depositions: Counsel should consult with XYZ before scheduling, noticing, or otherwise initiating any depositions other than those already approved in the initial litigation plan. Similarly, Counsel should consult with XYZ prior to attending any depositions initiated by other parties.

[NOTE: PLACE OTHER RESTRICTIONS HERE]

- **Billing: Rendering Billing Statements/Invoices and Billing Rates**

General: XYZ reserves the right to review all charges for services and disbursements for legal work conducted on its behalf, without limitation. XYZ reserves the right to conduct on-site audits and to review Counsel's files and/or billing statements/invoices. Counsel agrees to comply with all reasonable requests for information and documents. XYZ further reserves its right to decline to pay charges that violate these Guidelines, and which are not fully explained, approved, or documented by Counsel after inquiry by XYZ.

Timing of rendering invoices: Invoices must be submitted not more than ninety (90) days after the month in which the time was accrued. The timing of the invoices is necessary for XYZ's budgeting and matter management. Counsel are advised that any time entries or invoices that are rendered outside this period will not be paid by XYZ without approval by the General Counsel.

Billing rates:

- Counsel agrees that billing rates set at the beginning of a matter will remain in effect unless Counsel submits a written request for a change or revision, and the written request is approved by XYZ. Such written requests must be submitted to XYZ at least sixty (60) days in advance of the effective date of the proposed change or revision.
- If Counsel's firm is comprised of multiple offices whose lawyers' (and other approved personnel's) billing rates vary by office, then for XYZ's matters, Counsel agrees to charge XYZ the lowest of the firm's rates for lawyers of the same level experience as those assigned to XYZ's matters, regardless of where the lawyers assigned to XYZ's matters are stationed.

Any other requests by Counsel for increases in compensation rates must be made to XYZ in writing, and XYZ must agree to such increases before such increases may appear in Counsel's billing statements. XYZ will not agree to such increases more often than biannually.

- **Billing Entries and Descriptions**

All billing statements/invoices shall be supported with details of the work performed. The details to be included are:

- A narrative description of the work performed for each specific task by the attorney or other professional performing it. The descriptions should set forth clearly the task performed and why it was necessary. For example, the following billing description, "Conference with ABC re: status," is not sufficient.
- Name or initials of the person who performed the task.
- The time spent on the task, in tenths of an hour increments.
- A summary by each attorney or other professional who performed work for XYZ during that month, showing the total number of hours billed by that person, his/her billing rate, and total charges for that person.

Single entry timekeeping is required: Each activity performed by a timekeeper must be set forth separately from other time entries. "Block billing" entries and entries that otherwise combine multiple tasks into single entries are not acceptable to, and will not be paid by, Samsung.

Use of standardized forms and pleadings: XYZ encourages Counsel to rely upon standardized forms for the creation of documents, where appropriate. XYZ may only be charged for Counsel's time to revise and modify such documents for the particular task for XYZ, and not for time spent to create the original forms.

Travel time: XYZ will reimburse Counsel for the reasonable cost of Counsel's actual time to travel to an appropriate case-related event.

- **Invoice Format**

Please address invoices to XYZ at _____ and send a hard copy of each invoice, with all documentation of disbursements made on XYZ's behalf, to _____.

- **Expenses/Disbursements**

Each disbursement shall be billed at Counsel's actual out-of-pocket costs. No markups or administrative fees may be added.

Approval by XYZ: Counsel shall not make any single disbursement of $500 or more without procuring prior approval from Samsung.

Documentation of disbursements: Counsel must provide documentation for each disbursement made on XYZ's behalf, including receipts and invoices. Such documentation must be provided to XYZ with the hard copy of Counsel's invoice sent to XYZ.

Interstate and long-distance travel: XYZ defines "interstate and long-distance travel" as travel between and among more than one state and/or intrastate travel outside a seventy-five (75) mile radius from Counsel's office. Counsel may not travel interstate or long distance without prior approval from XYZ.

[NOTE: YOU CAN PLACE MORE RESTRICTIONS ON TRAVEL HERE]

- XYZ expects that Counsel will undertake reasonable efforts to secure the most cost-effective fares possible. XYZ encourages Counsel to book travel arrangements as early as possible to take advantage of discounts for early reservations.
- Airfares: XYZ will reimburse Counsel only for economy or coach fare for approved flights within the continental USA, Asia, Europe, and Latin America; business-class airfare may be reimbursed with preapproval for overseas travel.
- Rental cars: XYZ will reimburse the charges for rental cars of midsize class or lower only.

- Meals and hotels: Counsel should use his/her professional judgment in selecting hotel accommodations and incurring expenses.
- XYZ will not reimburse counsel for the costs of travel agents.

Local and intrastate travel: XYZ defines "local and intrastate travel" as travel within Counsel's state of domicile, and other travel within a seventy-five (75) mile radius from Counsel's office. XYZ considers local and intrastate travel to be part of Counsel's ordinary overhead, and as such, XYZ will not reimburse Counsel for expenses related to intrastate travel.

Automobile travel (for other than local or intrastate travel):

- Charges for automobile travel must be accompanied by the following information: date(s) of travel; purpose; number of miles; per-mile charge; and the amounts and nature of other expenses (tolls, parking, etc.). XYZ will reimburse Counsel according to the Internal Revenue Service's maximum mileage expense rate in effect at the time of travel or Counsel's internal rate, whichever is lower.
- XYZ will not reimburse Counsel for the costs of fines and penalties related to driving and parking violations incurred by Counsel during business-related travel for SAE.
- XYZ will not reimburse Counsel for the cost of towing and repair services incurred to service an automobile during business-related travel on behalf of XYZ.

Photocopies:

- Photocopies numbering fewer than two hundred pages per billing period (usually monthly) are part of Counsel's overhead, and the cost of such photocopies will not be paid by XYZ.
- If Counsel determines that it must copy single groups of documents numbering more than one hundred pages, then Counsel must seek prior approval from XYZ, and endeavor

to secure the most cost-effective means of making such photocopies. For approved photocopy projects completed internally by Counsel's firm, XYZ will reimburse Counsel at a rate of up to ten cents per page.

Legal and technical research; computerized legal research services:

- Performance of legal and technical research: XYZ hires Counsel based upon their experience and expects that Counsel will be highly specialized and experienced in his/her field(s) of expertise. As such, XYZ expects that it will be rare for legal research by Counsel to be required. Before undertaking any legal research, therefore, Counsel should obtain permission from XYZ, using the approval form attached hereto. In the few cases in which it is impractical for Counsel to procure prior approval, Counsel should inform XYZ as soon as possible after research has begun.
- Computerized legal research: XYZ considers charges related to the use of computerized legal research services (e.g., Westlaw and LEXIS-NEXIS) to be part of Counsel's overhead, and such charges will not be reimbursed by XYZ.

Charges for messengers, couriers, and express or overnight delivery services: XYZ discourages the use of such services and will reimburse Counsel only for such charges that are reasonable under the circumstances and directly related to the defense or prosecution of the case.

Other non-reimbursable expenses: XYZ will not reimburse Counsel for the following expenses:

- Photocopies (except as delineated above)
- Computer, e-mail, and word processing fees
- Support staff pay
- Overtime pay and shift differentials for staffers
- Charges and rent for conference rooms
- Office supplies

- Postage
- Library use and library staff charges
- Clerks (billable time, expenses, etc.)
- Proofreader charges
- Meals and food service (except during approved business-related travel)
- Taxis/limousines to and from office (even at night, except for approved business-related travel)
- Telephone charges
- Facsimile charges
- Cellular/wireless/Blackberry service charges
- Document scanning charges (unless pre-approved by XYZ)

[NOTE: YOU CAN ADD MORE RESTRICTIONS]

Experts, consultants and other professionals: Counsel will consult with and seek approval from XYZ before retaining or otherwise incurring expenses for work performed by experts, consultants, investigators, translators, or other professional service providers.

Agreement

_____ hereby agrees to abide by and follow "Requirements for Legal Counsel Retained by or on Behalf of XYZ Co Ltd."

_____ (firm)

By: _____

Dated:

Bibliography

Basri, Carole. *International Corporate Practice*. New York: Practising Law Institute, 2011.

Basri, Carole, and Irving Kagan. *Corporate Legal Departments*. 3rd ed. New York: Practising Law Institute, 2004.

Berstein, Jonathan with Bruce Bonafede, Managers' Guide to Crisis Management. New York: McGraw Hill, 2011.

Breen, Michael. *The Koreans*. New York: St. Martin's Press, 1998

Buchholts and Carroll. *Business and Society*. 7th Edition: South-Western, 2006 at p 2003

Care Mark International, inc. Derivative Litigation, 698 A.2nd 959 (Del-Ch 1996)

Clayton Act (1914)

Collier, Paul M. *Fundamentals of Risk Management for Accountants and Managers*. Oxford, UK: Elsevier, 2009

Coyner, Thomas. *Doing Business in Korea: An Expanded Guide*. Seoul, Korea: Seoul Selection, 2010.

CPSA, 15 USC Sec 2064 (b).

Donovan, Donald. *Introducing Clients to US Civil Litigation (International Litigation Strategies and Practice.* Washington D.C.: ABA Publishing, 2005

Eisner, Rebecca S. *European Union Data Privacy Requirements: A US Perspective*

Family Medical Leave Act

Fink, Steven. *Crisis Communications: The Definitive Guide to Managing the Message.* McGraw Hill Education, 2013

Fisher, R., W. Ury, and B. Patton. *Getting to Yes, Negotiating Agreement without Giving In.* 2nd ed. New York: Penguin. 1991.

"For Asian Companies the New EU Laws can be a Headache", https:// seoullegalriskmgmt.com, April 24, 2017

Fujitsu Ltd. v. Federal Express Corp., 247 F 3rd 423 (2nd Cir 2001).

Graham, Jon L. *The Japanese Negotiation Style: Characteristics of a Distinct Approach*, Negotiation Journal, April 2, 1993.

Harrington, Scott E and Gregory R Niehaus. *Risk Management and Insurance.* 2nd ed. New York: McGraw Hill, 2003

Hart Scott Rodino Act, Sec 9

Hopkins, Bryan E. *A Comparison of Recent Changes in Arbitral Laws and Regulations of Hong Kong, Singapore and Korea.* Seoul, Korea: *KLRI Journal of Law and Legislation* 3, no. 1 (2013).

Hopkins, Bryan E. *Legal Risk Management for In-House Counsel and Managers*. Singapore, Partridge Publishing, 2014.

In re Alleged Abuse of Market Dominance of Qualcomm Inc., KFTC Decision No. 2017-0-25, January 20, 2017.

Koltran, Phillip. *Keys to Managing a FOSS Compliance Program*, The Linux Foundation, www.Linuxfoundation.com

Korean Commercial Code, Art. 382 (3), 399 (1)

Jacobson v. Katzer, 533 F 3rd 1373 (Fed Cir 2008).

Lewicki, Roy J, Bruce Barry and David M Saunders. *Negotiation*, New York: McGraw-Hill 2012

Losey, Ralph C. *Introduction to e-Discovery*. Chicago: American Bar Association, 2009.

Monopoly Regulation and Fair Trade Act of Korea (1981), Art. 1, 29

Morrison, Terri and Conway, Wayne. *Kiss, Bow or Shake Hands: Asia*. 57 Littlefield Street, Avon, MA, Adams Media, 2007

Personal Information Protection Act (PIPA) of Korea

Quinley, Kevin M, *Litigation Management*. Dallas, Texas: International Risk Management Institute, Inc. 1995

Restatement of Torts (Second) Sec 402, 1964.

Restatement of Torts, Sec. 757 (1939)

Rich, Cyntia, *Privacy Laws in Asia*, BNA Insights, Vol. 14, No. 20 (2015)

Smith v Van Gorkom, 488 A. 2nd, 282 (Del. 1985)

The Act on Prevention of Improper Solicitation and Receipt of Money (Kim Young Ran Act) of Korea.

15 USC Sec 1-2

15 USC Sec 13 (a)

15 USC Sec 72 (a)

UCC–Sec 2-316.

UCC–Sec 2-607.

UCC–Sec 2-715.

Unfair Competition Prevention and Trade Secret Act of Korea, Art. 2 (2)

Uniform Trade Secrets Act (USTA), 1979

www.europa.eu/dataprotection

Zubulake v. UBS Warburg LLC, 217 F.R.D. 309 (SDNY 2003).

Zubulake v. UBS Warburg LLC, 229 F.R.D. 422 (SDNY 2004).

Index

Lightning Source UK Ltd.
Milton Keynes UK
UKHW011839110220
358569UK00003B/24